THE OPEN BOOK OF EMPTINESS

A COLLECTION OF PUBLIC TALKS AND TEACHINGS

BY JAMES LOW

Published by Simply Being www.simplybeing.co.uk

British Library Cataloguing in Publication Data. A catalogue record for this book is available from the British Library.

ISBN: 978-1-7399381-7-8

Edited by Barbara Terris

Revised by James Low

Cover photograph is courtesy of Robbie Terris.

Content

Preface

Although the word 'emptiness' can seem a bit intimidating, in the Buddhist traditions it is the key to freedom. Our mind is intrinsically empty of self and any fixed or defining content. We are not defined by anything which has occurred, that is occurring now, or will even occur in the future. Being empty of fixed content allows us to open to all that occurs without being trapped in reactivity. By resting in the intrinsic openness of our mind it becomes clear that we are not a thing amongst things. The sky-like openness of our mind as it is neither grasps at arisings nor effortfully discards them. No occurrence can touch or affect the mind as it is. Occurrences do contact and impinge on patterns of interpretation and identification that we, as ego-selves, have come to rely on.

By opening to our own unborn openness we are freed from the delusion that our transient patterning points to the truth of who we are. The chapters in this book offer fresh ways of viewing our situation so that we can awaken to our true essence and to freedom.

Getting to know how we are

Let's start by thinking about our ordinary everyday life: all the things that we rely on and take refuge in – the places where we stay, the warm bed where we sleep, our clothes, our cooking materials, our books – everything that we rely on to create our sense of who we are and our safe, familiar world. One view within buddhism is that these things on which we rely in our ordinary life are somehow dangerous for us because they pull us into attachment. If we follow this view we try to lessen and renounce our attachment to these things by explicitly taking refuge instead in the Buddha, Dharma and Sangha. We use our reliance on a buddhist refuge to protect us from our tendency to get caught up in the things of this world and our attachment thereby increasing.

Another view in buddhism, the mahayana view, is that the idea and fact of emptiness helps us to understand that all the things that we are attached to – all the things we take refuge in as a support for our ordinary life – are devoid of inherent self-nature. We then want to take refuge in the Buddha, not as someone apart from the world, but Buddha as the spirit of awareness – the attitude of awareness which recognises the essential emptiness of all things. This view does not restrict our freedom to be in the world. It is not a path of renunciation. We continue to make use of all the things that we ordinarily make use of, but without becoming tied up in them. In fact, the view of emptiness encourages using all these ordinary objects of attachment as a means of opening ourselves to deeper and deeper understanding of the dharma. Using our attachment onto everyday objects as the path leads to understanding that our grasping is what is creating the duality of subject and object.

One of the particular qualities of mahayana buddhism, and of tantra and dzogchen, is the tension between a confident certainty that a direct realisation of the integration of samsara and nirvana is possible, alongside the humility of recognising that this is very difficult to achieve!

Tantra requires of us a paradoxical or double movement. Through the experience of the meditation we develop a full faith in the realisation of the world as a buddha field of perfect enlightenment, whilst at the same time deconstructing our tendency to solidify that view. We want to develop faith, respect and devotion to the buddhas and the bodhisattvas whilst at the same time using the vision of full enlightenment to deconstruct the attitude of faith that might be solidified into a kind of endless helpless humility.

We seek not to establish hope and humility as two polarities in dualistic opposition, but rather to see them as two points in a dance whereby they deconstruct and open each other as they play and unfold. The kindness, which is the hope that all beings will awaken, is inseparable from the clarity that all beings are inseparable from emptiness. We develop kindness towards illusory beings. This is the warmth of the two truths: the relative truth of diverse appearances and the absolute truth that emptiness is the nature of all phenomena.

The text by Chetsangpa in *SIMPLY BEING* says that you must believe that whatever the guru does is good. It is good because it is empty of inherent existence. This is the absolute nature which offers no actual basis for judgement. If you don't understand that it is empty, then whatever he does will just strengthen your judgement: this is good, this is bad. The practice of emptiness is for grown-ups; it's not for children. Insight into emptiness creates a subjective experience which will free us by shifting our experience from a dualistic paradigm to a non-dualistic paradigm. We use devotion to the guru or the deity in order to experience our helplessness, our vulnerability and our neediness. We hollow out our ego self so that we can merge with the deity. The more empty of self we are, the more we are able to become the deity and thereby access the qualities required for liberating all sentient beings. True kindness arises from emptiness and does not stray from it.

In the mahayana Tibetan tradition, we believe that if we pray to Padmasambhava[1] he will come and save us by letting us experience our true nature. This is a method for understanding the nature of our mind by using the dualistic power of devotion to open the door to non-duality. This method is even more helpful if we can see Padmasambhava in the form of our own teacher. This is because our habit of seeing somebody as their flesh and blood body is dissolved by directly encountering their light body. It is our own attachment to the idea of materiality that obscures the actual nature of phenomena. Tantric visualisation allows us to see that materiality is simply a dull and thick way of experiencing light.

Let's say you want to emigrate to America. You need go through the American embassy. Imagine you are living in a very poor country, perhaps you are an Indian farmer in Bihar, and you decide you want to go America. You would take the long, local, cheap passenger train all the way to Delhi, sitting in a hard wooden seat. Then you would walk through the streets of Delhi – it's very hot, it's very tiring – out to Chanakyapuri, and you would go to the American embassy. You'd go through the front door, if they let you in, and enter an air-conditioned room. There's a very comfortable seat. You think, *"Ah I'm in America. I want to stay here forever."* Just then the doorman says, *"We're closing for lunch, you have to go out now."* However, you remember that when you went

---

[1] Tibetans generally refer to Padmasambhava, the Lotus Born, as Guru Rinpoche, the Precious Guru.

to school in the village, they told you that America was a wonderful democratic country where they announced that they would welcome people from all over the world, the sick, the poor, the downtrodden, and so you reply, *"I am exactly that. I am a poor downtrodden peasant from Bihar. I want to stay here in America."* But then the doorman comes and puts you outside the door. So the business of actually getting to America itself is very hard. You need if possible to have some friends who are already in America who will help you. Auntie Tara. Uncle Amitabha. Grandpa Chenrezig. *"Please send me a letter of invitation so I can come too."* Then, if you have good karma you get a green card and you can go and settle there. If you have less good karma you can go on a tourist visit! Whether or not you have good relatives over there who will help you, you still have to go through the embassy. And the embassy is both friendly and unfriendly. Often it operates according to rules you don't really understand. You imagine that something is clear. You hand over your passport, you expect to get a visa, but they come back and say, *"Sorry, some mistake. You have to go back to your village and get the headman to stamp it."*

So the guru is very much like the American embassy. Sometimes looks very nice, sometimes looks very not-nice. Sometimes helpful, sometimes not so helpful. Not a place to go and live. The guru is not a place to live; it is just an embassy. The ambassador lives in the embassy, but for other people who are travelling it is just a place of transit. You go to the embassy for a purpose. You go to the guru for a purpose. If the peasant from Bihar, falls asleep while waiting in this beautiful air-conditioned embassy, he may dream that he is already in America and that everything is safe but at a certain point he'll have to wake up from the dream.

You hear people saying such things as, *"When I met this Lama I felt so good. I spent some months with him in India and it was really wonderful. But then I had to come back to the West and it is so difficult for me now. I just want to earn enough money to go back to India and hang out with this Guru. Then I'll feel very good."* The danger in this is that you turn the guru into a kind of embassy hotel in which you have the false illusion that just by hanging out there, you are in the place to be.

When you go to dharma centres, or you go to see lamas, or you go on pilgrimage, or to India or somewhere like that, it is very easy to mistake the embassy, the transition point, for the final destination. You have lost your purpose or intention. Dharma centres, or dharma places as they exist in the world, always need work to sustain them. If you become part of a dharma centre it is very important that you participate in the work and help it to thrive. Yet helping dharma centres to grow, or building monasteries, or printing books, can easily eat up all your time and become a way of avoiding looking at your mind.

Dharma texts use many terms like 'path', 'way', 'vehicle', all of them referring to journeying and travelling. A path leads somewhere. In dualistic terms 'there' is better than 'here'. Nirvana is better than samsara and so I have to keep my eye on my goal. There are many pitstops along the path of duality, but none of them is deeply reliable because we are looking to the other for help. People and places can give us the energy, enthusiasm and commitment to continue our journey. The guru becomes the point of entry or transition into a deeper understanding of our journey.

If our peasant from Bihar who had saved up a lot of money for his ticket to America, got his visa and then was so grateful to this wonderful embassy that had given him a visa, that he went to the market and used all his plane ticket money to buy lots of butterlamps and put them all around the embassy – if he did all that, with a great puja to worship the glorious embassy of the United States of America; if he did all that, he wouldn't be able to get on the aeroplane!

People can become so intoxicated with the presence of a teacher that in worshipping this person they forget that they actually need to make use of this person to get somewhere. Teachers are methods. We need to learn how to make use of this method. If the guru is used well, the journey becomes very short.)

THE TWO TRUTHS

The Two Truths are usually referred to as relative truth and absolute truth. Essentially, relative truth means whatever is constructed using the organisational frame of a perceiving subject and an object that is perceived. Relative truth is subdivided into pure relative truth and impure relative truth. Impure relative truth is the relative truth in which you perceive objects as real *and* you have attachment to them. Pure relative truth is when you perceive objects as real, but you have *no* attachment to them. Absolute truth is when you neither perceive objects, nor have any attachment to them.

'To perceive an object' means to perceive something which appears to exist in truth, in and of itself. Here I have a watch, one which I am very attached to. We can see it and we perceive it as something existing in truth. We know what to do with it, we can read the dial and it makes sense. We have a lot of mental constructs which can be located around this object. I have a particular attachment to this watch because it is *my* watch. But even if this isn't your watch, you have an attachment to it as something which supports whatever attitudes you have that let you know that it is a watch.

So we have an attachment to the *concept* of watch and we strengthen that every time we look at the watch and think we know what a watch is. We are attached to both our concepts which allow us to identify this as an object, an entity, a thing-in-itself, and to our skills of identification and signification by which we focus on the specific characteristics of this particular watch. We might be able to free ourselves from attachment to concrete entities like watches – we might decide that we will go and live in a cave, living very simply and renouncing the world. However the method of conceptualisation we employ for making sense of the world is one which has attachment embedded in it. Not only that but we are attached to the meaning-making patterns of signification that exist in language. It's through our attachment to language as a meaning-making device that we create the identity that we have as a separate phenomenon, taking up a place amongst other phenomena.

This level of attachment is very difficult to recognise, because it's so normal for us. In using language we are dealing with an intangible, metaphorical constructive system which creates the illusion of real things existing in truth. Language as a system of signification creates a particular world of meaning which we imagine to have a precise correlation with objects that exist in the world. A watch appears to be what is here. But we have to remember that the watch we see is inseparable from the concepts we employ to 'see' it. The watch doesn't exist in itself. It is a site of interpretation and cannot be contained within any specific definition.

Our education leads us to believe that language has a direct relationship to what is 'out there' – indeed that language is derived from objects that exist in reality in the world. What we encounter in the world, what appears to be a series of discrete separate objects having their own qualities, is actually an interplay of language and conceptualisation which is moving and shifting and creating the boundaries between one identification and another. So in saying *"This is my watch"*, I am both making a statement referring back to me in terms of my possession of this object, and I am also talking about the object as something that exists in truth, that can be recognised as a real object, recognised by everyone here. Thus my belief that this is 'my watch' is a statement from within impure relative truth. There is my sense of the watch itself, taken to be an independent entity. This is an aspect of mental dullness and lack of insight. And there is my sense of ownership of it which generates desire for it and aversion towards anyone who might take it or damage it.

Sometimes when we come out of our meditation we look and it is as if something is there, but what it is we don't quite know until we start the business of attaching thoughts and language again to experience. When we come out of meditation, we may sometimes have had the experience of a kind of a gap, that we just kind of open, and then the world becomes a bit more concrete. Similarly, if we run very fast until we get out of breath and then stop – there is a kind of an openness. Or maybe in sex you can have that kind of experience of being just a little bit knocked open. It's that kind of moment. There's a gap and then language, conceptualisation comes in to fill the gap.

In buddhism as in most religions there are spiritual practices designed to encourage this disruption. For example, the practice of silence in zen monasteries. When you practise silence something arises and you may want to tell it to someone to confirm the nature of your experience – as a kind of feedback loop that strengthens the reality of things – but if you are unable to speak because you have taken a vow of silence for example, something arises yet you can't turn it into some-*thing*, you can't solidify it, so it tends to remain rather thin.

TANTRA AS A METHOD TO PURIFY IMPURE RELATIVE TRUTH

The tantric tradition makes use of mantras. Although the syllables of the mantra can be ascribed meaning, the meaning of the mantra, syllable by syllable, is not the main thing. The main thing is that on one level they are meaningless sound. That is to say, the meaning of these sounds does not belong inside the matrix of meaning which we ordinarily use in the world.

The word mantra means 'mind-protector' because it stops the mind from getting woven into the web of dualistic meaning which is embedded in language. On the level of ordinary meaning, when you recite a mantra you are saying something that has no meaning. If you have done mantra practice for any length of time you may have experienced feeling a bit spaced-out. Saying mantra and using a mala does have signification on a cultural and sociological level, such as being a Tibetan Buddhist or whatever. That is an ordinary level. However, in doing the practice there is a disorientation because thoughts rest on words and mantra is using sound to disrupt the ordinary use of language, which is to appropriate and colonise the world into samsaric, dualistic meaning.

This desire to own the world by making sense of it is very profound. This arises as the process of the unfolding of the *four-stage development of ignorance.* The *first stage* is the forgetfulness of the openness of our presence. Thus, 'being here', fresh and open, is lost to us as direct experience since we cleave to the more dense sense that 'I am here'. This leads to the *second stage,* where I have a sense of being other than you while still being connected with you. Self and other are born together, two seeming entities whose actual absence of autonomy binds them together. From this arises the *third stage.* The third stage describes how once openness is lost and the mind starts to look for something, the vast array of entities is organised by the use of signs, generating a competence in identifying specific entities by employing their name or designation. This is the seductive intelligence which can name all things, yet not penetrate to the true nature of how they are. We are absolutely convinced that this is reality because we have been brought up to believe that each phenomenon is just itself, due to this specificity being the expression of its unique essence.

Moreover, this sense of the knowability of everything is the ground or basis of karma. Being unaware of how karma operates is the **fourth stage** of ignorance. Karma is generated through the alignment of the following four factors: being sure that both I and you are real; an intention, good or bad, towards you arises in me; I can then act this out; and then review what I have done. If these four factors are all aligned the full karmic force of this action will manifest at a later date and I, in whatever form I am then, will experience the force of that karmic formation. When this process is not understood, it is called ignorance or unawareness of being dull regarding the operation of karma.

As meditators our aim is to reduce the intensity of the five afflictive emotions: mental dullness, desire, aversion, pride, and jealousy. With this we can start to see appearances without being carried away by strong reactions. Then we can begin to focus on the empty nature of phenomena – the startling fact that there are actually no self-existing objects although we talk as if there were. The more we see the actual impermanence of phenomena, the more the delusional nature of the beliefs we have been operating under becomes apparent. We have been grasping at clouds, falling in love with echoes, feeling aversion towards mirages.

This reframing, or re-identification, of the nature of phenomena as they arise moment by moment, gradually loosens our tendency to solidify and reify. Subject and object are experienced as playing together. The world arises again as revelation, revelation *in* emptiness, *as* emptiness, *of* emptiness. Through that one enters into the experience of absolute truth in which, although we say that nothing is occurring, clearly everything *is* occurring, but everything is occurring as nothing. It is the revelation within mirror-like awareness. This is the real focus of dzogchen meditation: to experience the world as a continuing spontaneous revelation which never becomes born as this or that with subject-object separation.

FINDING A METHOD THAT WORKS FOR YOU

Having got to know ourselves a little bit we start to know what our real problems are so that when we talk about the five poisons, anger, desire, stupidity, jealousy and pride, these are no longer just general concepts or interesting things to think about, but we recognise ourselves in them. We know our own pattern of stupidity, we know how our own desire ties us in knots, we know the kind of situations we get pissed off with. At that point, when we know ourselves a bit and we have some clearer understanding of who we are, we can have some clearer understanding of the dharma. We can start to fit ourselves – our particular karmic shape in this life – into the menu of potential that is the dharma and find the best possible fit.

It is useful if we have a teacher who knows something about the dharma and also something about us so that they can give us some guidance on that fit. The kind of advice we need from a teacher will change as we know more about ourselves, as we know more about the dharma, and as we know more about the fit. At first we are very dependent, but as we get to know more we can be more independent and we can then have a kind of consultation with a teacher to get more understanding about where we understand ourselves to be.

Let's revisit the word 'Buddha'. 'Buddha' is translated in Tibetan as '*Sangs rGyas*'. '*Sang*' means purified, all obstacles and difficulties are removed. '*Gye*' means rich, full, complete, spreading out all good qualities. So the more we know ourselves, the more we know the things that have to be purified or removed. If we are a very angry person or a very jealous person, or very stupid, or proud or don't do the practice – whatever our own particular pattern is – we can have a sense for ourselves what is our next task. If I have to work on my anger, what is the best way to do that? Now that we know what buddhahood is like, we realise that we have these problems that we have to get rid of, since we have read that buddhahood is free of anger, jealousy, hatred and so on. If I am a very lazy person, for example, although I keep having the thought that I'd like to practise the dharma, I often feel tired, or I need to go to bed early, or at the end of a busy day I just want to watch television. In the morning I have got to rush to work because I don't like to get out of bed early. In this way it is never the right time for doing dharma practice.

Now, I might be able to motivate myself to do something by thinking about death, by thinking that my life will end, that I don't know when it will end, that it might end very soon, and that if I die now I will have achieved nothing. *"Oh my God, I'd better do some practice!"* I could reflect on impermanence and death and use that to frighten myself. I could use fear to motivate myself to meditate. However perhaps I grew up in a family where my parents were often trying to frighten me into activity and so I have grown resistant to fear. *"If you don't do your homework, then you won't pass your exam, and you won't get to college and so will never get a job. Look at you, you will be like these jobless people sitting on the park benches. So, get on with your homework. It's a very dangerous world now and only your education will protect you!"* For people who grew up hearing this sort of message, frightening yourself into meditation will not work. For some people meditating on death does motivate them but if this method does not work for you then it makes sense to use another line of thought. For example, you might think, *"Well, if I practise the dharma and I purify all my bad karma then I will never have to be born again in a household where I have to do homework every night!"* If you understand yourself a little bit and understand something of your own karmic habits as they reveal themselves in your past experience, you might decide that this approach suits you better.

Both are just methods to get you motivated to practise the dharma and once you know more about yourself, you can start to find what is a good fit for you. You can see what is effective in getting you mobilised and what depresses you and takes your enthusiasm away. A big supermarket sells all sorts of food, but if I have diabetes, many of the things are not food for me; they are poison. So although all of these things are classed as food, many of them, such as jams and cakes, are actually poison for me. They are not a fit.

So, method is very important and nobody else can really tell us about that. Even if I am a diabetic and my doctor tells me what not to eat, until I have eaten that food for myself and experienced the consequences, then I do not really appreciate how this 'food' is now a poison for me. It may not have been a poison for me when I was younger, but now it is.

Sometimes we eat something and we don't like the taste, but actually it's good for us. Other times we eat something and we don't like it and it's *not* good for us. It can be difficult to know the difference, which is why it is important to talk to teachers, to read, to reflect on what we read and hear, to talk with other practitioners and try to think together about what is going on. *"Why is it that this doesn't seem to help me? Is it because I am being resistant to something? I tell myself that I want to change but it seems that actually I don't want to change. I know that if I really do this practice it will change me. Is that why I don't do it properly? Because I don't want to change?"* Is it that story? Or is it the case that this practice doesn't fit with me just now?

That's why it makes sense to do some of the preliminary practices *(ngondro)* and through that to recognise the ways in which we may sabotage ourselves. Some people, for example, are so greedy that they want the best thing immediately: *"I want only to do dzogchen, the highest practice."* But they don't understand dzogchen and because they are full of greed and pride they feel ashamed at not understanding it. So they pretend they understand, and keep up this pretense for some years until finally they drop the whole thing. It's very important to learn how we sabotage ourselves. If we know a lot about that, then dzogchen can make a lot of sense since the main practice of dzogchen is to be able to dissolve the points at which we self-sabotage. In fact, that is the real essence of dzogchen.

When we visualise a ball of light, or Padmasambhava, or Tara or any other deity we are trying to have the sense of it as transparent. We are seeing it, but in the moment of seeing it we want to have the recognition that this is simply an image, like the quality of image that you would get in a mirror. What we are trying to do is have the sense of colours organised into particular shapes that resemble the form of a deity, Padmasambhava, Tara or whoever, with their specific ornaments and robes, but all of that being light. You have form or shape but no substance.

Our habit is to think that when we see something, there is actually some substance there. But what we are trying to do in tantric visualisation sadhanas is see something, whilst knowing that there is nothing there. But it is not that there is nothing there at all. Nothing is appearing as some-thing, just as when you look in a mirror and you see something, but you can't grasp it. There is nothing to grasp. There is no substance to the reflection in a mirror and yet it is there.

I hope you can see how this is very important – and how it links in with the purification of relative truth – because you are purifying the notion that when you see something, there is something there. This practice is saying, *"No. Every time I see some-thing, nothing is there."* But nothing is revealing itself as something, without the something becoming something as such.

14

This is very important and it is why an intellectual understanding of emptiness is also very important.

DECONSTRUCTING OUR ASSUMPTIONS

The heart of our practice is allowing the deconstructing of the habit whereby we perceive substances as existing in truth, as being really there.

I am holding up a match. When you look at it, what can you see? You have all seen matches before; you may even have used them many times. When we look at it, it's a match. We can see a wooden stick with some coloured chemicals on the end. This exists, doesn't it? This is definitely a match. It's not a magician's illusion. Here is a match. Now I'd like you to watch this match very carefully. What is happening to the match now? *[James lights the match.]* Where has the match gone? The *idea* of the match may return but this particular match itself will not return. When we see the match, we forget that the match is made up of substances which are held together due to the presence of particular conditions in the environment. Matches are manufactured in a particular way. We are used to opening the box and seeing matches looking a certain way, maybe with red heads, maybe blue heads, but anyway looking roughly like this.

In order for the match to exist like this, many thousands of millions of conditions have to be in place. There needs to be a planet, there needs to be a habitable climate on the planet, there need to be the things that have developed through time to grow as trees, there needs to be people who plant the trees, who fell the trees, people who make the metal that makes the saws that cut the trees. There need to be vehicles to put the trees on, there need to be boats to put the trees on, there needs to be a factory where this match was made and cut up very small. There needs to be a whole petrochemical industry that makes the chemicals on the

15

head of the match. There are millions and billions of factors resting in this one thing. This item holds the whole world together, this match!

So many billions of factors have brought this into existence in this room at this time, and then all sorts of other factors will lead to its destruction and where it will go when it goes into the rubbish. It is moving through time, held in place in its particular momentary form as a meeting place of causes and conditions. I think that it's very important to remember this when we look at something in our usual way. *"Oh, it's a match."* Somebody asks us, *"Have you got a light?"* It's very automatic. We see this item existing in itself and we don't see the whole incredible infinity of circumstances that have to be in place for it to exist. Its 'existence' is a dependent existence without the least inherent existence.

The same applies to everything else. It applies to our own bodies. Think how many complex factors have created and sustained our bodies as they are in this room at this time. Just think of the position your body is in and all the things that cause it to be in that position. Habits, maybe not being used to sitting on a cushion, maybe being tired at the end of the day, all sorts of factors are involved in our posture.

To return to the example of the match, in relation to buddhism what is important is the sense that if this match is existing here as the momentary coming-together of all these causes and conditions, then it has no essence in itself, there is no match-ness in the match. It is simply the play of an infinite multitude of factors. If we change the causes and conditions we actually change the thing. If we let the match get damp, and then try to light it, it is a bit difficult because water doesn't burn. Matches burn. What other use do we make of matches? Only for burning. When it is wet it doesn't burn but if we dry the wet match then because the causes and conditions of the heat are greater than the water, the water will dry off so that the basic quality of this particular combination will reveal itself for a moment when it is lit. Having burnt itself out, it burns no more.

As a further example, supermarkets display food in different ways according to the susceptibility of specific foods to changes in temperature. Some food is kept in a freezer, some is kept on an open shelf. So here we have a beautiful fish, but if it is not kept cold it starts to go off and we think, *"Oh I don't really want to eat this fish, it's not so fresh."* When we were small we maybe had a drawing book or a first reading book with a little picture of a fish and the letter 'F' for fish. Then one day mum says, *"Tonight we have fish for supper!"* and she cooks it and puts it on our plate. Now, we seem to know what a fish is, but a fish is lots of other things as well. Fish is this biochemical composition which disintegrates under certain circumstances. Once the fish is killed the energy recycling force that was keeping it healthy and fresh is cut off and a new process starts, which is the process of rotting and corruption. So what we have to do is get the fish out of the sea and into the shops and onto our plates as quickly as possible before this other decaying process takes place, otherwise, *"Ugh I can't eat that!"* It is the same with the ego. It is held in place by circumstances. Somebody says, *"You're no good at this"* and the ego deflates. Somebody says, *"Oh you're so wonderful..."* and your ego expands. Due to causes and conditions we change our shape, yet we imagine that we are essentially the same person.

Usually we act as if there were a true essence or a self-substance to the things that we see and to ourselves but in fact what we have is a ceaseless play of the infinitely complex interplay of causes and conditions bumping off each other and transforming and transforming and transforming... What we take to be an existent, a being this or that, is actually part of the ceaseless process of becoming.

This is why contemplation on impermanence is so important as a means to keep us in touch with the dynamic, moving nature of the world, watching how things form and un-form according to their interplay with the environment. With this practice we can start to get a conceptual understanding that although we perceive something, there is nothing there other than the play of forces. We have the erroneous belief that there is something with inherent existence. It is this belief that is to be deconstructed through the meditation.

Seeing things as real and being attached to them

Attachment is the quality of impure relative truth, the second and more dense aspect of relative truth. We develop our attachment to something that does not actually exist and then invest it with value according to our own proclivities. So here we are sitting in this meditation hall saying our prayers to Padmasambhava as the manifestation of nothing!! *"Nothing, nothing, please come here and get rid of something!"* It might seem quite mad to be trying to turn all the richness of the world into nothing. However, the fact is that it has always been nothing: form and emptiness, sound and emptiness, everything and emptiness.

The tantric method is to be as devoted as possible to this 'some thing' which is nothing. Ordinarily we take each thing to be something. Padmasambhava, the precious guru, Guru Rinpoche, is the divine apparition, the illusory form who makes contact with our illusory forms so that we can see that our self-identity has always been an illusion. Through merging with him we come to see nothing as something and something as nothing. When you have attachment to something as something you like, such as a nice watch, you will have a similar attachment to something as something when you go to the doctor and he tells you that this lump you were concerned about is cancerous. Then you think, *"Something is something and I don't want this something! Get rid of this something!"*

18

We free ourselves from attachment by developing faith and devotion. The traditional texts say we should have such devotion that the surface of our skin is rippling, the hair stands up on our neck, and tears run from our eyes. We cry out in desperation, *"You, you who are nothing, come and save me from the delusion of something!"* This is the purification of attachment through the application of attachment to nothing. It may sound a strange thing to do but remember that the reason for us doing this practice is to recognise that suffering arises from attachment to delusionally reified nothing. If we can turn the focus of our attachment on to nothing rather than onto something, then nothing, nothingness, emptiness, openness, radiance will become the most empowered 'object' in our world and it will then be able to antidote our attachment to imagined somethings.

To practise this transformation, try to visualise the open clear blue sky. Arising in it is a ball of shining light, or the form of Padmasambhava or any another deity you wish to use. Visualise this as clearly as you can as the manifestation of light in a form which appears to be something but which is actually nothing. The true essence of Padmasambhava is emptiness – this is the dharmakaya nature, infinite emptiness.

Focus on Padmasambhava and recite the mantra, *"OM A HUNG BENZA GURU PEMA SIDDHI HUNG".* Be aware of your own thoughts and feelings. Be aware if you are making this image too strong or weird or distorting it in some way. Try to stay with the visualisation, recite the mantra and relax free of any thoughts and feelings that are covering it over. Do this with devotion. *"Padmasambhava, you are the essence of all the Buddhas. You represent whatever is enlightened in the world. I have total faith in you as the radiance of nothing."*

At the end of doing this, this form comes to the top of my head and dissolves down into a ball of light that goes down through the top of my head into my heart. My body then dissolves as light. During the practice rays of light have been coming from Padmasambhava's three places into me, filling me with light which dissolves all trace of my body as a substantial entity. My body is now a light body. The Guru, as a ball of light, comes into my heart, my body of light dissolves into that ball, so now subject and object have come together. There is just one ball of light. You have the sense of going in and in and just dissolving and then there is nothing...

Gradually, through these rays of light that were coming from Padmasambhava into me, I have gone from being something-as-such into something-as-nothing, into the radiance of light. Then the something which was nothing, the light form, has itself dissolved into nothing, and out of that nothingness something arises – thoughts, feelings images, colour, whatever it is.

It is at this point that we want to recognise that all that arises is the form of Padmasambhava, that is to say, it is something-as-nothing and nothing-as-something. Whatever is arising is actually nothing, just the play of nothing. We don't need to be attached to it or frightened of it; we don't need more of it or less of it, because it is just nothing. It's just play, like clouds in the sky.

After some time you will become aware that your mind is wandering off after some thoughts. This is when you can focus on the thoughts in order to recognise that the nature of all thoughts is ungraspable. By becoming conscious of what distracts you, you can see the ways in which the five poisons are operating through you and the ways in which you are most likely to let them sabotage your ability just to relax and be open.

Gradually the forms that are arising for you manifest in the familiar forms that are around you. At that moment keep the clarity that whatever is arising is nothing as something-ness of nothing. If your experience starts to get a bit solid and you find lots of thoughts are arising that are pulling you back into seeing something as something, you can briefly close your eyes and imagine everything dissolving back down very quickly to nothing, and then just let it arise again. You can repeat that dissolving, arising, dissolving, arising, and keep softening the tendency to turn something-as-play into something-as-something. This is one method for integrating the two truths in our meditation practice.

MIDDLE WAY: AVOIDING EXTREMES

The Buddha's dharma is often referred to as the Middle Way, the path which lies between the polar extremes. The two extremes that the Buddha frequently discusses are the belief that things are truly permanent and last forever, and the belief that things exist only for a moment and leave no trace at all. Each some-thing arises out of nothingness and is itself nothing in the moment when it appears to be something. To see this is to follow the path between the extremes.

Form and emptiness is the way in which these extremes are often expressed. The view of permanence is expressed in the notion of form and the view of annihilation is expressed in the notion of emptiness. Just as we use deities such as Padmasambhava and Tara to help us understand the way in which form and emptiness are present together in one place in one moment, we also use the view of non-duality to understand that the emptiness of the mind is not different from the arising of thoughts in the mind. The central focus of all the meditation practices is to dissolve the belief that objects are strongly real in themselves, and to relax the mind that grasps at these objects as real.

The mind has two main tendencies, to be too tight and to be too loose. The Buddha likened the mind to a stringed instrument. If the string is too tight then the pitch is too high, if the string is too loose then the pitch is too low. You have to tune the instrument. A sitar has strings on the front which are actually played. Behind them are the sympathetic strings which vibrate in resonance with the strings that are played. These sympathetic strings have to be tuned accurately so that they will be able to vibrate in harmony with the main strings that are being played. We could think of our meditation as being like these sympathetic strings. What we have to do is subtly tune ourselves so that we are able to pick up the vibration of what is around us and resonate with that. We don't want to use an intentional egoic energy out in the world. Rather we use the energy of the world to evoke our potential as required.

Too tight

We want to avoid being too tight and rigid. This would take us into the realm of anxiety, of standing back from situations and being cut off from the world by a self-protective withdrawal. We also want to avoid the other extreme of being too loose. We don't want to be chaotic, all over the place with no boundaries, tumbling through life without any direction.

The dzogchen approach to meditation is to observe ourselves in relationship to the world. For example, you may have come here this weekend with some uncertainties about your own dharma practice, your meditation, or about Tibetan Buddhism in general. You have questions but you have not asked them yet and you are wondering whether you will get a chance to ask your question before the weekend is over. You have a very interesting piece of research to do here. How do I sabotage, or block my ability to get my needs met? What do I do in my own head to stop my mouth opening and the words coming out?

This is also part of meditation – watching how mental patternings block our easy play in the world. We may be anxious and in our anxiety we look at the world extremely carefully and see so many opportunities however in the very intensity of seeing the opportunity we are somehow separated from the opportunity and so we cannot make use of it. If you find yourself being like that then it is important to learn how to relax. Relaxation means letting go of attachment to fixed ideas, ideas about ourselves, and ideas about others. We might think that other people are more important than us, that other people are critical of us, that other people are like our mother, our father, our school teachers and so on. All kinds of fearful thoughts stimulated by our past can arise. Their causal circumstances vanished a long time ago yet we continue to be attached to them.

We can spend a lot of money going to therapy to learn how to relax or we can use the Buddha's very cheap and simple method of mindfulness meditation. It is known as shiné (Tib. *Zhi-gNas*) or shamatha (Skt. *Śamatha*). Shiné meditation calms the mind by focusing on something simple such as our breath. Thoughts still arise and we may find them very interesting but we practise not paying attention to them and we just let them go wherever thoughts go off to. Again and again, we return our attention to something so very simple, so very boring: to our breath going in and out. When practising shiné meditation it's very important not to pay attention to thoughts when they arise, as they surely will.

Through this practice, we gradually dissolve our attachment to the thoughts that take us into situations of tightness and restriction. We all suffer from fears such as fear of death, fear of rejection, fear of humiliation, fear of being thought stupid, fear of pain... The Buddha clearly said that all suffering arises from attachment. If we accept this as a working hypothesis, it will help us to directly see that our own attachment to ideas arising in our mind creates these various fears. The fear of abandonment arises from the anxiety that other people won't like me, that they'll reject me, and I will feel lonely and destroyed. Because of this kind of fear people put up with many unhealthy situations they don't like such as oppressive situations at work and oppressive relationships. Such situations shrink our capacity to open to life.

We all know that we were born out of our mother in blood and slime and that when we die our body will rot and smell and be eaten by insects and people will want to get rid of it because dead bodies putrefy. Moreover, when we waken up in the morning we have sticky stuff in our eyes, wax in our ears, snot in our noses, poo up our bums, and we smell sweaty. This is the reality of all human beings. Even the people who might humiliate us, the people we idealise and give power and authority to, these people also will fart and smell and ooze secretions. In the dharma it is considered very helpful to reflect on old age, sickness and death. However much of human culture is designed to disguise the realities of our embodied existence. So it can be helpful when you find yourself getting stuck in a situation where other people, or situations, seem overwhelmingly powerful, to remember that just below the layer of skin of these people, all these things are going on in their body. This imposing person dressed in a suit behind a big desk is just a skin bag of pus.

We can use that awareness to deconstruct our own projected fantasies about what this person can do to us. We can use the classic contemplations of the dharma and the meditation systems of the dharma to deconstruct whatever heavy, tight, rigid assumptions keep us feeling anxious in a world where there seems little room to manoeuvre.

Too loose

On the other extreme we have movements into chaos where we don't really know what is going on at all. Chaos can be depressive or manic. When we get depressed, we become

24

confused. We don't know what to do with our lives. All our thoughts keep returning to the same few topics. Everything is just too much for us and we can't find a way out into the world. We shrink back from others, sinking and sinking and sinking under the weight of thought. It is very common for people to feel that depression is something that is happening to them. They might say, *"I don't want to be depressed, I wish I wasn't depressed, I don't know why this happens to me."* It seems to arrive unexpectedly and take them over.

But if we have been practising a little bit of shiné, we know that this is a lie we tell ourselves. We come to recognise that thoughts come and go and that it is possible to separate the thought from the thinker of the thought. We can observe without involvement. In shiné meditation when we get caught up in something, we simply recognise that this has happened and go back to the breath. Although we got caught up in a thought and fused with it, we know that this is a transient event. We can waken up and return to focused attention on the breath for a while. And then it gets lost again... and then we see what is happening... So it continues.

From the point of view of meditation, the statement *"I am depressed"* arises as the conclusion of a process. The concatenation of various sensations and feelings, including anxiety, hopelessness, heaviness, dread, and confusion is interpreted as an indication that something is wrong with me. Moreover, the name for what is wrong is 'depression'. The term 'depression' is a wrapper which gives shape and substance to the effect, misinterpreted as the cause. Thus, I didn't experience hopelessness because I have depression, but rather 'depression' is the name I give to disparate experiences that I feel oppressed by. Depression becomes the defining mood of my identity and then no matter how hard I try, I cannot think my way back to health. It is our very reliance on thoughts and feelings as vehicles of truth which has trapped us in this restrictive identity.

Therefore, in shiné practice we direct our attention away from the depressive thoughts that are arising and on to the sensation of our breath at our nostrils. The breath is not a thing; it cannot be pinned down and therefore it is an ideal object of focus for our attention. We are resting our attention on the dynamic, thin experience of the sensation generated by the breath at our nostrils. It is easy to slip away on to another appearance, one which generates more interest and a sense that it offers something to adopt or discard.

We are replacing the distracting power of objects which activate our emotions with nebulous objects which will only support our attention if that attention is calm, fine and consistent. Focused attention conserves energy and protects us from the dissipation that comes with being pulled this way and that by the transient pleasures of unstable enticement. When we practise within the view of duality, it is important to adjust our engagement with what is occurring for us. We should aim to adopt what is virtuous and reject what is unvirtuous. We do this with regard to both external situations and activities and internal thoughts, feelings, memories and so on. Habitual patterns are difficult to change because they are triggered and become operational before we are conscious of what is happening. Therefore, the first requirement is to maintain a state of calm mindfulness in the midst of provocations.

How do we become calm when we are already excited? First we have to recognise that, *"I am not excited."* How can it be that I am not excited when clearly I *am* excited? If we take the sensations of excitement to be ourselves, then this confusion of identity will render us powerless. However, if we have practised shiné in quiet peaceful times, we will believe and know out of our own experience that whatever arises passes away. Moreover we will have noticed that if we become attached to what arises, we will get caught up in it and that fusion will continue for some time.

Attention has no content of its own. It is the simple availability to attend to whatever is our chosen focus. This could be sensation at the nostrils, a small image of the Buddha, whatever occurs, or the actual emptiness of the field of appearance. The more we are simply attentive, the less of an agenda we are burdened by. We start to experience a basic freedom when we see that *"I could, but I don't have to."* We are becoming free of the felt necessity that we have to respond. We can simply remain calm and uninvolved. Then we find that our egoic identity is built from identifying with certain aspects of the field of experience. Moreover, when I do not identify with these aspects, nor with any others, I find that I am present as a simple state of attention. I am free of defining content constituting myself and am simply available. And so neither external nor internal arisings can elicit any involvement.

This is the fruit of shiné. We are calm and unruffled, like the depths of the ocean. If we stick with this practice and open our focus to be open unbiased attention to whatever occurs, then we find that the calm depths are unperturbed by the turbulent surface waves. Now we can function in the world without loss of clarity.

However, if this basic calm is not achieved then on the basis of the stupidity of believing that I am real and that, for example a cigarette is real and that the connection between us is very real, there arises desire for this cigarette which can lead to anger towards those who take away my cigarettes, envy of those who still have some cigarettes left, and pride at the fact that I have a little secret stash of cigarettes left just for myself afterwards! In this way, on the basis of cigarettes, the five poisons increase endlessly and we wander in samsara looking for a tobacconist! With the various manifestations of dispersed manic excitement, the important thing is to learn to fix a clear boundary between attention and the objects of attention.

The practice of calm-abiding belongs to the general teachings of the Buddha and are a vital component of the path of renunciation. Without calm and a spirit of renunciation, it is difficult to let go of the many factors which constitute our egoic self. No matter how strong our habits of involvement are, each moment of involvement is a choice. The freedom to choose is, for most of us, achieved through the struggle not to succumb to the familiar. We need to try to identify our habitual patterns of thinking and to recognise that these are constructs. They may appear given, they may appear true, but they are actually just patternings of thoughts. They are impermanent social constructs acting as causes and conditions.

When we practise with a dzogchen view, we start from the basic completion or perfection of everything. There is nothing to improve and so no need to adopt or reject. Thus, when thoughts and feelings arise, we don't pull back and observe the thoughts as if they were something other. We stay present in openness and do not interfere in anyway with whatever is arising, neither analysing, nor accepting, nor rejecting.

We move from a situation of control into one of acceptance and playfulness, of being able to respond. This means that the one who is tuning the string is not outside, but it is as if the string is tuning itself through its own movement.

Sometimes you may be so confused that you can't find the string to tune it! That's why it is useful to have a range of other meditation techniques to help you get in touch with the string and then get back into the practice. The two main things we focus on are firstly the shiné to calm down and increase the ability to stay with the separated observing self, and secondly tantric visualisation with mantra recitation which uses devotion to promote purification and awaken us to non-duality.

Attachment to appearances as if they were real leads to liking and disliking, desire and aversion. There are so many projects to get involved with, so many seemingly important things to do. Life goes by and then we are old and tired. When will we find the time for dharma study and practice? So it is very important to accept that we will die and lose all the opportunities of this life. Our body will turn into food for worms. That is the truth. We imagine that our body is a safe little house that will keep us cosy forever, but this is not true. When we believe that our body is a reliable point of reference and security then we spend all our time and energy making it as comfortable as possible – nice clothes, food and warmth. We live in a culture that avoids facing the fact of death. Many of us have never seen a person dying or a dead body. There can be a lot of emotion around death which obscures the very natural transition that is happening.

Imagine you have booked a package holiday abroad for a week and it turns out that the hotel is horrible. You decide to go straight into town to a furniture shop where you buy a new bed, tables and chairs. Then you go to the decorator's shop and organise for workers to come immediately and paint the room, put up wallpaper and lay down some good carpet. You spend lots of money *"because I am worth it"* and also because *"I have worked very hard all year and I am entitled to stay in a nice place."* At the end of one week you leave to go back home and all your energy, effort and money is gone. This is how ordinary beings spend their time in samsara, going from life to life decorating hotel rooms.

And that's why you have to save up all your good karma and put it down for a mortgage to buy a permanent home in buddha-land.

Teachings given in Frankfurt, 11 March 1995. Edited by Barbara Terris and revised by James Low in 2022.

Love and impermanence

Generally speaking, in western culture we believe in love, and we even believe that another human being can save us. *"Only you. You're the one. When I am with you I feel whole."* For a while. It's a common feeling. *"Without you I'm nothing. You fill me up."* There are many love songs with words like that. This raises the important question 'Who am I?' What is the lack in me, which I seek to fill by finding you? Who are you and how do I imagine you to be? What qualities do you have? We have ideas about ourselves and ideas about the other.

One of the functions of meditation is to bring us close to the actuality of what is manifesting so that in experiencing phenomena as they are, we can see if our idea about a phenomenon actually brings us close to how things are. Usually we think that if we have the name for something and can describe it, then this bring us to what is there. Actually it brings us close to our *idea* of what is there, but not to any reality. We live in a jungle of concepts which do provide illumination of a kind, but the clarification is established inside our belief that the concepts we hold speak about how things are.

When we start to meditate we become aware that our mind is full of thought. We find ourselves caught up in an ongoing commentary about experience: judging, developing opinion, reinforcing our assumptions. The better we notice this the better we see that our view of the world is mediated through, or veiled by, this network of interpreted concepts. It's not that concepts are wrong or bad, it's about applying them in the right place. For example, unless you are a rock star, you probably won't wear sunglasses indoors. If you wear your concepts all of the time, your view of the world might be a bit tinted, which means your relationship to other people will be a bit tinted.

Tibetan buddhism has many styles of practice. They are referred to as vehicles, or ways of travelling to the goal of awakening. Each is organised into view, meditation, behaviour and result. One meditation, from the first vehicle, is saying, *"I'm wandering in confusion. Whenever I sit to meditate, I notice that I easily get distracted. I'm all over the place and so I have to learn to control my mind."* That view is linked to making decisions about behaviour, such as avoiding stimulating circumstances. The aim is to be calm so that I can develop my potential. In some ways it's a path of mastery. The assumption is that if I get rid of all my limitations and develop my full potential then I can become like the Buddha. It's all up to me and if it doesn't go well, then there's no one else I can blame. To follow that kind of dharma path, you have to develop very broad strong shoulders, because you have to carry everything yourself!

There are nine different vehicles and here I will be focusing on dzogchen, the ninth vehicle. 'Dzogchen' means 'the whole' or 'the great completion'. When we sit and meditate we soon notice that our mind is moving. My 'self' then decides that I don't want my mind to move by itself since, after all, I am the boss of my mind. If my hand were to suddenly jump up and grab my ear, I would get quite upset. My hand should behave itself! So, whenever we begin our practice from the position of the ego, we are in an ongoing struggle to get ourself back on track.

The dzogchen view is not to jump into judgement. We simply observe. Lots of things are moving in the mind: hopes, fears, memories, sensations and so on. Things arise and pass. They're there for a while and then they're gone. There are many things in my mind and they are all moving in all different directions. It's going to take a lot of energy to try to control them. What happens if I don't control them? I get angry for a while, I get jealous for a while, I'm sweet and friendly for a while. My moods are not predictable and reliable so why should I expect other people to be reliable?

The mind is not an animal to be tamed. In some of the Buddha's teachings the mind is described as an elephant or a buffalo and it gradually comes under our control. But when we observe what is experienced, there are experiences outside, and sensations inside. This movement doesn't come to an end. That is just how it is. So movement is not seen as the enemy, not seen as something to be constrained and controlled.

When you start with an idea of how you should be or could be, then this idea or image becomes the point that you try to align yourself with. Dictatorships often have public art works of paintings or sculptures of good citizens and good workers. That's because structures of dominance always have a template. Whether the template is in religion, or in politics or your own individual idea, then fitting the template is decisive. If you fit the template you are 'good'; if you don't fit the template you are 'bad'.

From the point of view of dzogchen this kind of framework is stupid, blind, blunt and cruel. It's blind because it doesn't invite you to see. It advises you to see what you're told to see, *"This is what the Buddha is like and if you want to be like the Buddha you have to become like that."* How do you get there? Who is it who is trying to get there? *"Don't worry about that, just try to get there."* You don't know who you are, you don't know how you are, but you do know that you should be somewhere. This is called fascism. Let's not do that. Our interest is to be present with ourselves and let the actuality of existence reveal itself, however it is. The more you start with an image of how it should be, the more you are introducing a prejudice, a pre-disposition, which means that you're trying to become something.

So how can we see in the most simple, neutral way? If you notice there's a lot going in your mind when you practise, you might have the thought that your mind is very disturbed. You can have that sentence with or without mustard! If you apply the mustard – 'My mind is very disturbed! That's clearly wrong, it shouldn't happen!' – then I want to scrape off the mustard. Am I disturbed by my disturbed mind? Well, yes. Sometimes I'm happy and sometimes I'm sad. When I'm happy I'm happy, when I'm sad, I'm sad. I am unreliable, unpredictable, inconsistent, and yet, if I am sad, when I am sad, what else should I be? What's wrong with being sad for a while? I taste happy, I taste sad – different tastes but both are tastes. A painter uses a palate of different colours. If they only used one colour, they might sell their paintings for a few years maybe but after a while people would ask them to extend your range of colours. Some colours you might want to be seen and others you don't want to be seen. We don't want people to know that our colour is envy or jealousy or failure. These colours make us feel bad and we don't want to feel bad. So you can see that any judgement about our situation blinds us to the actuality of our feeling since our tendency is to merge into the feeling or recoil from it.

In meditation texts these two positions are described again and again. Don't merge into what is arising and don't shift away from it. Just be present with it. Whatever is arising is the flavour or the colour that is filling your life at this moment. It's not always going to be like that since all phenomena are impermanent; they arise and pass. If you merge into the feeling it becomes the totality of your experience and it feels as if it is going to last forever. In Buddhism this is called illusion. We take patternings of experience – which are impermanent - and act towards them as if they were an eternal truth: either *it is true and real* or *there's nothing to be done because it's true and real*. In the meditation practice our main focus is to stay present with whatever is arising, while avoiding these two extremes of merging or enforced separation. We will see that our experience is ever-changing, that life is dynamic.

When a baby is born, it's given a name. People come to see it and are told that this is Magda. They may be shown lots of photos of Magda. Look at what Magda can do now! Look how Magda lifts a spoon! Look at Magda taking her first step! Magda exists. Does Magda exist in Magda? The mother sees Magda, but who is there? The baby is not intrinsically Magda. It's not produced in a factory with the name of the product stamped on the forehead. The name is a convention. We happen to call this child Magda, but it could have been called many other names. Due to causes and conditions – maybe a saint's day or some family tradition – it was named Magda and when we say that name, we know who we mean. She is Magda; we refer to her with that name. Someone is there. First a non-walking Magda, then a walking Magda, then a walking and talking Magda. Is walking and talking Magda the same as non-walking Magda? The face of a baby at three months and at three years is very different. The sensory and motor skills are changing, the expressive range of emotions is changing. The use of language is developing. Is this still the same person? Yes! How do we know? *"Because it's Magda!"* The truth of Magda is the name. The most enduring factor in Magda's life is the name. Since you've been born you have been thousands of people but generally the name continues. The name is abstract, conventional, assigned.

Is a signifier what it signifies? No. When we say 'Magda' and we look at the girl are we describing this form, this phenomenon, or are we describing my idea about Magda? *"No, Magda, don't behave like that. Be the proper little Magda that I know so I can love you, because if you are your own Magda then you became a delinquent Magda – and you know how long the waiting list is for child therapy – so please fit in. Be the Magda that I love and that I know you really are."* 'Magda' is an idea just as 'myself' is an idea.

35

Each of us exists in two different planes. The first is the unfolding of our potential moment by moment in conversation with circumstances. How we manifest, how we show ourself depends in who we are talking to and where we are. If you were in a Catholic church you would not sit yourself on the floor. If you were in a Buddhist temple you would sit yourself on the floor. It is a situational thing; your body takes on this particular posture according to the idea of where you are. When you are not being a buddhist you won't be sitting on the floor. You have a mental frame and an environmental frame and you find yourself sitting on a cushion on the floor. As you enter a room, you look around and see where other people are sitting; your relation with this field of experience reins your body into a particularly position. You are co-emerging with the environment.

Each of us is here for all kind of reasons. We are doing the activity of being here together according to the co-arising of circumstances. I am here talking with you about buddhism because I have been involved in this for many years. There is no inherent buddhism in me. I've been swimming in the ocean of buddhism or dharma for a long time, so what I can share with you are streaming pathways that arise through me while I am with you. There is not a box inside me labelled 'Buddhist James' that I keep closed when I go to the supermarket. I don't need to be 'Buddhist James' to buy potatoes. I need to be 'James with some money in my pocket' to buy potatoes. But if I am going to be here talking with you I need to be 'Buddhist James'. Is that a particular identity inside me or does it arise through me being here with you? What is arising is something which belongs to all of us.

In buddhism this is called dependent co-origination: on the basis of this, that arises. On the basis of me studying Tibetan and so on, certain things can arise to this life stream which I manifest at the moment. After some time, as I get older, I probably won't do this the same way or as much. Due to the fact of not being dead yet, I am here. I will be dead. When? I don't know. We don't know when we are going to die. How can we plan for our life if we don't know when we are going to die? We have no idea of the shape of our existence. We don't know what thought is going to arise in our mind in the next moment, we don't know what sensation is going to arise in our body. We know a lot of things, but we don't know much. The important things we don't know. The reason we don't know them is because they are unknowable.

I am a stream of experience yet I imagine that there is a continuity to 'I, me, myself'. *"As far as I can remember I have always been me."* That is a sentence we can all say. It seems a meaningful thing to say. It seems to be obviously true. *I am me and not you.* I've always been me. I was not you yesterday and me today. You have always been you as far as I know, but I definitively have always been me. However, when I look for the ingredients of me – my beliefs: they have changed a bit – my memories: they have changed a lot – my plans: always changing – my thoughts, feelings, sensations: always changing. We also are relational in our value. My buddhist knowledge can be of some use now to you, but when I apply for a job it will not be important to an employer. We believe that this is important. Whether it is important or not is our mental activity.

We have the chance to stay immersed inside our dream time or become curious: where is the dreamer? Who is the one that believes that I am me? We have the content of our mind: memories, plans, everything we know, arising and shifting in endless permutation. We are aware of something occurring. The continuity of this clarity about been alive seems to be generated by the content of our mind. Am I present because I myself is the one that is present? Or is presence an illuminating quality which shows me being here? These are not philosophical questions. These are ontological questions about the nature of our being. This is the most intimate sense of ourselves we can have. When I tell myself a reassuring story about my existence am I enlivening the feeling tone of my life or I am singing a lullaby putting myself to sleep?

We want to look at the fixed sense that we have of ourselves and of the people we love and get involved with. Can love be eased out of attachment towards a more open appreciation? Very often if we appreciate something we want to get it. *"You are special so I want you with me. If I add you on to my life I'm going to improve."* But that only works if I see the other as an apprehendable object and because I can think of myself as an apprehendable object. Can we have a clarity which is non-conceptual, so that instead of simply building up images and storylines of who we are, we can direct fresh presence experience to the illumination of what we take to be ourselves and others.

There are the many different approaches in buddhism. Many of them are concerned with the path to awakening, going from here to there. In dzogchen we want to go from here to here. We are already here but not quite here. We are not quite where we are because we don't quite see it. In the traditional example, when you look at a mirror you see reflections. The reflections are in the mirror. They are how the mirror shows itself but are not the mirror itself. In the same way, our mind shows itself as thoughts, feelings, memories, plans and so on. This is the radiant display of our mind. This is the flow of experience.

Very often we are not aware of this because we sit inside a separation or a division: *"I am me here, I am looking at you there. You are not me, I am not you."* Our starting point is often separation, isolation, autonomy, individuality. But of course if I say *"I am here, you are there"*, that is a proposition, that is a statement, it is a sequence of concepts: that there is an *I* which is here, that there is a *you* which is there. We can only have this kind of discourse because of the arising of thoughts mediated through language. These are experiences. We experience talking and listening, moving and sitting. This is what is revealed.

What is the basis of the revelation? Clearly, a mirror has a clarity which a piece of wall doesn't have. When you look at the wall, you see the wall. When you look at the mirror you see the reflection, which is not the reflection *of* the mirror but is the reflection *because* of the mirror. That is to say, the mirror shows itself through displaying what is not itself. Although a particular reflection is not the truth of the mirror – because the mirror has the capacity to show many different reflections – the reflection is inseparable from the mirror. They are not the same. They are not one thing, but neither are two things because there is no way to extract the reflection from the mirror. The mirror and the reflection are non-dual, not two. Not one, not two, but in the middle.

In the same way, we have a mind that is our awareness, or the basic illumination capacity that is how we know anything is there. Just as the mirror reveals the reflection, so the mind reveals thoughts, memories, plans and so on. It also reveals motorcars, factories, houses, trees, plants. Every kind of experience we have is revealed through our mind. Now, a mirror is able to show many different reflections because of two main factors: one is that no reflection defines the mirror itself, and secondly, reflections arise as co-emergent with an article placed in front of the mirror. One could say that the potential of the mirror is evoked by placing the object in front of it.

The potential of the mirror is not like the potential of a seed we may plant in the garden. The seed is a potential. When it is put in the earth, watered, protected from frost and gets some sunlight, it starts to germinate and you get the plant. That is to say, the plant has a specific cause which was the seed from which it manifested. But the mirror doesn't have little packages of seeds at the back. It doesn't have a particular capacity for showing a tree or a car. Its potential is not the potential of *something.* It's the potential of the openness, or the lack of predetermination in the mirror which allows these different reflections to arise.

It is the same with your mind. Since you are born you have had many experiences that you understand as *my* experiences: *"I have these experiences because I am me."* This is the egocentric story we can tell ourselves: *"I am the maker of my experiences",* but a little enquiry will indicate that this is false because if we look, life happens through us, to us, with us. I find myself being like this. I am aware of myself in the moment of the revelation of myself. *This is to say, 'I, me, myself' is an aspect of disclosure, not an aspect of causation.*

There is a lot of writing nowadays about the self as a performativity, but in fact ourselves is part of the performance. When we are walking, walking movement is me walking. *"I am walking"* is a commentary, a conclusion and an act of colonialism. Walking is going on. Who is walking? Walking is walking. *"No, no, no, no, I am walking!"* – but how do you do this? Is there a little puppeteer inside me pulling all the strings to make a walking me? What is the agency of walking? Imagine if every movement you made with your body was a conscious one which you had to prepare for before you did it. That would not be very nice. You would be so preoccupied with all the micro instructions: *"Elbow down, no too far, up again..."* You find yourself co-emerging with the situation.

You can see it directly by yourself. This is the meaning of the term *non-dual.* My life is *with*, I am always *with*. I am with the sit; if I get up I am standing with my feet; if I step down I am with the movement of my hips as I put one leg at a lower level than another. *My body is always dancing with the shape of the environment.* Always. If you go to a Chinese restaurant and get chopsticks your relationship with eating is very different from having knife and fork. There is a different kind of finesse.

According to the chopstick, my hands take on a particular formation. Different patterns of muscles are being employed. You may say, *"I am using the chopsticks"*, but it is the chopsticks that are causing my hand to take that particular formation. You have to do what the chopstick says. If you haven't been to a Chinese restaurant for a while you forget how to hold them however after some time you can even pick up a single grain of rice with your chopsticks. You are trusting the connectivity between the grain of rice and these two sticks in your hand. You are collaborating with the chopsticks. So, who is in charge?

Let's return to the image of the mirror. The indeterminacy of what the mirror itself is, is the basis of its capacity to show many different images. Because the mirror is ungraspable, there is no identifiable essence to the mirror. This indicates that there is no restriction on the potential of the mirror. If we look at the wall, there is some potential for fascination in that wall. If you were locked in a prison cell you might be able to get many hours of fascination from the marks on wall. If someone had made a painting on the wall the painting would direct our gaze more than random marks on the wall. As we look at the painting, our eyes move around tracking colours, combinations, contrasts and so on. We are participating in the shaping of the formation of the image. We are helping to give the painting an identity. If we were to see the painting in the gallery it would have a title and a frame which would help to establish its validity.

The mind is not like a painting. The mind is showing more and more and more. However, you also have the patterning of what you take to be your identity: your likes, your dislikes, what you are drawn towards, what you hold back from. There is a shape to you and we often take this shape as being somehow determined by myself. *This is how I am. This is what I like to eat and this is what I don't like to eat.* On the basis of choice – which is always determining a line between included and excluded – we establish the periphery and the contouring of ourselves. This is a description of your potential. Identity, especially anxiously maintained identity, becomes a foreclosure on accessing the potential of the mind.

This is why once you have established your basic competences in life, not knowing is better than knowing. Not knowing dissolves the boundaries of identity to open it to fresh input from potential. If you have a highly formulated identity, for example if you have been imprisoned for ten years, or you've been in the army for ten years, when you leave these settings it is often very difficult because the choreography demanded by closed institutions is very precise. Outside in the big world there is a lot more freedom. In prison you know how you must behave. If you go out and walk in the streets here in Warsaw, you don't necessarily know how you should behave. You could sing, hop and walk backwards and you wouldn't be arrested. You might be embarrassed! That could be a very good way to test how anxiously contained your identity is.

Moment by moment our life is an effulgence, a radiance of experience, some of which looks object and some of which looks subject. That is to say, experience – the content of my mind, what is revealed in, through and as the mind – is ever-changing, inseparable from the mind but not the same as the mind or definitive of the mind. Let's say that I am habitually quite angry, you may then say that James is an angry person. That anger is an ongoing trait or flavour or colouration of the person who is known as James. But could I say *"my mind is angry?"* What would that mean? If you put something which you find disgusting in front of a mirror would you say that it is a horrible mirror. It may be a horrible reflection, but it doesn't determine the mirror. *"I am angry."* That is the reflection, that's the showing, that's the display. If you impute from it some essence of James, you collapse the openness of the potential of awareness into a self that is identifiable as having fixed enduring characteristics.

That is a key point to investigate for yourself. For example, you are talking with a friend about some problem: *"I don't know, I feel so stupid, why did I do that?"* You seem to be establishing something about yourself, but you are speaking with someone, you are relating, you are creating a moment of connectivity with that other person. It is an intimate moment because something is being revealed that might otherwise be concealed. But what is being revealed? *"I feel so stupid, how could I be so stupid, I am really stupid."* Who is the one who is stupid? The conversation carries on and soon you are laughing together; now you are feeling happy. Before you were self-blaming. What has happened to the one who felt really stupid? Now your friend asks you for some advice, and you respond with something quite wise. Surely there is a contradiction, how can you be really stupid and also really wise as one and the same person?

Novels and dramas often show a person with inner conflicts. The flawed hero is the anti-hero. A lot of literary criticism explores that theme. The novelist creates a complex character, with nuances, a polyphony. It is a very helpful idea because so many voices arise as us, not just ten or a thousand, we have access to millions of voices. Millions of different combinations of facial expressions, gestures, repetitive speech and so on. The permutations are infinite.

When we relax we show more of ourselves. When we go for a job interview we have a more intentional presentation of ourself. What we call our ego self is a patterning arising moment by moment with circumstances. It is not guaranteed or established or certified by any enduring self-essence. This is amazing. I am emergent in a situation and this emergence is arising from the connectivity of the field whose ground or basis cannot be caught. To put that in formal buddhist language, *the ground of everything is emptiness.* It is unsubstantial. It doesn't mean that there is nothing at all because this emptiness is the openness of what is yet to be shown.

Children play together, at work you work with colleagues even if they are not in the same room. We are always in intercourse, in interplay. Just as in the ocean the wave has a crest and a depth, up and down, up and down, when you are having a conversation with someone they speak you listen, then you speak, they listen. Like waves going up and down, expressing, receiving. You get up in the morning, you look out of the window, you see how the weather is and then you decide what coat you need to wear. There is fashion of course, but there is also weather. If you are eighteen you might not mind being cold but as you get older it feels better to be warm. In that way you are in ceaseless conversation with factors. Weather, age, health, confidence in your sexuality or not, so many factors could occur on how you present yourself. *I decided to wear my blue sweater.* What does that mean? A thought arose in my mind: *this sweater is warm* and I followed the thought. Did I make the thought? No. I caught the thought. Or did the thought catch me? In any case, now I am wearing the blue sweater. Again and again, start to see how your mind is operating.

Buddhism identifies three stages of practice: hearing, reflecting and meditating. When reflecting, we can, for example, look at how we hold the spoon when we are eating our soup. If you don't collaborate with the spoon, the soup will go on your clothes. The spoon has a shape and if you don't get the angle right it won't hold the soup. Just observe how you are picking up the spoon. You put the spoon in the soup and in the soup there are some vegetables that hang on the edge of the spoon. Will they fall off or not? It is very immediate. Maybe you have to put the spoon back in the soup and take fewer vegetables. Moment by moment our existence is very precise because there is a conjunction of circumstances coming together. Not me over the world, not the world over me but a collaborative emergence. I am revealed to myself through my participation.

We now have a sense of the particularity of the moment, this particular expression arising within a field that is open, which contains self and other. What is the field resting on? What is the ground or the base of the experience? We can call it the mind but that is just a word. If you stay present, there is a showing. Who sees the showing? We call it the mind or awareness. We are here together in this space; each of us has a particular perception because of where we are sitting and what is opening up in front of our gaze. We can interpret what is going on, we can describe to ourself what is going on, but prior to that, there is this. The commentary comes after the fact of the showing.

THE SHOWING IS INTRINSIC, THE INTERPRETATION IS CONTINGENT

Normally we have a duality of showing and shown but when we look at the mirror the show-er of the reflection is the mirror. What is showing is the reflection but are they two different things? Can you take some scissors and cut between them? What shows and what is shown are inseparable. In the same way, here in this room everything is revealed. On top of that showing you can run your own particular identifications, commentaries, likes and dislikes and so on. But before the mind moves, before these formulations occur, there is *this*. Each moment is *this*. Then you can make sense of it – but what is *this*? All comes together.

When you think about it you might conceptualise, *"I am inside my body looking out at you."* That is a story, an interpretation. However if I stay with the immediacy, feeling my hands on my knees, the hardness of the chair I am sitting on, the slight tension in my shoulder, seeing all of what it is in front of me: red blanket, man, woman, chair and so on. That is already halfway to an interpretation. I don't see a man and a woman. I see shape and colour. The interpretation 'man and woman' comes after what is here. The field discloses itself as light and sound. Within that, the movements of interpretation arise indicating a particular kind of meaning to the pattern.

The showing was intrinsic, the interpretation is contingent. As soon as you go into the particularity of the people you see in the room, you have liking and not liking. Some people may look threatening or boring or sexually interesting; there is some kind of charge or energetic vitality in what you encounter. Before that there was just *this.* Undifferentiated light and colour. Undifferentiated in the sense that although there are different colours it's all at once. All at once. Immediate. Not mediated, not passing through some process. The processing comes after.

From the point of view of dzogchen these are the three aspects of our mind. Mind is open empty; if you look for the mind you can't find it. However it is not a dull empty. It's an openness which allows everything just as the indeterminacy of the mirror allows every possible reflection. This openness is uncontaminated.

Maybe you have had this experience? It can be very annoying if you are angry with somebody and you are really trying to say something important and serious to them but they respond in a way that makes you laugh. *"Why am I laughing? I am pissed off with you! Stop making me laugh! This is really annoying."* It is important to see that we can be taken out of ourselves quite easily and that is because there is not a self to begin with. Our relatedness is ceaselessly transforming according to circumstances. That is to say, *self-ing* is a showing. None of us here has a fixed self. We have many selves or many potential selves. They are non-definitive.

The empty open ground of the mind is never determined or marked or shaped by anything which has occurred. This is referred to as *kadag* (Tib. *Ka Dag*), primordial purity. It's an unchanging, indestructible purity. The capacity of the mirror to show reflections is not altered by any particularly horrible reflection. If you were to take the mirror away from your bedroom and hang it in an abattoir for a whole day in front of lots of animals having their throats cut and so on, then when you came to collect it at the end the day would you have to take the poor mirror to a doctor? Would the mirror be very upset? No. The ego self is very concerned with good, bad, right, wrong. The openness of the mind is not. It is indifferent. Mind is just open. It sees everything. Everything is revealed.

Dzogchen meditation texts use the term *rang bab* (Tib. *Rang Babs*) free fall, like a waterfall tumbling down a hill. When you are sitting in the practice let the mind just come however it comes. Don't try to channel it or edit it or improve it. This doesn't mean that you are going to act out your worst tendencies, rather, it is an encouragement to release the anxiety which interrupts the immediacy, the spontaneity, the intuitive connectivity of how we manifest.

Let's now do some practice. Make yourself comfortable. There is nothing in particular to focus on; the focus of our practice is whatever occurs. We relax, open, open and allow whatever comes to come. The key thing is not to merge into the moment and try to hang on to it. If you don't like whatever is arising, don't try to push it away. Remember the example of the mirror – no reflection damages the mirror. No thought or feeling or memory damages the mind. When you realise that, any need to edit experience ceases.

We will do this kind of sitting again and again for short periods of time. At first when you do this practice it may seems strange, a bit pointless and meaningless. When you have that experience it is an indication that you are tilting over to your ego self that wants to know what is going on.

TWO PATHS

It is important to know the difference between clarity and knowledge. In this context, clarity is the basic facticity of what is occurring. Just *this*. What it is, what it means, is something you are introducing into what is occurring. You are selecting and editing and organising from this field of experience something that makes sense to you. So you are employing your interpretative matrix as the validator of truth.

Here we have a crossroad. Two pathways: one is to stay open and relaxed with whatever comes, even if it seems mad or stupid or meaningless. See it almost like a dream. Dreams are often very strange. Patterns arise and go. If you stay with non-intervention you start to see this is the intrinsic lucidity of the mind, this is the mind's way of showing. Because it is not *my* mind, it doesn't have *me* as the central focus. The mind is open, ungraspable, and not a personal possession. Like the mirror it shows hospitality to whatever is occurring. This basic hospitality of the mind is very important because it allows the unimpeded clarity to show itself. Otherwise, if you apply your own frame of reference to this clarity it may not make much sense because you are trying to pull experience back into the familiar constructs that reassure you that you know what is going on. The key thing is to just relax, be open and be with whatever it is.

Buddhism describes six different realms of existence. We can and have been born in each and every one of these realms. The culture we are currently living in may not be the culture we are reborn in. If you are reborn as a woman in Afghanistan, you would be accustomed to wearing a burka. Our values, who we take ourselves to be, is created in this historical moment. The political scenario could change very easily and people who have found freedom may find themselves back in a box. Who is keeping us safe? We are hanging on threads all the time. When we see this, we realise that this construct of ego identity – of me knowing who I am and how I want to live and what I want to do – we realise it is all theatre.

What is the ground of my being? If we take it to be a socio-political-economic construct – that due to the actions of many people over many lifetimes we find ourselves in a culture which at the moment allows certain freedoms and makes certain demands – you can see that this is not firmly established. That is why buddhist texts say that you can have a human life now but in the next life, who knows where you will be. If your sense of yourself is as an identity, a construct, a narrative story line, then it is dependent on all these factors staying in place. When they shift....it's very different.

Buddhism is concerned to go beneath and beyond the limitation of our personal identity, to see that awareness – the clarity which illuminates every moment of our existence – is not a construct, is not an aspect of our personality, is not something generated by brain chemistry. It is the intrinsic light of the mind. When we rest in that, we find an indestructible refuge that is unchanging; it is the clarity of the openness of the mind. The energy of the mind, the potential of the mind, shows many different patterns. None of them is stable. None of them has a true essence. What you take yourself to be is the interplay of your potential within this energetic field.

You can experience that for yourself. For example, look at how you make choices. A choice could be quite neutral such as, *"Oh, I'll eat that"* or it could be *"Oh! I'd really like to eat that."* or *"Yuck I would never eat that."* It is good when you notice a strong reaction to the object. When you decide that something is good, it is because you like it. The goodness of the object is in your liking of the object. If the object were inherently good everyone would like it but they don't. Although you think that the goodness is in the object it is actually in the mind. When you stop projecting values onto the objects of the world, then you see the simple clarity of everything.

When the mind is forgetful of its own ground it arises as ignorance and is permanently involved in selecting, attributing value and so on. This is mental activity. When you relax the mind and don't project meaning out onto the field, the field starts to show itself. This also is something that you can start observing for yourself: how busy you are judging, assuming, defining. The more you define the object the more you define yourself, and the more you define yourself the more you cut yourself off from your open potential and get limited in a very narrow bandwidth.

STUPIDITY

From the buddhist point of view our problems arise because we have adopted a central point of reference in the self. For example, in this room the ceiling is held up by pillars and we can say that the pillars are strong and hard. We know that because if we push them or punch them they are stronger and harder than we are. So my embodiment becomes the checking framework for the qualities of the pillars. The pillar is not hard for some machines. The hardness of the pillar is relational. If the time comes to knock down this building it won't take long because they will use machines which are much stronger than the concrete. So, the pillars are hard and strong relative to my human body but not to the steel tip of the destroying machine.

Knowing this helps us to see that whenever we make a statement about anything, it has always got a missing part. The soup was good *for me.* If I was an insect and flew into the hot soup, the soup would be my death. Not so good. So, the soup is good *for me. For me. For me.*

This is not to emphasise that I am an important person but merely to point out that all experience includes me. I don't have access to objective truth. My world is irreducibly subjective. Subject and object arise together. As I participate in the world, the world is revealed to me through my participation. So, if I am hungry the food is likely to taste better. The world is flavoured. The colours of the world, the moods of the world are revealed through how our experience arises for us. This unique specificity of *my* flavours is *my* existence. This is why if you want to understand another human being you have to spend a lot of time with them. If you don't do that you just put them in a category.

Here in Warsaw I am staying in a flat with several cats. I don't know about cats, I just think "cats", but the owner can explain about their psychology, how this one is shy and this one does this and that other does that. Because of her loving eye towards the cats, the different qualities of this cats are revealed. Farmers know that their different cows have different characters, different qualities and different modes. When I see a cow in a field, the cow is just a cow. This is my stupidity. It is enough for me to say, *"It's a cow"* and put it in its box. Because I know it is a cow and I know that I am not very interested in cows, my curiosity ends here.

In buddhism this is what is meant by stupidity. Buddhism talks of the five poisons. The first one is this kind of mental obscuration that functions as an assumption. 'A cow is a cow.' This is my obscuration. If I were interested in the cow, I'd watch how it walks, how it breathes, how it is relates to the other animals. Most cows don't mind having sheep in the field but some cows are not so happy. It makes a big difference, but not for me; it is just a cow. Once you start observing your own mind you see how you make yourself stupid in relation to the world. The world shows itself as a richly textured experience, full of detail, but when you put it into a little box and you stop looking.

In this context, stupidity means falling asleep in the concept. If I know that this animal in the field is a cow, I am satisfied that I know what it is. Maybe I don't know anything about cows but if I know it is a cow, that is enough. The label obscures the specificity of the individual animal so that we do not need to attend to the details of its life.

Projecting names onto objects make us blind. In Gonpo Wangyal's text he says that everything we see, everything we would ever encounter, whether living or not living, absolutely everything is simply a name put by our mind. There is no inherent existence in any phenomena. We have the potential of what is arising as shape and colour, then the concept allows us to add adjectives and adverbs and do all kind of associations, but it is *your* mind. What you encounter is the movement of *your* own mind.

WHAT AND HOW WE LOVE

To see things as they are is the heart of buddhism. To see people as they are, warts and all. It is not an insult to people to observe that they have some bad qualities; we all have limitations. If you are honest about the patterns and limitations of the people you encounter then you can work with them, but if you deny the limitation – if you want to pretend to yourself that this person is other than what it is right in front of you – then you are deluded. This is the relational form that Gonpo Wangyal speaks about. Everything you see is only a name put by your own mind, therefore you just have to really see what is the relation between the name and the form which is there. If you take the name to mean what you believe the name indicates, then is difficult to see the actual phenomenon. The phenomenon is what is showed.

Sometimes women in my therapy practice talk about their partners. If I ask what their impression was on their first date, they say something like *"Oh I didn't much like him, but then as we went talking, I though well... maybe there could be something here."* So you were seducing yourself and once you were seduced by yourself it was very easy for him to seduce you? Your guts said *"No"* but then you thought, *"Oh well, I've nothing to do this weekend, so why not give him a chance."* Then thoughts start going around and around, you self-hypnotise and you become convinced that he is who you think he is, that your thoughts have got direct contact with the truth of this person. In fact, your thoughts have covered this person with your projections.

This is why relationships between people are often very difficult: we imagine and project rather than check out. Your own mind is always part of your experience, you are not experiencing the objective truth of what is there. What arises for you is your experience of this building, this tree, this flower. This person is my imagination of this person. The *you* that I encounter is 'you for me' and you are not only 'you for me', you are 'you for you', you for your mother, for your boss, for your friends. Each of these people gets a different you.

On the basis of this partial perception, which has already been wrapped in your hopes, fears and assumption, you think you've really seen the person. *"I know you don't like him but I see something different in him, he is really nice when you get to know him."* Of course, when you get to know someone you are not exactly getting to know them, you are getting to know your image of who you think they are. We don't love other people; we love images of other people as created in our mind. That is very strange.

Who are you? Who I think you are. Even if you tell me who you are, I would only hear that in terms of how I can hear. Which is to say, if I hear what you are saying, it is not that I am a piece of paper that is having something written on it. I hear what you are saying with *my* ears. My dishonest twisty editing ears. My selective ears. The purpose of this is to ask you to investigate whether you really have objective access to the world? Because if you don't have objective access, if you only have subjective access and your subjectivity is very cloudy, then you are lost in the forest and granny's house is far away. Night is coming, wolves are howling, *"Oh, this is a nice guy, he is really cute." "Oh, Little Red Riding Hood!"* This is what is meant by reflection: seeing how you cheat yourself. This is not an insult; it is an invitation to start to free yourself from the burden of assumptions.

Assumptions can be personal and they can be national. It seems that nowadays there is a return of nationalism: my country, right or wrong. My country is called Great Britain, 'great' as in big, but we also think of it as 'great' as in 'very good'. However historically it has not been very good and like most European countries we are discovering many skeletons in the cupboard, things we cover up, things we don't want to know. From the buddhist point of view is useful to reflect and see that the constructive factors which give rise to identity are often not very healthy. So how are we going to be honest? By getting access to that which is not conditioned by thought, the mind itself.

FIVE QUESTIONS TO POSE ABOUT THE MIND

What is the mind? Is the mind something similar to all the other things I know? If we look around this room we see that everything has a shape, a colour and a size. If we go outside and walk in the streets we see the same, everything has shape, colour and size. So the **first question** is: does your mind have shape and colour? The **second question** is: does your mind have size? Everything in this room has come from somewhere, everything in this room is situated somewhere. We are all located somewhere. When we go outside everything is in its place: the bird is in the sky, the car is on the road, the car has come from some place, the bird has come from an egg. The **third question** is: where does the mind comes from? Does it come from anywhere? Everything is somewhere, rests somewhere, seems to stay somewhere even if only for a short time. The **fourth question** is: where does your mind rest? Is your mind inside your body? You've been told that your mind is inside your head, in your brain. This is an idea. What is the truth of this idea? Who is having the idea? The mind reveals the idea. I know that in my mind is arising the thought that my mind is in my brain. Where is this awareness that reveals the thought? The **fifth question** is: where does the mind go? Everything goes some place. The day goes into the evening, the rubbish is collected... does the mind go somewhere?

These are the five questions by which we can investigate if the mind is a thing like every other thing. Can we catch the mind? Can we categorise it? Can we see it as having defining features? If the mind is not like that, and the mind is not caught, is not a thing, then grasping cannot catch the mind. We grasp at things and the things we grasp at are concepts. When you go outside onto the street you'll see a car. It is obvious to you that you see a car; the concept 'car' and the object are married together. The concept 'car' is linked with language since different languages have different words for car. 'Car' is a conventional term. What is actually there? Some people think cars are polluting the environment, other people think they are very useful. What you call a car is revealed through interpretation. If you don't apply a concept to the car, what is there? How would you describe it?

To describe something is to pull it into concept, but the shape is there even before the concept. You don't have to believe what I am saying, it is just a suggestion, you can investigate for yourself. There would not be 'car' without your mind doing 'car'. When a fly lands on a car, it is not landing on a car; when a bird shits on a car, it's not shitting on a car, not for the bird. How much longer are you going to be a human being? Maybe fifty years if you are young or lucky. For many people it is less. Another twenty, ten, five? After that, you won't be looking with human eyes. It is a different world. It is amazing. If you were a cat, would you like cars? Cars are very useful for cats because they hide under them looking for small spaces where other people can't see them. If you start walking through the world as a cat it would be completely different. This is a basic dzogchen practice: spend the day as a cat, for example. Then the colours and shapes of the world are reconstituted according to cat-ness, flies become very interesting because you are a cat. Cars are interesting because you are a human, and you are a human for a while. As a human, this is how it comes together, it doesn't come together like this for a cat.

There is not inherent truth in the object; there is not inherent existence in the object. If you watch a TV programme about elephants you'll be amazed at how they operate together as big families; they seem so amazing. While you are watching this on the television someone in Africa with a chainsaw is cutting the tusks off a living elephant. How is this possible? Because they look at the elephant and they see money; we look at the elephant and we see something different. The truth is not out there, because if everybody feels what I feel about the elephants they wouldn't be stealing their tusks and selling them. It is relative, which is why dharma practice usually begins with taking refuge. Because when you come out from behind the veil of your assumptions, samsara is a very scary place.

On the level of manifestation everything is relative, which is why we apply these five questions. We want to see if the mind itself is relative. Is it shifted by the emergence of other phenomena? So we sit for a while with these questions. We are here. This is the revelation of our awareness. We are present and this presence seems to be self-illuminated by the brightness of our mind which reveals whatever is occurring. Where is this? Is it resting in some place? Is it inside the body, outside the body? Above the body, below the body? In another planet? Where is it? We are here. Mind is here. When you are investigating these questions you may get a little bit distracted or sleepy. Don't get lost in that. If you need, take a big breath and slowly breathe out to energise yourself a little.

They main thing is not to go into thought stimulation. We are very biased towards relying on thoughts. Our tendency is to trust thoughts, but from the point of view of this practice the thought is the child. The child is the display of the mother; it comes out of the mother. The mother always knows more about the child than the child knows about the mother. Awareness is open; the thought is a formation which is arising and passing. It is unrealistic to think that child-thought is going to tell you about the mother. Stay with the mother, with mind itself. Your mind is here.

Don't confuse the mind and the content of the mind. The mind doesn't move, the content of the mind is always moving. When you are enquiring about these five questions some propositions arise for you and they seem to be true. Just stay with them. If it's the child, it will be in movement and it will vanish. The mind doesn't move. The mirror doesn't move, the reflections move in the mirror. Does the mind go anywhere? If your mind really vanishes you would have no experience at all. Something is occurring. The mind is here. It is going away? You can return to these five thoughts again and again. You can find many discussions about these five questions in dzogchen texts. They talk about the nature of the mind and how the mind is.

With these five questions you can get very close to yourself in the moment of being here. The mind is present; it shows its presence as your presence. Who is the one who is here? Is it a who, is it a what? Is to be present to be present as someone? We all know how to be here as ourselves: I am me, in my body, with my thoughts, my memories... that's the familiar way in which we weave together the shaping of our identity. But identity is movement, it is activity. If you don't *do* then you won't get the identity. The mind is not doing anything, in the same way as the mirror is not doing anything. The mirror doesn't get tired, it doesn't get worn out by showing lots of reflections. The mind doesn't worn out because it is not working to show; it is just showing. Illumination is how the mind is. Inherently bright.

This is your mind; it is not the Buddha's mind somewhere else. So if you sit down and you fill tired or a little heavy, this is an experience arising. If you go to the theatre and the lights don't work it's not much of a show. No matter how good the dancers are, you have to be able to see them. Likewise feeling dull and heavy and stupid is the play of your mind. Put the lights on. You know you feel dull and heavy and stupid, but if you merge into the arising feeling of being oh-so-tired then you are blinding yourself to the fact that tired is an experience that is emerging. It wasn't there before; it arose due to circumstances and after a while it will vanish. It is not who you really are.

So, in that very moment when feeling arises, whatever it is – happy or sad, expansive or contractive – don't merge with it; don't stand apart from it, just be present with it in the way that the mirror is present with the reflection. At first these instructions may not mean very much, but if you spend some time getting to know how you are – not *what* you are but *how* you are – you will see that the clarity of the mind is a constant display of movement.

DEFINING OTHERS AND BEING DEFINED BY OTHERS

The more we experience ourselves as an unfolding process and see how there is no fixed essence or substance to ourselves, the more we see that the same applies to other people. People are not things, they are not discreet entities, despite the fact that when we notice people we 'clock' their physical shape and how they stand and move in the environment so clearly that they seem to be separated from it.

We are certainly not in a fixed location in the environment, like a tree or a lamppost, yet none the less, we are always in the environment, we are always somewhere. Our somewhere-ness is part of how we show in our different forms, our different moods of closeness or distance. We are dynamic energetic forms moving in a field of energy. You can't 'get' other people; they are not commodities, even though some may be trafficked for sexual purposes, for cheap labour and so on.

There are many subtle forms of slavery. To enslave someone is to limit their freedom. The first thing that you need to do is to collapse their dignity. In the old days when there were public slave markets the slaves were often displayed naked; they had no way to hide. Everyone else was clothed and they were naked. From observing family structures, we know that often when the parents are very invasive and judgemental the child feels exposed, that they have nowhere to hide and they can collapse inside. When you collapse inside, the heart sinks and the spine becomes weak. The rigidity of the skeleton is not in dialogue with the wonderful, soft pliable nature of muscle and skin. If you become too plastic as a person you become moulded by circumstances. So, such children often get bullied when they go to school. They have gone under the power of the idea that somebody else is able to define them.

Usually in that kind of structure what people are saying to you is that you are useless, that you are ugly, that you are stupid and so on. However if someone tells you that you are wonderful, you are beautiful, you are amazing, that is also a form of enslavement. *"You exist and I can, in my perception of you, know you so well that I can come to a conclusion about you."* In terms of the content of the communication, it may sound quite positive, *"You are so beautiful"*, but implicit in that is that if you stop being beautiful I won't like you. So, when someone says, *"You are so beautiful"*, you should give them the bill for all the face cream and makeup you use to maintain your beauty! Either way, criticism or praise, you are being bound into an image and that always has its difficulties.

What we have been looking at is how our embodied existence is shifting according to circumstances. We are available and then unavailable; we are happy to meet and then maybe not so happy, but we want to feel safe with the other person. Child development therapists speak about the need of what they call 'object constancy'. They say that if the behaviour of the parents is predictable, if the child has meals at regular times, gets up early and goes to bed early, this creates predictable rhythms which allows the child a sense security in the world. Nevertheless other people are not always reliable, and as an adult if I still feel that my security and happiness depends on another person, then in order for me to feel safe, the other person has to behave in certain ways which I can anticipate and rely on. Such people often become very jealous. *"Why are you looking at that woman? Do you like her better than me?"* This kind of insecurity is really telling the other person, their partner, that they have to control their life and their world and not respond to circumstances in a way which makes them less predictable to me. So, we end up with this attachment: *"I love you because you are the one I need so that I can be me."* *"I need you so that I can feel like me. You make me feel like me. I don't feel like me if you are not there."* This is the situation of a three-year-old child. When mama is not available anxiety arises; the child only settles when it is child-plus-mama.

Many people retain the same structure as adults. They have never planted their selves vertically. They are not centred and grounded where they are in whatever circumstances. They are structurally off-balance and looking for someone else to keep them upright. It need not be another person, it could be alcohol, an intense habit form like anorexia, bulimia, self-harming, getting into abusive relationships. These can function as self-soothing activities, although they are disturbing as well. They are ways of try to settle oneself when one is upset or overwhelmed by what is going on.

"I use you to make me feel okay and so my relationship with you is that you are a means to an end." Such a relationship is functional in terms of a psychological need. So, if I say. *"I love you"* it may sound as if this is just about you but it is actually disguising the fact that I love you *because of the function that you play* in maintaining my sense of self. I have incorporated you into my sense of self. This is what small children do with their mothers. The mother is like an artificial limb for the child. Mama becomes a part of me. Mama is like an additional brain outside of oneself. Small children communicate like that a lot.

However if this dependent attachment is carried over into adult life then it makes a deeper spiritual independence unattainable because I have become so dependent on someone else that I have lost my integrity. When two people collapse onto each other it is sometimes described as an A-frame relationship. An alternative healthier form is described as an H-frame relationship, where two people are grounded in themselves yet linked. They can get close and fuse and separate and do whatever they need to do and meet together again later. There is the sense of *"Here I am and I am with you."* If somebody goes away and their partner asks, *"Did you miss me?"* hopefully one can respond, *"No, I was fully doing whatever I was doing. Why would I miss you? I hope you didn't miss me."* However this doesn't sound very romantic!

ALONE YET NOT LONELY

If you want to be mindful and present you are mindful and present with what is showing. If the beloved is far away then what is showing is something different. You do your work or you talk with a friend, you are there. Paul Young sang, *"Every time you go away you take a little part of me."* This is tragic, ridiculous, why would you want to lose part of yourself? Projecting your life into other people creates a pseudo closeness, a fusion which denies the fact that you are born alone, you live alone and you die alone. You might be married to someone for fifty years and spend every night in the same bed and yet you are alone. Alone is not necessarily lonely, if you are at home and at peace in yourself, what is lacking? Lacking gives the sense that something is missing.

The basis of my presence as this form in the world is the openness of the mind. Awareness is infinite. Although I say *'my awareness'* it is not my possession. Awareness is the mother of me, I emerge within the field of awareness as a movement of energy with other movements of energy, and if I don't forget the ground then the open spaciousness of the mind is always available. So we can be relaxed and at ease and then, without losing the spaciousness, we manifest interpersonally, getting close to people, engaging in different ways for a while.

What do we need? We need contact because contact is where we experience the non-duality of self and other, but if I need 'you' then we have duality. I am separate here; 'you' are there with your qualities. *"I need you. I need you because I know you are so good for me."* That is not something to be believed, that is the imagination. Why? Because you are unreliable. You mutate, you change. You are not a stone. Hopefully this is true in all of us. If you want something immutable, marry a stone. People are always shifting and changing. You can enjoy contact, but you can never 'get' another person. Relationships go wrong when we start to collapse on each other. *"I built my world around you."* Why? Why would you do that? *"You are the basis of my existence."* This is ludicrous, laughable. How could you be the basis of my existence?

That is an idea of fusion. When you put food in your mouth, *my* stomach doesn't get filled.

—Oh James, you just don't understand these things, is a *feeling.* I need you.

—What do you need? Me? What do you know about me? 'Me' is what you imagine. I can tell you ten things about me that would make you run away.

—But I won't. I need you too.

It is a bit of a cover up: the drama of romantic love. This is not to say that we shouldn't fall in love, some of us can't help falling in love, but if you can catch it in the moment it is a movement of energy. It is a wish to engage in a dance, to have co-emergence, to have synergy. It may not last very long but is very filling and life affirming. Just as you don't know what sensations will arise in your body or what thoughts will arise in your mind, other people are also unpredictable. So when we say *"I love you"*, this implies that there is a reliable 'you' to be loved. *"I will always be there for you"* – sometimes you are not available because you are just not in the mood.

ROMANTIC LOVE IS TRANSFORMED INTO DEVOTION

In buddhism when we recite, *"I take refuge in the Buddha, Dharma and Sangha"* we are taking refuge in the idea of the possibility of liberation, of being free of reliance on hopes and fears. We open into the path by becoming aware of the limitation of our deluded notion that we exist as a thing. I am not a thing; you are not a thing. Taking refuge means awakening to how we are but first we have to be able to look. We say that love is blind and when you are blind you don't see too much. In tantric practices romantic love is transformed into devotion. Our longing for an other who saves us is removed from the human domain and centred on a deity. It could be a peaceful deity like Tara or a dancing deity like Vajrayogini; there are many types of deities out there.

When you have a connection with the practice you always have access to the deity; they won't betray you or let you down. You might betray them because you'll possibly forget to do the practice. You start with the high idea that you will do the practice every day, then it becomes once a week and then once a month. But the deity is always there, available. They don't need you, you need them. You need them in order to find out how not to need. Then you are free. That is the tantric transformation of the desperation of devotion into the dissolving of the whole mandala into emptiness.

We are social creatures, we live together, and so surely we can help one another. That is a good idea, but help each other to do what? To be grounded and centred? To live with dignity? To find out more about how we are? To be curious? To work with circumstances? To work with how inner feelings and outer situations change? These are all important tasks but they are not linked with romantic love. The most important thing between people is workability.

One way of describing how we relate with others is chakra energy. We have genital energy, the drive towards seeking the other. We have the energy of the navel, which is the point where the inner duality of subject and object meet. We have chakras in the heart, the throat, between the eyes and in the top of the head. We might meet someone and have a very strong sexual connection but no real heart connection. We might have a very playful energy from the navel but no real communication in terms of discussion or conversation. The possibilities of our relating are not volitional. You find someone sexually interesting or not; it arises as a kind of given in the interplay of your embodiment. With some people you might have a lot to say, with other people you smile at them but there is nothing much to say. Our connectivity is revealed through our participation together and this availability shifts and changes.

Thinking like this may help us have more sense that the other is not an object, is not a thing. We cannot appropriate a person. We can be open to be with them in some way, for a while. To live like that we have to be honest because when different aspects of our embodiment engage with the other person, they may fit but later on they may not fit. If you come home and have a conversation like this with your partner,

—Something has happened today and I really need to tell you all about it.

—Well, I really need not to hear about it.

—But I thought you were interested in me?

—Yeah, well, I am, sort of, sometimes.

—Only sometimes?

—No, that's no good. I want you there all the time, fully available, on my terms.

This is a violence. It's not a personal violence, is not that you are being really horrible to each other, it's the structural violence of you not living with the freshness of energy.

If you want a reliable thing run some water from the tap, fill up the ice tray, put it in the fridge and tomorrow you have little ice cubes. They have a definite shape. If you say to them, *"I love you"* they just sit there, but when the ice starts to melt it flows out. Water is without inherent shape; it takes on shape according to circumstances. We are like water, fire and wind. We have the earth element but it is not dominant, so we shift and move. To expect always to have synchronicity of your energy with another person's is a very big ask.

This is why buddhism identifies grasping and challenges the expectation that there are things to get and that having got them, you can hold onto them. People change, we all change. How to live with that? We have to be fresh. How to be fresh? Dissolve into the space which is the ground of your being. How will I do that? By not grasping at yourself.

Grasping at self as something is exactly the twin of grasping at other as something. Your self-knowledge is a delusion. You wrap yourself in stories about yourself, but rather than revealing who you are, this is how you hide yourself from yourself and from other people. Our life is based on *'Let's see.'*

—What shall we do on Saturday night?

—Let's see. Maybe you'll be tired, maybe I'll be tired.

—But we need to make plans.

—Make a plan with the ice cube then. I don't know how I will be by Saturday night!

A plan is a violence, the future hasn't come and the future you imagine is unlikely to come. You will get a future, but it won't be the one you thought you were going to get. And you won't be who you are when the future does arrive. Who you are now will have dissolved.

Does that mean we don't know anything? We know how to stay relaxed and hopeful and responsive. We know how to work with circumstances, to not enslave other people in order to feel free ourselves. How would I know what to do? You won't know what to do, you don't need to know what to do. You will do something. *"But maybe I'll do the wrong thing!"* That is OK, then you say sorry. If you make too many plans you become extended out into the future.

In order to survive financially we often need to do the kind of work that involves planning, which is based on the mechanisation of human beings. We are expected to function in a mechanised way, every month we need to submit our report, we have to do this, and we have to do that. Have to? If you are taking it up willingly as your adult dignity then, fine. But if this *have to* is imposed on you, then it is a kind of violence.

Computers and algorithms are pre-figuring the shape of things. What keeps us fresh is enquiry, living on the growing edge of our existence, moment by moment. When we feel very alive, it is usually because we are feeling life just manifesting as us. Our life, our vitality, our presence, is here revealing itself as us, in this moment. So, to relate to other people in that way we don't need to ask them to pre-form themselves in order to fit into some template.

We are very far from that in our culture nowadays. In the old days when we were taking in the harvest, using a scythe, doing heavy physical work, there would be breaks in the day and the quaffing of beer and singing of harvesting songs. It would be an organic process. Tractors don't have organic processes; they have deadlines to bring things to the factories or to the markets. Forgetfulness or a lack of mindfulness can be a blessing some times. If we were more aware of the violence of our structures, we would be very unhappy. This unhappiness manifest as depression, anxiety, eating disorders, addictions and so on. These are symptoms manifesting in the individual but actually the problem is structural and pervasive.

We have created an inhumane world and we are starting to see the consequences. We don't know when to stop because we don't see what we are doing. To set fire to Amazonian jungle, is quite a thing. Huge trees burn down, so many birds and animals burn. They are sacrificed for the idea that it is of benefit to grow soya beans and maize. The maize is for the pigs, to make them fat, so that fat people can get even fatter. The intoxication by idea allows you not to see what is right in front of your eyes. Likewise, at work your boss may have an idea and wants you to make it into a project. You have to do it. Next week he will have another idea, and another, and another. Each project involves you projecting yourself into the future. You have displaced yourself from here to there. You take your mind out of your body and you put it into the future. Many of us are disembodied in this way.

One aim in meditation practices can be to re-inhabit our body. Only by actually being in your body can you start to know how the five elements are working as the body. A demand to do something is like wind and earth. Something solid is been propelled at you, like the roof of a house blown off in a hurricane and flying towards you. Wind needs space. As long as the hurricane is over the ocean it doesn't cause too much trouble but when it hits the island, then the trouble begins.

The mind needs space because the agitation of life sets up these various winds which operate through the prana channel. How will I find the space? We are always in space. Space is our mother. The space we move in is the form of the womb of the great mother. It is empty, and within the space all these energetic forms arise without inherent existence. They are here and then they vanish. Mental formations make them important and serious. We can loosen this. We can work hard, we can do many different things but in a very relaxed easy way. To strive and push yourself is not so good.

Energy arises from space. Thought arises from the open empty mind. So experiencing energy as the play of the wind in the open sky allows you to move easily as required, and the more you can do that, the less exhausted you are, the less in need of compensation. This means that you can relate to other people without having your need, your hunger and your emptiness as your calling card.

The open emptiness of the mind is not a lack. It is the basis of every experience arising to fill the space of the mind. Lack arises when the individual ego marks out territory with a boundary and then operates as an import-export agency, trading with the environment as if it were something outer. But we are *in* the environment, we are *of* the environment. The open ground shows the non-dual field of subject and object arising together, within which, moment by moment we take on different forms, connecting in different ways. From that basis, relating to other people is much easier because if you are sensitive to your own situation, if you appreciate the qualities of the many different factors of your life, then you can start to appreciate other people.

When you sit in meditation your mind may be very excited or anxious or dull. Do not enter into judgment, don't try to change the situation, just be with the mind as it is. I am dull, I am having a full cup of dullness, a full cup of anxiety, a full cup of loneliness, a full cup of *"I am wasting my time meditating because I can't do it."* Whatever is arising, if you stay with it, it will give you its whole flavour. This is how the energy of the Buddha's heart shows itself: ordinary hopes and fears. Hopes come, fears come. For the ego hopes are better than fears but for awareness it is all just stuff, one no better than the other, happy, sad, in love, in grief, arising and passing, arising and passing.

The more we are relaxed in the open spaciousness of awareness, the less demand we put on other people to conform to the image that we have of the ideal person who makes us feel safe. Finding this unborn ground of our own being is very helpful for being intimate with others.

RAW, FRESH AND NAKED

Dzogchen speaks about the mind and says it is primordially pure. 'Pure' means untouched by anything else. Our clothes get dirty through contact with the world, with our sweat and so on, but the mind is alone. This doesn't mean it is cut off or isolated; it is just alone. Like the side mirrors of a car, reflections after reflections arise and in each moment the mirror is fresh and able to show a new reflection. It doesn't became stained or tired. This is primordial purity. In our lives many things happen and we tend to accumulate certain patterns of experiences and tendencies. A mirror is not like that. Appearances continuously and instantly arise and instantly pass. The appearances are non-cumulative. The mirror doesn't grasp or hang on to or build up anything. The mind has openness – not a dull empty openness but an openness which is present and available.

It is described as being raw, fresh and naked. 'Raw' means not cooked, nothing has been done to it; it hasn't been processed in any way. It is fresh, completely like the first moment in every moment. It is naked because it is not covered over in any way. When you think of the mirror, the reflection arises in the mirror but the mirror is still naked. The reflection is not something hidden in the mirror; there is no mirror essence behind the reflection.

When we take up these five questions looking for the mind, what we find is that the mind is not some thing some where else. I live in my skin bag. Inside the skin bag is my heart and lungs and so on. This is the inner content whose function maintains the integrity of the skin bag. When people meet and have some contact, they are showing on the level of the skin but that is because there is something inside the skin bag maintaining and displaying the vitality and potential for connecting. Despite looking again and again, you'll find nothing behind the mind, and also that the mind is not behind anything. The reflection *is* the mirror. There is not more to the mirror than the reflection, however it is not really correct to say that the reflection *is* the mirror because the moment of the reflection doesn't define the potential of the mirror.

At every moment of your life experiences are arising and passing. They arise and pass because the mind itself is not sticky.

Nevertheless if you think about your mind and you think about all that has happened since you woke up this morning, then there is a selectivity in that memory. Some things stand out, others have already passed into oblivion. Your sense of self develops a contouring, like peaks and valleys in the mountain. When you remember an incident, you can tell that to someone else and it becomes elaborated into a story, but what was happening was not a story. It is exactly this, just this, and then gone. Your story is a representation, you are talking *about* something, you are thinking *about* something. It is not raw, naked and fresh. It is prepared, elaborated, edited, and presented.

The ego self is dependent on certain aspects of the world in order to function. They are necessary for the continuity of *me* in *my* life. If I lose my passport, it will be difficult at the airport. If I want to travel, I need to show people that I am who I say I am. A passport or an identity card is a re-presentation. If we don't have the re-presentation we won't be allowed to present ourself. This gives you the flavour of samsara – we don't trust presentation, we trust re-presentation.

ALL-AT-ONCE-NESS

Primordial purity means that moment by moment the mind is open. If a tragedy happens, if you feel terrible, if events turn your life upside down, these are patterns or movements of energy. *You* are still there. If you start to go blind, *you* are still there. If you have a leg amputated, *you* are still there. *You* are there as a presence. Your sense of self is altered. You are aware, and this awareness is the showing of the altered sense of self. When you feel angry or dispirited, frustrated at this change in your sense of self, the patterning of the content of experience is so intoxicating that you identify with it. It becomes who you are. What is lost is the awareness, the revealer of the experience.

71

The mind itself, your mind, is what you are moment by moment. Forgetfulness of how the mind is open, empty and pure from the very beginning leads to non-relaxation because your attention gets focused on patterns of movement, patterns of emergence, and you try to sort it out: *Which bit of this is me? Which bit of this is not me?* We go close to experiences, we identify, we merge in them, then something happens and we withdraw. If we can stay with the openness of awareness, what we experience is all-at-one-ness.

We are sitting together here in this room and whatever is happening is happening all at once. We stand up and we go out the door, turn right, pass through another room, turn to the right, climb the stairs and so on. You can know all that, tell yourself a story about that, but if you just stay open you'll see that what I call 'myself' and what I call 'my environment' arise together. All are experiences, all at once. Is not like a painting that it built up stroke by stoke, adding, rubbing out, building up an image. If you turn your head one way and then turn your head the other way, instantly everything is there and you with it. This is 'instant presence' (Tib. *Lhan Cig sKye Pa*), coming all at once, uncompounded. A compound is a gathering together of different things and the putting them in particular patterns and packages.

As you look around and see one thing and then another thing, one person and then another person, you are engaged in composition. Selective activity leads to liking and not liking. We want to look more at what we like and less at what we don't like because our attention is the medium for value in the world. We attend to what shines to us. The chi, or prana, or life energy, flows out with our sense organs and when we like something it starts to shine for us. If we don't like it, it doesn't shine so much. Our world is experienced as full of some important things and many unimportant things. This simplifies our experience as an individual ego-self because, if everything were interesting, how could I make choices?

It's through the ceaseless process of making choices that I shape and re shape my ego-self. What arises within what I take to be me – sensations, thoughts, memories and so on – is unpredictable. What I will experience through my sense organs is also unpredictable. So, the process of selectivity, which is going on moment by moment, is in a shifting field of interaction of great complexity. It's a lot of work and this is what is called 'karma'. Karma means activity. You say, *"This person is interesting. This other person is not so interesting. I want to spend time with the interesting person. I don't want to spend time with the not so interesting person."* But maybe the interesting person doesn't want to spend time with you and the not so interesting person really does want to spend time with you. This is our life, we all know this; this is the life of the ego self.

Observing this ceaseless process of selectivity we just relax, since we realise that this is movement inside a field that is already here. All-at-once-ness comes before selectivity. You get it all without effort but you don't know what to do with it because you are some-one and some-ones want some-thing; they don't know what to do with every-thing. In order to maintain your someone-ness you need to work out what sort of some-thing you are and what sort of some-thing I am. Are you my kind of something? This is how the ego manifest within the field of clarity. There are not two factors, someone making the good things and someone else making the bad things. Ignoring the given-ness of everything and the fact that we are always already part of this everything is what leads us to the limiting particularisation of our sense of self. Meditation gives us a chance to relax our relentless selective investment and avoidance.

In your embodiment you are organised for selectivity. You are selecting from the field and the field is the showing or the shining force of emptiness. Everything in the field is empty, this is to say, devoid of inherent existence. So when we make selections we are selecting patterns of energy. If you are offered a banana or an orange you can think of them as two different things. You can say both belong to the family we call 'fruits', but they have different shapes and colours; we can eat the skin of the apple, but we cannot eat the skin of the banana. The particularity of shape, colour, smell and so on, says that one is an apple and another is a banana, but how do I know it's a banana? It's yellow, it's curved, it has a tough bit at one end where it was attached to the banana tree. The banana reveals itself to me through colour and shape. 'Banana' is a name that I apply to that colour and shape. By calling it 'banana' I pull it in to the field of my interpretation and knowledge. Imagine if you were flying over a hot country and the plane crashed and landed in a jungle. You are the only survivor, wandering in the jungle, feeling hungry but not familiar with any of the plants. There could be many delicious edible fruits there, but there again, they might be poisonous. If they are poisonous, you may die. They may taste delicious yet be poisonous. So now you are both hungry and anxious! This is the human condition: our experience is mediated through knowledge. Knowledge keeps us safe.

Conclusions are good for the ego. The ego likes to know what is what. However it's already gone. Because life is dynamic and ever-changing, as soon as you get hold of something it has already dissolved into the next moment and the next moment and the next moment. The capacity to receive the unfolding revelation of how life is moment by moment, which is ever fresh and shiny, gets toned down, becomes muted by the anxious requirement to have definitive knowledge. Instead of attending to how, we focus on what: *"Oh! It's a banana."* End of story.

Within the field of clarity, in the immediacy of all the phenomena arising at once, we find ourselves participating as movement. This is a journey without beginning or end. This turns into this, turns into this, turns into this. When you stay with the *this* you have the freshness but if you try to catch *this* and make it into an entity to think about, then you step onto the path of comparing *this* with *that*. *"Oh yes! This banana is from Brazil, it tastes different from the banana from El Salvador."* When you are eating a banana, what is important is the texture, the colour, the smell. Is it from Brazil or El Salvador? Who cares? It is good, and that means it is good for me at this moment. In India there are many varieties of bananas and the very small ones, the sweetest, are often mashed up for babies. As you get older you don't need sweet tastes so much. It's like that. It is how I am, in this moment, in this context, like this. Can I say what I will be like tomorrow? Only if I speak about myself as an idea. Then I have an existential choice: to be like this or to be like that.

We operate in the world by telling other people what we are like. When we tell someone *about* ourselves we are creating, or helping to develop, a likeness of ourselves in their minds. There is an image of us developing in their minds been fed by the stories we tell them about ourselves. I tell you *about* myself so that you can think about me. This is the royal road to desolation and loneliness. *"Darling, I've been thinking about you all day..."* What should darling do with their thoughts about me? A thought is not a kiss. If you give me a kiss I get something. You can think about me for a hundred years but that's you, it's not me. That is what representation means: image building. This is where our mind is cleverly deceitful because as my image of you becomes ever more multi-textured and multi-dimensional the closer I feel I am getting to you. But I am not. When a person is packaged into a story, the concrete moments of their life, which are inexpressible, are re-packaged as something abstract which is expressible.

I am talking with you about dzogchen. Dzogchen can't be talked about nevertheless I do it and I am very glad you give me this opportunity to come here and talk. We have to hear the talking in a very gentle way since words are not going to help us to find out the truth. The function of the words is to soften us up, like a massage, so that we can be more pliable and allow more possibilities to emerge. Talking about ourselves is not showing ourselves. Of course we don't show ourselves like an actor on the stage; we show ourselves without showing – we just are and other people see. Their seeing will depend on whether they can receive.

This takes us back to the title of this teaching, *Love and impermanence.* If love or closeness or intimacy is based on attachment, the attachment is always to the idea of the person. The person - as disclosure, as the unveiling of oneself moment by moment - is like water running through our fingers: we have the sensation that there is something going on. Colour, shape, sound, movement. Self-arising and self-vanishing, self-liberating, moment by moment. Like being at the sea and watching the waves going up and down, up and down. We receive it, but what can we say about it? When I watch the waves and the sparkling light I feel softened inside; my thinking subsides and I am just with the emerging experience. I can't say anything about it. What am I doing? I am looking at the sea. Was I looking at the sea? I was being with the sea. What was occurring was not a *some-thing*, it was presence before the thing-ness processing began. Thing-ness processing, reification construction, comes after the immediacy of the all-at-once-ness.

The practice of meditation helps us to be here with the immediacy of the all-at-once-ness. As soon as you are with another person you are already into self and other. Being present with the field is also to be present with movement, endlessly, shimmering within the field. This is our authentic mind, a co-presence, with nothing to take away and nothing to gain.

Some people think that psychotherapy is about developing insight, see the structure of what is going on and then perhaps sharing that insight with others. It may be helpful to share our understanding of the structure. That is one way of perceiving it but when we are simply present together, this presence itself releases many of the structural tensions because tension, anxiety and defences cut us off from being in immediate connectivity. We open to the field without entering into judgement about what is good and what is bad. In conversation our judgement is often expressed as saying that something is important, and something else is unimportant.

Sigmund Freud understood this very clearly: don't commit yourself to a pathway of interpretation. An interpretation should be given when it is no longer necessary, when the patient is themselves at the point of making it. If you offer interpretations prematurely it is like hanging a thread in a copper sulphate solution – after some time crystals start growing around the thread. This is to say, the patient will crystalise themselves according to the interpretation offered by the therapist.

When we are longing for love, we seek to make ourselves lovable, we seek to become the one who the other wants, but if I become the one that the other wants, who will the other become? Who will I become? I don't know what the other wants and generally speaking the other doesn't know what they want either. So this attempt is very foolish nevertheless people do spend a lot of time thinking how they should be in order to make a relationship work.

BEING IN PLAY

Workability depends on an energy of co-emergence. It is something in the air and cannot be forced. When you come towards some people you shake hands, with others you share a little hug, with others a great big hug. Some people just smile. There are many permutations of how we connect; it is not a ritual, you just find yourself in different energies. We are participating within the field of experience as it is, in this moment. It is not about knowing, it is about having a feeling tone. You may have hugged someone yesterday but today be more distant. Why? You will never know. You can't say. It is just how it is, because this is the formation of energy prior to conceptualisation. Does it mean we like the person less? That is a concept. If we stay with the concept we will be in a labyrinth of thought and memories, wandering in the wilderness. It is just this and it does not predict how the next moment will be. This is a different way of living – raw, naked and fresh.

Make yourself available. When you are available you receive the emergent sensation of the other; you can go back or you can go forward. To be available doesn't mean to be a slave; you are not at the mercy of the other, but it does require that you receive the how-ness of the other person through your senses. Not the what-ness. What-ness is conceptual, already packaged, whereas the how is shifting and changing, which means that you need to be ready to shift and change. It means you should be light, able to move, un-burdened by expectation, un-narrowed by judgement. You are in play and that can invite the other to be in play. If they don't want to play, fine. You go away because there is always the next moment. *"But I can't let it drop. S/he is the only person who can make me happy."* That is an idea, not only an idea, but a neurotic idea! It's a great method for making oneself unhappy. To be present in the moment is to be in *this* moment.

EQUANIMITY

When we lose access to the openness of the mind we become immersed in the realm of polarities: good, bad, right, wrong, inclusion, exclusion. The view of dzogchen is the great inclusion, everything is included – including all the things that we ordinarily want to exclude. The way we find this great inclusion is through equanimity. Whenever you project a definitive meaning to anything you encounter, whether a person or a situation, you are giving it a value. The intrinsic value of everything is that is pure from the very beginning and empty of personal essence. So, if we meet people and we find that we like them, or even strongly like them, the fact is that we are seeing a face, two eyes, a body, we are hearing their voice, and these are all movements of patterns that are dissolving. This movement will never be repeated. How to avoid consolidating this into some fixed image of the other?

When we include everything it does not means that we homogenise it. Each person has a unique specificity, a quality manifesting with you in this moment. Two pathways of understanding this are: from the point of view of dzogchen this is the manifestation of the energy of the ground. Our basic openness brings us into this particular display at this moment and within this we have specific ways of connecting with different people, at this time, in this place. In other words, we have the diversity of the display of emptiness. Every reflection that comes in the mirror has its own particular shape and colours but each reflection is identical in being a reflection. It has no personal essence from its own. It is a showing of the clarity of the brilliance of the mirror in this one particular moment. So one pathway is arising with awareness and the other pathway is arising with assumptions. This is why in our practice we stay with how things are; we don't try to get more of the thoughts or sensations that we like and less of those we don't like. We want to have an open hospitality to whatever is occurring without bias or prejudice and in that way we have equanimity whatever is arising.

Equanimity is not dull and flat. For example, if we go to see a musical, there will be a large stage with people dancing on it. We expect the dancers to be moving about but if there is an earthquake and the stage starts to move about too then that is a different matter! In fact if the stage were moving about, it would be difficult to dance. Equanimity is like the stage, there is a basic calmness, spaciousness, openness. There is a free movement of whatever is arising and in this field we arise as subject and object. Sometimes you feel like subject and someone else is the object, and sometimes they appear as subject and you appear as the object. Sometimes subject and object are moving inside yourself – you may have a thought about what you did yesterday, *"I went to see my neighbour and told them that...."* That is a subject-object formation. Because you have equanimity you can feel this thought arising, have the taste of it, but it is not the total truth. If you merge into the thought then you get the emotion *"Oh, no! Why did I say that!"* and then you start moving this way and that way, acting and reacting, confirming your sense of being isolated and unsure how to behave in the world.

Relax and open

We relax and open. In the openness many appearances arise. They are uniquely just this, just this, just this and then they are gone. There is no path. There is no person. When I think, *"Oh no! Why did I do that yesterday!?"*, this is now, you cannot go to yesterday. The thought of yesterday is a perverse thought of today, a cloudy form of now, because you are thinking about something which is not here but by your emotional identification with your thought about it, it is as if you have gone there or it has come here. The past is gone.

If you've been in a relationship and it got difficult and they vanish, they are not here. Where are you when you are thinking about them? If there is a lot of emotion linked with the thought about the absent person, you are stupefying yourself because you are here and what is arising is a thought. Lots of them. Like little white summer-time clouds passing and going. *"Oh, but why did they leave? What did I do wrong? Maybe I need to find out."* Now you have a lot of thoughts. Are they helping you? Who are you? *"I am a troubled, inadequate person."* Thinking like this takes you into activity, so just relax, open.

From the point of view of dzogchen all is relaxed and open: be with the thought, and see what the thought is. When you buy a second-hand car the seller might say, *"Drive it for a week and if you don't like it, bring it back and I will return your money."* But they give you a false address and at the end of the week when you take the car back, you knock on the door and no one is there. It is the same with thoughts; the thought comes in the mind, the thought tells you something about your life: *"I should have been more kind. I should have supported their fragile ego."* That is a thought. Where is the thought? Already gone. Why would you believe a vanishing thought? You are still here, that thought has gone, but if you follow the thought you will not have a sense of being here.

This is the fundamental crossroad in life: if you stay here, everything will come to you but if you go chasing memories and thoughts and elaborating plans, you will be displaced. You will be on the train of thoughts.

How we are in the world with other people is not something separate from the practice of sitting. We don't use sitting merely to go deep inside ourselves because when we go into this openness, this openness is inclusive: all the people we meet are already inside the openness of the mind. If we stay with awareness there will be plenty of thoughts, however if we follow the thoughts there will be very little awareness. Awareness is inclusive; it includes thoughts, feelings, sensations and so on, but thoughts and conceptual elaboration are exclusive. They exclude awareness because they are formulated in terms of duality: *"I am thinking about you, I miss you."* Subject-verb-object. Who is the *you* that I miss? This is a concept, but now with this concepts of you I have even more memories, how we were, all what we did... Every time you meander down one of these little pathways of concepts there is not space for awareness – although paradoxically, every little pathway of conceptualisation is itself moving within the space of awareness because awareness is the basic space of existence. Every finite is within the infinite, but if you go into a finite moment, although this finite moment is not different from its mother-ground, the infinite, it cannot show openness.

DOING NON-DOING

This is why, again and again, when you find yourself caught up in something, identifying and fusing into a particular emotion or sense of what is happening, don't try to change it. Don't do anything at all. Just stay present with it. That may seem an odd instruction because you have to *do* non-doing, which is actually very hard. You have to not do the doing which would interrupt the non-doing!

Awareness doesn't do, conceptualising ego does. 'Not doing' means just letting it go, not interfering, not mobilising. Some people's character is to quick mobilisation; they find their power and energy in doing something, but here there is nothing to be done. This may feel very odd and you may feel uncomfortable not knowing what is going on. That is because our sense of self is a construct which we maintain by our activity. We have to go through a transitional phase in which we relax the habitual actions which confirm our sense of who we are. We are like a caterpillar that at a certain point has to stop moving and make a cocoon and then after some time, out of the cocoon comes a butterfly! Our meditation is us cocooning ourself. This is what we do.

Imagine you have a little crystal hanging by a window and in summer time a ray of light comes from the sun, goes into the crystal and then dancing on the wall are rainbow colours. These colours are the potential of the clear light revealed. The movement of these vibrations together will show as clear light, and when separated out they show as red, green, blue and so on. When we look at a reflection we say, *"This is red."* That is a very different experience from just seeing the redness before the naming of red. Dzogchen uses the term *tsal,* (Tib. *rTsal*) to describe both the creative energy and the display. When you are sitting in the practice, what we call thoughts, feelings and sensations emerge; there is a showing. This is the showing of the potential which is revealed in this particular moment as if it were being reflected through a crystal.

The empty mind has the potential to show many different forms, but in this particular moment, because of the angle of the light and the configuration of circumstances, it brings forth these particular thoughts, sensations and feelings. If you stay with this what you will be experiencing is the emergence of the mind. The mind doesn't emerge as itself. Just as when the reflection shows in the mirror, this is the mirror emerging but it is not emerging as itself, and yet it *is* emerging as itself. This is the non-duality of emptiness and appearance.

When you grasp at the colour and you say it is red, perhaps a particularly intense red, it is as if there is something there, something has been born, something has come into separate autonomous existence. If you put a piece of board in between the window and the crystal the coloured light will immediately cease; the coloured light is a showing, a movement of energy. You see red, you see orange, but they are not there. These are your concepts; this is the grasping mind. The grasping consolidates what is there and, in doing that, hides what is there.

MEDITATION ADVICE

So the instruction for meditation is that when experiences, thoughts and so on are arising, if you grasp at them as being something, this involvement will disguise from yourself what is actually there, which is ceaseless display, unfolding, showing. Like light flowing, it is not a thing, it is like a river of experience. Therefore, we have the basic instruction: *"Don't go after past thoughts. Don't wait expectantly for future thoughts. Don't identify with the emerging thought. Don't hold yourself apart from it."*

When you are sitting in the practice, what arises in your mind is your mind. It is not definitive of its potential but is precisely itself in the moment. So, whether we are sad or happy or angry, however the mind is, don't change it. It is just like light coming through the crystal. If you stay present with whatever is arising it will vanish because it is movement; there is nothing substantial there. When you conceptualise, the addition of the thought to the appearance creates the illusion of something being there. The illusion is a form of experience, something that is real for us because we believe in it.

It's not that concepts are bad or wrong; we wouldn't be able to function in the world without them, but when we attach them to everything there is a congealing, a thickening. This disguises the fact that thickening too is a form of movement. We seem to arrive somewhere, we look at the colour of the wall and we say that is red. Something is there, the light goes through the crystal onto the wall, reflected on the wall into our eyes. This is only a circle of movement. Our conclusion brings the experience into culture, into human conceptualisation, but what is it in its nakedness? In its rawness? In its freshness? Concepts are like adding monosodium glutamate to food; they bring a particular kind of taste to everything. We end up with the taste of something-ness because of the additive.

In the buddhist tradition the qualities of the fully enlightened Buddha are described as dharmakaya, sambhogakaya and nirmanakaya. The mind of the Buddha is referred to as dharmakaya, which means that the presence of all potential, of all possible dharmas, are within the awareness of the Buddha.

Sambhogakaya means that within this space everything can be enjoyed. But how could you enjoy sadness? Sadness is an experience, a showing. When you see that it is the showing of the potential of the mind, that it is a form of radiance, then by staying with it, you have a particular patterning of resonances, flavours and qualities. We often think that sadness is a state, but sadness is a movement. When we feel sad the muscles on the shoulders and the neck usually go down a bit, we collapse a little bit into sadness. The diaphragm is a little tense, there is a constriction. This is something we can examine in ourselves: what happens to our posture, our gestures, our capacity for eye contact, our breathing... We are living sadness. Sadness is living through us. Then we have some happiness, we feel envious – these are all modes of experience and all can be appreciated and enjoyed because of their unique specificity.

Within dharmakaya is equanimity. You are settled enough to be with what is arising. If we get very excited by the joy of one thing or the horror of another, then we are into desire and aversion, adopting and rejecting. Human beings have many different ways of avoiding being sad. If sadness is unpleasant, why stay with it? But what is sadness in its phenomenal aspect? In its conceptual aspect we all know that we don't like sadness, but when we position ourself starting from concepts we don't go near the phenomenon, so we are not open to the phenomenon. In fact, that is the last thing you want to do – so you are in aversion. How would you taste sadness? The soup is in the bowl, but you don't want to eat it; it's horrible. But you didn't try it. You don't want to try it because you have decided that it is horrible. This is regression to us being four years old. Most of our life is structured in this way – we turn away from many of the potential experiences of life.

When you feel sad, lonely or confused, don't merge in it and make it your identity but appreciate it; it has a texture and it's coloured. Sour is a taste. We usually don't want to have too much sourness although we may prefer it to bitter. But what is bitter? Bitter is not an abstract concept, it does something to you. What? *'It is horrible.'* That is a value judgement. It's bitter and bitter is this. Sad is this. Loneliness is this. This is what we do in meditation: we try to remove the conceptual package from experience because the concept is both constructing a particular dimension to the experience and is providing the basis for apprehending the experience, for taking hold of the experience.

So, again and again, however the mind is, let the mind be as it is and then observe how you enter into judgement, how you take up a position. *"This is good, I want more, this is not good, I want less."* On an ordinary dualistic level this is a sign of your intelligence, however from the non-dual point of view this is the mark of ignorance because judgement is blocking experience. It is also blocking enjoyment because you don't know how to enjoy everything. That is the meaning of the sambhogakaya: everything is okay, it can all be enjoyed.

The name of the founding Buddha of dzogchen is *Kuntuzangpo,* always good, everything is good. This does not mean that you always have to choose what you experience as horrible. It's not a heroic path. You are not striving to overcome your limitations. Bitter is bitter; if you really know what it is, that is what it is. Sad is sad. So when sadness occurs you experience its arising as a flow, moment by moment by moment. If you stay with the sadness, in the sadness, but not merged with the sadness, then sadness suffuses you the way that the reflection suffused the mirror – and then it is gone. When you are really open to it, the paradox is that it doesn't leave a trace. When you close yourself against the experience, you put up a barrier to the experience and the experience opens its bag, takes out the spray-can and sprays graffiti all over you: the mark of existence. This is very wonderful. In fact, that the more you open to everything the less marked you are because the ego cannot open to everything; only awareness can open to everything.

By relaxing and opening you make the invisible transition from being wrapped in self-identification and being present as open awareness. If you refine this in your meditation practice, then when you are with other people you are connecting with them and you can have the full experience of how they are. You are very clear that there is no one there to catch but that we all have the capacity to reveal. The more we are open to the revelation of ourselves and to receiving the full revelation of another, the more we have the vitality of contact. When we are self-protected, we become inhibited and thereby we become unavailable and therefore we don't get what we need.

Life is contact. Our vitality can help other people to feel vital and we can live without fear, without hope, just in the vitality of the moment. Then we experience directly the self-liberation of each moment. Of course we can maintain our work, our family life if we have that, we can develop and maintain a relationship. In fact, this will help us to do that, because we realise that we can never be complacent. We never feel you've arrived some place. If we think, *"Now we are in a relationship and I know you are going to be with me forever so I don't need to worry about you so much."* then of course it will get difficult. But if you see that you are always living in a moment of time, you can't fall asleep into the situation because you want to be alive, you want to be present. That can help the other person to be present, so you have co-presence. That is a pretty good way to live. If we are here with this, this is as good as it gets.

Our brief time together comes to an end. Whatever merit there it is from our study and practice together we dedicate to all beings. Although it has been a short time we have covered some of the main points of dzogchen. This approach is helpful in its depth, it is helpful in its radiance, and it helps to make us more aware of our intrinsic connectivity. I hope you stay with the flavour of it and bring it into your lives.

Teaching given in Warsaw over the 14th to 15th Dec 2019. Edited by Barbara Terris and James Low.

Open to life: the heart of awareness

Dzogchen (the great perfection) is one of the most beautiful expressions of wisdom that has come from Tibet and India. Its essence points to the inherent freedom and clarity that is our natural state. Free from religious or spiritual dogma, it offers a way of being in the world that allows a deep sense of ease, relaxation and spontaneous awareness. The day will focus on the advantage of trusting relaxed openness, rather than anxious mobilisation. It will be grounded in the dzogchen view and there will be meditation practice and time for questions.

INTRODUCTION

The view and practice of dzogchen enables us to relax into an easier relationship with ourselves. We are returned to where we already are, free of alienation and centred in the stream of our experience.

The focus is on recognising our innate freedom from ignorance. Ignorance in the Buddhist sense is not a cognitive problem. It's not that we are ignorant of a particular kind of knowledge or information which we need to acquire, and that if only we build up a better database we would somehow give a more substantial basis to our individual existence. Rather, ignorance is about not being at home in our spacious openness, not being relaxed and in our own skin. There is a kind of ill-at-easeness, a disgruntlement, which causes agitation to manifest in various ways, sometimes as depressed, sometimes as anxious, sometimes as lots of thoughts and so on. Feeling that something is wrong we try to make sense of our lives – but this leads to endless activity as there are many problems to be addressed, issues to be solved and unravelled. There's no end to this type of conceptualisation.

The root problem is our misapprehension of our situation, that we take ourselves to be an entity living in a world of entities. We have learned how to solve certain problems such as changing a bicycle tyre and then apply this way of thinking to the question of our identity and how to find meaning in life. But life, our experience, our existence is not a problem to be solved. It is important to recognise that trying to solve insolvable problems is a waste of time. So in dzogchen we simply attend to our existence as it manifests moment by moment by maintaining an openness to what we take to be the subject and what we take to be the object.

Our lives tend to be grounded in basic assumptions, basic presuppositions. Thus we start with the idea *"I am me, this is my body and through my body I engage with the world outside me." Although everything changes in the world, there seems to be some constant factor to my experience and that's 'me'. Wherever I go I'm just me, the one who I know myself to be and the one who has to make sense of what is going on."* The notion of having a particular, definable, understandable identity is, from the point of view of dzogchen, the basic site of alienation. For our being, our presence, our aliveness, is not something which can be grasped, it's not a thing and is never caught by any meaning or quality we might ascribe to 'it'. Our presence, the immediacy of our awareness is prior to and beyond concepts, knowledge, memory, judgement, and all the other means of establishing identity. It is neither revealed nor created by effort. Rather it is always already here and available, if only we attend to it. The artificial confectionary of our self-narrative, the stories that we tell about ourselves, all that we wrap ourselves in in order to feel safe, can be let go of without loss or harm. We relax our fixation on our usual sense of the world, not to wipe it away because it's bad or wrong but simply because we've become so hooked onto a particular take on the world so that it's as if everything else goes into the darkness. Not the darkness of being ignored but the darkness of being taken for granted.

Dzogchen is an encouragement to look with fresh eyes, with a fresh heart. We come to see the nature of experience, not by telling our experience what it is, not by layering it over with more storylines, but by simply sitting in open receptivity, allowing experience to reveal itself as it is. So this is not a system of interpretation or a new kind of belief; we're not seeking to add anything onto our lives. It's more like a spring-cleaning, a ceasing to invest our accumulated assumptions and habitual interpretations so that we can directly open to what is.

Thoughts, feelings and sensations are the basic ingredients of our existence as we know it. We pull them together into familiar, habitual patterns and use this construct as our basis of relating to what seems to be going on. As an alternative, we can stay open to what is there. Open is a word much used in the language of dzogchen. Open indicates emptiness, that all the phenomena that we encounter has no fixed, inherent self-nature. Moreover who we take ourselves to be, the structures out of which we construct ourselves, are also not fixed. The outer stories we can tell about ourselves, the inner experiences that we have in terms of the streams of our thoughts, feelings, sensations and so on, all of this actually occurs only in the present. Experience presents itself in the present to our presence. It registers, it has an impact, yet you can't catch or say something definite about it. Even when you describe 'this is how it is' in this moment 'it' has already gone. The truth of our existence is that it is momentary. Each moment there is a unique specific pattern, a particular configuration arising and passing. It is an impactful, concrete appearance devoid of substance. It is what it is, and is both inside and outside our sense of linear time. To locate a moment in the arc of meaning running across time, you have to apply an interpretive structure which disguises the immediate actuality of the moment. The busyness of making sense of what is going on directs our attention so that we do not open to the immediacy of the momentary structure.

Moment by moment life is astonishing, it's very strange, and it's very surprising. If you weave the moments, or at least their echo, into your narrative then you can make them more and more understandable. This brings a reassuring complacency but at the loss of fresh aliveness. Generally speaking, life is easier if you put the blinkers on and just do more of whatever you have found out works for you.

Our life is very much like that, you go to work because it is what you do and you need to get some money and you need to pay a mortgage, and so on. We develop all sorts of rationalisations to keep the show on the road but I would suggest that the particular structure of your life has no innate meaning at all – it's just the happenstance of your existence. For some reason at a certain age you decided to study something or you met someone and you fell in love, or you decided to take a lot of drugs and this took you off in some particular direction. Then we spend a lot of time and energy trying to maintain that structure while visited by thoughts of *"Is this how I should be living? What does this mean?"* These waves of anxiety, depression and hesitation arise because we can never be quite sure this is enough: *"Is this all there is? Is this really who we are?"* Our personal narrative describes what we have done, what we may do, opinions we have held, things which have happened to us. We join these in various patterns and create different kinds of stories that we tell to different kinds of people. The stories may seem quite true as we tell them, yet we can't quite escape the knowledge that they are constructs, that in the telling we are creating the ground we are standing on.

Through this process of storytelling, of relating, we can weave ourselves into the social body, we can find a place in the world, we can connect with people who feel similar enough to us that we don't feel strange when we are with them. All of which is quite reassuring, but somehow there's not much substance to it, for the gestures which support it have to be repeated again and again.

The Buddhist idea of emptiness indicates that there is no intrinsic or inherent self-existence in any phenomena. For example, beside me there is a little wooden table. It's quite a loose structured table made of various pieces of wood which are screwed together in a pattern, such that these bits of wood placed together makes what we see into a table. If we have a screwdriver, we can take out the screws and lay out all the pieces of wood, and then we wouldn't have a table. When we bring all the pieces of wood together and screw them back into place, we have a table. So what has been added to the pieces of wood to make the table? Nothing material has been added. The same bits of wood and few screws can be laid on the ground or put together in this pattern. The thing which is added to make the table a table is our belief that there is a table. When you add the concept of the table to this shape formation, the concept, in a very instant and magical move, jumps from inside your head to the piece of wood. It is the seamless union of wood and concept, which generates the experience of seeing 'a table'. You don't see a bunch of bits of wood which you happen to call 'table', you see the table as out there existing in itself. But the table is not existing in itself. Its seeming existence arises due to causes and conditions, and if these are changed the table is also changed. The table is both something in the world and simultaneously an interpretation. If you take the interpretation out of the table, then there are many more possibilities for what you can do with it, but you won't attend to it in the proper way that a 'table' should be attended to.

If there was a two year old child in the room and they pulled on the table we would say, *"Oh, careful the table's going to fall over, it's not very stable."* The child is not thinking about stability but is exploring whether they can make it move. That's their area of interest, how they impact the world. Gradually we induct the child into the world of socially agreed conceptualisation. This is a table and because it's a folding table we say, *"Don't put your finger in there, it could get trapped. You could get hurt, and you don't want to get hurt, be careful."* Many, many messages of this kind have been massaged into you for years and years and years by your parents, until you are absolutely glowing with this powerful knowledge that you know how the world works, you know what it's all about!

On one level that's very true, very helpful and very useful. Yet what it also does is to make us believe that the world exists out there, in and of itself. When we do that it's as if we have a pair of scissors and we cut the direct connection between ourselves and the world. Then the world is full of self-existing phenomena, I am also a self-existing phenomena, and I wander around on my own two feet a little bit lonely, a little bit insecure, in a world full of stuff. There's an awful lot of stuff and somehow we never know enough about stuff. There's always new stuff to be dealt with and often we have the wrong kind of stuff in ourselves. We have regrets, *"If only I had taken the right kind of stuff from outside and put it into myself then I would be ok."* It's like the journey to the Wizard of Oz, some of us are looking for more heart stuff and some are looking for more head stuff. Something is missing and it seems to be 'out there' which is why humans have developed many, many different kinds of practices. There are practices for the body, yoga, tai chi and so on, practices for the voice, practices for the mind, all to develop ourselves because we feel that we are not complete and we want to be complete.

If you look in the wrong place for completion you will never find it, and trapped in the delusion that something is missing, you will be kept busy and dissatisfied for a long, long time. When we look outside we can always find things that we don't have, we can see qualities in the personalities of other people we would like to have, we might see how their house is structured or the job that they have or the way that they raise their kids. There's always something that I think I could extend the shape of myself in the direction of, and through which I would be more fulfilled. I would be more like me if I had more of what you have, which is a rather strange notion. Of course, on the level of personality, in the development of our individuality, this is exactly true. In psychological terms we become ourselves through our interaction with other people. We are constituted dialogically, we are constituted in conversation.

The kind of parents we have, the kind of school we go to, creates certain possibilities of speaking and certain ways of being silent, and so we find ourselves seeing other people doing things which we can't or are not allowed to do. We look at them and they are not so different from us: they've got two legs, two arms and so on. They walk about in the world and they eat and they drink, yet we are not like them, and often we can't understand how they can do what they do. This is very interesting because it illustrates how we have become identified with a particular patterning of ourselves which we take to be definitive of ourselves.

However when we look at it historically, our particular pattern has developed through our interactions with other people in the world; we have become our particular shape through interacting. We have taken on ideas, beliefs and behaviours, for example, how to hold a knife and fork, whether one makes some noise when drinking soup or not. The habitual is felt to be normal, to be how it is, and so when we see someone who has a different behaviour, we say, *"Whoa, why are they doing that? That's wrong, for I have to believe in my rulebook. If anything goes what will I do? In order to be me, I have to follow my own rulebook, yet I didn't make the rules in my rulebook."* This is the basis for many conflicts in relationships as our assumptions clash. You might go to psychotherapy to examine your rulebook and decide, *"Ah, this is wrong, it is what my father said. From now on I never follow this rule."* So then you have to have another rule, but where will you get it from? The world is full of people selling rules, and perhaps we also quite like converting others to our rules to ensure that we are not the only one in the world holding our particular belief system.

Enquiring in this way it would appear that our sense of self is a construct although it feels innate. Next to me there is a small table. When we look at it it's obviously a table. In the same way when I consider myself I am obviously me. However the table is just the happenstance of wood being cut in a particular way. When the tree was cut down the wood could have been sliced in many different shapes, it could have gone into making housing beams, bits for ships, all sorts of things. Yet it happened to be cut in these kinds of strips and then for some reason somebody decided that making this kind of table is something people would be willing to buy and so they produced this. Then, for some reason, somebody bought this table and it ends up here. There's a happenstance to this table existing here, and there is a similar happenstance to our being ourselves.

As we get older we have more opportunity to look back and see all the crossroads that we've met in our lives. All the choices and decisions we've made which have taken us on the somewhat random and circuitous route to end up with our particular shape of life. If we feel there is something wrong with this shape we might think, *"Oh, something has to be done. I would be better off, happier, if I was another shape, and in fact other people who know me would be happier if I were another shape too."* So in terms of both wisdom and compassion we had better change. This is a fairly mainstream belief and you see it running through most religions, certainly in mainstream Buddhism.

BE CAREFUL – DON'T FALL ASLEEP IN ASSUMPTIONS

Dzogchen is suggesting something slightly different. It suggests that before you proceed into the effortful process of trying to change yourself, maybe you should look at yourself to see whether you have truly seen yourself before you try to change. So in this case the function of meditation is to create an environment in which we can attend to the experience of being and how it stands in relation to the way in which different movements are occurring. We directly open to our presence and then we can see what is going on. We are observing the contents of our experience: perceptions of the external world coming through our senses, sounds, colour, shapes, taste, tactile sensation and so on. We also experience the internal sensations of our body and our feelings, memories, thoughts and conceptualisations. As this stream of experience is arising we can see that we designate some of this as 'self' and some of it as 'other'.

For example, if I look out the window I can see a winter tree with all its leaves gone. I 'here' see the tree 'there'. The sense of here and there, of me and it, is an interpretation.

Actually, directly, the whole field of experience is arising at once. When I relax the interpretive process there is experience, direct ungraspable experience. This creates a space within which the facticity, the actuality, of unfolding experience is revealed – it is what it is. This is always available yet is unattended to when I am focused on telling the world what it is. These two aspects or modes are simultaneously present yet one, the direct, is invisible while the other, the conceptual, is highly visible and seems to be a given.

If someone asks you, *"What's that building over there?"* as you answer their question they have very gently wound you into the world of conceptions, a world in which they function and you function. You have the freedom to perform your existence as a human being with other human beings, an interaction mediated through language, but what is the experience prior to the interpretation provided by language, memory and concept? Something occurs; if we don't conceptualise our experience we still have experience. In conceptualising experience we think about what is happening 'out there', and what is happening to me 'in here', and this activity confirms to us that I am the one to whom it is happening. These are all conceptual elaborations, interpretations.

The point of view of dzogchen is that we need to be careful not to fall asleep in the assumption that 'I just am', 'I'm just me', 'this is who I am and these are the kind of thoughts I have'. It seems to be a common belief that there is nothing to be inspected: *"I'm over 21. I'm entitled to lead my own life. I claim autonomy."* Yet no matter how much autonomy we claim, we hear noises, we see appearances, the world intrudes, enters into 'us' before we have chance to control it. To be in the world is to have the noise, so where is the autonomy? Experience and our first response occur before we make a conscious choice. To be alive is to be part of the unfolding field – our manifestation is always within the shared field – autonomy and individuality are deluding concepts which help us to ignore the actuality of the non-duality of manifestation. People get to you, they disturb you, they annoy you, why is that? *"Why can't they just leave me alone?"* Because you don't leave them alone. If you can guarantee that you will stop thinking about other people and having judgements and opinions about them, and stop looking at other people when you walk down the street, if you can guarantee to seal yourself completely in a bubble of yourself, then we'll accept your autonomy.

However, nobody can do that because to be alive is to be related. It's not that I am related to you as if we were two separate entities which just happen to be linked by circumstance. Rather what I call 'I' is the vehicle of relating. What I call 'you' is the vehicle of relating. There is an interplay between both of our experiences of being in the world with others. I am constituted out of the stream of experience and everything I encounter through my senses is also a stream of experience. From this point of view, there is no firm boundary between self and other. 'Outer' and 'inner' ceaselessly commingle, so how could we not expect to be disturbed by other people? Some people disturb or impact us in ways that we like, and some people disturb us and impact us in ways that we don't like. Either way we are going to be impacted.

We are part of the movement of the world, as is everybody else. We are all moving in a field of movement, there is no individual self-substance. This is not in itself frightening. It might feel a little strange but actually it is the guarantor of our freedom: the freedom to relate, the freedom to participate, the freedom to be part of what is going on. We do not live our lives from a clear vantage point, observing, then deciding on the basis of rational choice. No one lives like that, that's just a fantasy. It's an anti-phenomenological story, a story that goes against the direct experience of being alive. We are breathing in and breathing out, we are moving within the world, the world is moving within us. Blood is going round our body, hormones are communicating – many, many kinds of communication are happening all at the same time. In fact we can say that our human body and all living bodies are nothing but communication.

Communication is the energy exchange which maintains the fairly self-regulating forms which constitute our world. We, and everything around us, are patterns of energy manifesting in communication and interaction with other forms. At certain points we get a bit sick, eventually we die, and then some of the regulating factors cease to operate and the body starts to decompose. Being alive is the operation of the factors which maintain a certain patterning of other factors which manifest as our body. The balancing of these dynamic factors is unstable and is always under threat. For example, we get colds like the one I have now. We meet with other people and talk and something comes out of their system and comes into our energetic field, and we respond to that and find that we have a cold. It stays for a while, we do certain things because of it, and then it's gone. That is to say we are called into our current pattern of becoming by events in the world. When you walk up the stairs the nature of the stair is determining how you walk. Our sense that, 'I am climbing the stairs' is a statement of individual agency. *"I know how to climb stairs, I've been climbing them for years, this is just another set of stairs, watch and I'll show you how to do it."* Yes, I am the one who climbs the stairs, but I am climbing *these* stairs and the particular shape of these stairs determines how I move my legs. So, the stair and our body are in conversation. We can't just climb these stairs as if it was any old stairs, for some stairs have a higher step than others and that will make our body move differently.

If you start to see the world in this way, you get a de-centring of the sense of being an individual agent who is in control. People who drive cars are out on the road with other cars. You can't just drive your car as a first person singular event for you're driving with other people. You're sharing the space of the road, and how they drive will also determine how you drive, how much space you want away from them, whether it seems safe to overtake them or not. If they become a bit erratic you become a bit wary. This sort of event-reaction is going on all the time.

When you're chopping vegetables, how much force you use depends on the kind of vegetable you're chopping. If you're chopping up a turnip then you need more force than with a parsnip, and a tomato needs less force than a parsnip – this is pretty obvious. Who is determining that? Again, you can tell the story, *"Oh, I know how to chop tomatoes,"* but the tomato is making you chop it in a particular way. The tomato is speaking to you, it's saying, *"If you hit me hard I'm going to splash you,"* so we listen to the tomato and we are very careful because the skin can be quite tough and if we cut it at the wrong angle, the knife will slide off. The world is communication. The world is the revelation of shared existence, the shared experience that we have.

This is the particular dzogchen reading of the general Buddhist notion of the absence of inherent self-nature in phenomena including people. The aspects of our experience are always in communication. For example, some people here are sitting on the floor and are less used to sitting cross legged, so every now and then they move because their knees tell them something is not quite right. Others are sitting on seats which are a little bit hard and so they move around because the back gets sore and the bum gets sore. In this simple way being alive is ceaseless communication.

APPROACHING DZOGCHEN

OBSERVING THE NATURE OF OUR IDENTITY

The first approach in dzogchen is to start to listen to yourself in the world as part of the world, rather than listening to yourself about the world. We're very, very good at telling stories about our experience, that's what we do all the time. Someone says, *"How are you doing?"* and we're off telling a story, *"I was here, I was there and then I did this and did that."* Whereas in dzogchen we focus on observing the co-emergence of the energy of openness. The arising of what we take to be outside and what we take to be inside are not two different things. Subject and object exist in non-duality, which simply means there is not just one thing nor are there many different things: the non-dual is the intimate co-emergence or co-presence of all our experience and its ground.

However, our education has pointed us in another direction. What we learned when in school and later indicated that we have to take care of ourselves: *"It's a hard world out there and if you don't look after you, who's going to do it?"* So, we can often become a bit weary, for sometimes we have painful love stories or a painful work experience and then find it difficult to trust people: *"What are you up to? How can I work out who you are? Or what's going on?"* These are the bruises round the heart which can lead to a kind of hyper-vigilance, a sense that the only way to be safe is to be in control. This is very sad especially because actually we can't be in total control, which means there's no way to be safe. Now you can hear this in two ways. One way is, *"There's nowhere to be safe. Shit what am I going to do? This is really not nice and I don't want all this, this is horrible."* Another way is to hear it in a more neutral way, as a simple fact that there is no way to be safe just as it is a fact that today is called Sunday – *"This world is not safe."* This is not a punishment nor even a sign that we should improve our situation. Rather it is an encouragement to stop looking to the object for the answer. If what is occurring is unsatisfactory perhaps this has something to do with how we experience it. Perhaps we need to observe ourselves instead of focusing on manipulating events.

Who is the one who wants life to be safe? *"Me. I've got to protect this body because this is who I am."* This seems obvious yet we might benefit from observing the nature of our identity? Who is the one who says, 'I am me'? 'I am me' is a string of words, and when you start swimming in the ocean of language, these gentle, warm waves break over your face like swimming in the Mediterranean on a beautiful summers day. The sky is blue, the sea is warm, *"I am me ... I am me ... It's so easy being alive."* But we are swimming, which is an activity, and if we stop swimming we drown. You've got to keep language going, you've got to keep thinking. We are keeping ourselves afloat by thinking and speaking. We are the active maintainers of the bubble of ourselves. Just as children have little water wings on their arms when they learn to swim, so we have the bubble of our self which seems to keep us afloat, maintaining our identity – but only if we keep inflating it.

Meditation helps us to enquire whether we actually need the water wings. Do we need to keep swimming? Who is the one who keeps swimming? Who is the one wearing the water wings? That is to say if I don't make meaning, if I don't make my life meaningful, will it be meaningless? If I have to keep generating meaning, it will be conventional, it will be according to certain shared rules. This is clearly the case because if somebody entirely makes their own world on their own terms, they tend to end up in contact with psychiatric services.

A 'reasonable' life tends to be one which has a degree of conformity with social convention. By aligning ourselves with the patterns of interpretation which organise our in our world, we feel ok. Every now and then something might happen where we meet people with whom we are not quite sure what the deal is. For example, if you have to go into hospital or have contact with lawyers, that can be a bit weird because these situations are very clearly defined worlds, worlds which operate on their own terms. In encountering them you have to leave your thoughts about what's reasonable and what's not reasonable at the door.

Generally we prefer to hang out with people where we feel at ease because their assumptions and behaviour confirms our own. But clearly this will keep us in quite a small world, like a little clearing in the dark forest. Uncertainty lurks in the shadows which we avoid. *"When I get old what will happen to me? Who will look after me?"* Encountering the unknown our self-construct starts to crumble and we become anxious because it can't be maintained. Once you move into retirement, what's the basis for your identity? As the economy gets worse and many people lose their jobs, anxiety increases. We know that redundancy is a big cause of mental distress, generating depression and anxiety. Why?

Well, on an outer level, there's a loss of money and so on, which alters our behaviour. But this is also a loss of identity. The sense of who we are can no longer be maintained. There's a howling space around us. *"What will I say to other people?" "How will they think of me if I can't show them the nicely defined little box of my life?"*

SEEING HOW LOST WE ARE

In the practice of dzogchen we want to look to into 'who am I?' The foundation point of these teachings in this world is a teacher called Garab Dorje who made three simple propositions. The first states that we can meet our actuality, we can be what we already are, which is our presence. This is not about being something in particular but simply being what we are, prior to any constructions about who or what we are.

We live in our flow of experiences, thoughts, memories, structures and so on, out of which we are continuously constructing a sense of our identity. We are always becoming someone new and yet we imagine that we are always just 'ourselves'. So who is the one who is becoming? All the things that we become exist just for a moment and then pass ... and then pass ... and then pass ... all day long, all night long, day after day, and yet there is a continuity of ourselves. There are different strands to this continuity. One is through our memory. For example, somebody might say, *"How was it for you when you were 10?"* You start to tell them your story, *"It was a really bad year, my dad was sick,"* or *"I remember, I got my first bicycle, I was zooming around."* We all have some story to tell.

In this way we join the moments of our life together to create patterns, usually through a very selective attention, sometimes a self-aggrandising selective attention and sometimes a self-deprecating one. Some people like to tell stories that shrink them and put themselves down. This may seem strange yet it is a method of generating a reasonably stable sense of self, for it offers me a definition of 'who I am'.

However in the approach of dzogchen we leave our thoughts, our feelings, our sensations to do what they do. Not interfering with them nor appropriating them to create a narrative of 'myself'; not pushing away the ones we don't like, not trying to hang onto the ones that we do like but just relaxing and letting the movement of our experience move. Staying at peace, at rest, as the one who isn't moving – what is this presence? This is basic facticity of openness, the spacious awareness which is inseparable from what is occurring yet is not the same as what is occurring. They're not two different things, neither are they the same thing. In fact there are no 'things' at all – only luminous space and the ceaseless play of illusory experience.

The traditional metaphor used to illustrate this is that of the mirror and its reflections. The reflection is in the mirror, it's not somewhere apart from the mirror. You can't take the reflection out of the mirror, but you also can't say that the reflection 'is' the mirror. You won't find a mirror that doesn't have a reflection in it, yet because the mirror can show many, many different reflections, each particular reflection is clearly not the mirror itself. The specific reflections do not define the mirror, though the quality of the mirror is to show reflections endlessly. Similarly, when we look at our lives we probably have some memories that make us happy and some memories that make us feel sad or shameful or regretful. They seem to have a concentrated or distilled quality to them. They could even seem to sum us up: *"Oh my God, I hate myself for that. I wish I had never done it."* The event itself, good or bad, is gone, yet its impact can still register forcefully in the present moment. The event has been incorporated into our on-going sense of self, expressed through our self-narrative. On the basis of this self-construct our open potential is functionally reduced to a very limited repertoire of behaviours. For example, if

I feel that I did some very bad things, I might feel I have to spend the rest of my life in reparation. Or if I feel people have hurt me, I now believe I have to be careful all the time.

These are patterns of experience generating the patterns of our individual sense of self. Yet do they really define who we are? Perhaps inside our head, but outside, they don't. Yet we often live within our beliefs and resist attending to facts that might undermine these beliefs. For example, in my work as a psychotherapist I often have the following strange and rather sad experience. When and I meet people for the first time ... *"Hello?"* ... anything is possible. Yet within half-an-hour they have convinced me that almost nothing is possible, for they have shown very clearly, 'this is who I am, this is what I do and this is what I don't do'. So now the work has to commence in a very restricted space generated by the person's belief that 'this is who I am'. It's not true but it feels to be true. They are being internally defined by a belief system and this determines their interactions with others.

When we start to practice meditation we get a chance to see the emergence of our own familiar building blocks. We can experience how we, our open potential, gets tapped into them. We start to see how we slide into them, how it seems so obvious that this is who I am. When we merge with a thought, when we believe it to be true, we board it as if it were a train and it takes us on a little journey. Then that journey ends and here is another train with our seat reserved!

One of the useful yet alarming aspects of meditation is that we start to see how lost we are, that day by day, moment by moment, we are merged into identification with transient phenomena. The sun shines in the window and we think, *"Hey it's a lovely day."* Last week when it was raining and the sky was grey we felt, *"Ohh, it's awful, it's been like this for a long time."* When the weather can make us expand or contract, where is our freedom? We actually do feel better when the sun is shining and worse on a grey day. This is not something added to us or something which influences us – this is us in the moment. There is no self-substance to be added to or subtracted from.

Our mind itself is open and spacious and what appears both is and is not 'us'. There is no castle we can wall ourselves in, in order to protect us from experience. **[1]** The mirror has the reflection right inside it, right inside it, right inside it. The sun shines and we're happy. This doesn't mean we're stupid or mere puppets. It means we don't have border guards; we are not a separate country. There is no immigration department stopping the sunshine and saying, *"Ah, have you a visa? How long are you going to stay?"* The sun comes in our eyes and the heart goes, 'oooh' … it's free, immediate, just like that. Or you hear your phone ring, you pick it up and somebody starts to tell you a sad story and you feel terrible, *"Oh sweetheart, I'm so sorry."* A sad story which you have no defence against; it's just there immediately, the immediacy of our open being. The empty nature of the mind is like the empty nature of the mirror in offering an instant response to whatever is occurring.

This has major implications for the practice of meditation for rather than try to develop a particular content to our experience, we allow whatever is occurring to occur. When an ugly object is placed in front of the mirror, the mirror will show the reflection of the ugly object, and then if the ugly object is taken away and something very beautiful is placed in front of the mirror, it will show that. The mirror is not marked or harmed by the quality of the reflection. Similarly in dzogchen practice we relax and release our identification with the structure of our personality, our memories, our hopes, our fears, our intentions.

Releasing the identification, we see that the mind itself has no shape and so is intrinsically safe. Our thoughts, memories and so on have particular shapes and therefore can be impacted by another shape. This is why the aspects of our personality, our identity, are intrinsically vulnerable. How I am as a person is truly going to be upset if somebody tells me bad news because I'm not made of stone. We're not aiming for some kind of technical neutrality where everything is just the same known and predictable. That would be a kind of madness, for although you might attain a sense of calm you'd be a pretty poor kind of human being – for compassion means that we're touched and moved. We laugh when other people are happy and we're sad when other people are sad. Our body moves to help someone if we see them stumbling in the street. We are part of what is going on, we manifest in the world with others. Yet dzogchen indicates that the basic presence which we are is a quality of being, unaffected by our sense of being an individual. Our 'individuality' is a manifestation, a quality of energy; it is not the ground of our being.

So it's not that you have to choose one or the other: that I'm caught up in all this reactivity running hither and thither, driven by events, or that I'm sitting very calm in the meditation and nothing gets to me. That would just be a form of duality, of setting this against that. Rather the spaciousness of our awareness is unchanging, like the mirror it shows whatever is occurring, free of the turbulence of gaining and losing.

This awareness is the ground or basis of all that is manifesting at the moment, including what we take to be 'ourselves'. We are all aware of this room, we see everything here, some people we might know and others we don't. Some people look more interesting to us because we have the particularity of our gaze. The world we inhabit is always, uniquely, 'our' world. This is both the infinite aloneness of presence and the ceaseless interplay and communication of all phenomena. Our sense of loneliness arises from disregarding this non-duality. Within the field of experience, inseparable from the ever-open ground, we manifest in unfolding particular forms. You might be interested in what I'm talking about just now or not. You might be full of memories, you might be thinking about what you're going to do tomorrow. All kinds of experience can arise for us, but they all arise only within the wider field of experience inseparable from emptiness.

When we, as it were, get 'lost' it's through forgetfulness of the field – although we are always within it. For example, say you're sitting here and you suddenly think, *"Oh tomorrow's Monday, I've got to do this, this and this"* and you get really wound into the pattern they generate. In that moment you're not here, although you have not gone anywhere else. Through the practice we open to the non-polarised possibility of attending to the arising thought of Monday within the open presence which is always here and now. When caught up in the duality of identification, it is as if we suddenly go into this blinkered caught-up-ed-ness: *"I'm here, where am I?"* We then are stuck in a pulsation of open and closed, like the tide going in and out. Rather, the actuality of true openness is always here, the dynamic field of experience is always here, and our way of manifesting is always changing. Thus movement and stillness are inseparable; they're not two different things with an either/or structure.

All the movement of our existence is within stillness. Basically, we're at peace at and in the ground of our being. With this we are fully in connection with other people in the turbulence of interaction and yet at peace. When we directly taste that these two are not in opposition, life gets less tiring and no-one can steal your peace. Even when you, as a person, feel disturbed and upset, this is an experience arising within the calm open sky of awareness, your own presence. If you have a relative peace, if you think, *"Sunday, a day to myself,"* and then suddenly the kids want to come home or whatever, it will then be, *"Oh no, why can't I just have a little time for me?"* In this way, the peace that I have is based on the exclusion of disturbance and difficulty. It is a very relative and vulnerable kind of peace and it can always be undermined. Whereas in dzogchen our simple practice is to directly rest in the openness of awareness which receives whatever is happening without being conditioned. It doesn't have to protect itself because it's invulnerable. That doesn't mean that you run around without taking care, for our body is vulnerable. On the level of the person many things can go wrong while on the level of awareness everything is perfect just as it is. You can make mistakes at work and lose your job. This will change the structure of your life, the form of your identity. Yet awareness, the experiencer of both the old and new structuring is unchanging, uncontaminated, fresh, naked and hospitable.

On the level of manifestation you need to have precision, being in the world with others is the practice of compassion, finely attuned and precise. This is inseparable from wisdom which is to remain open to and with all changing patterns of movement.

PRACTICE: MEETING OUR ACTUALITY

In order to directly taste this we enter the practice. So just sit in a comfortable way, you can sit in an uncomfortable way as well, that means you just get a bit more sensation. Either way something will be happening. Whatever's happening we allow it to happen. Our awareness is open, relaxed and balanced without bias to subject or object. If we stay in the familiar conceptualisation, 'I am me having this experience, my familiar sense of myself is the experiencer', you're starting with a prejudice, with a limiting identification.

We relax into our basic state of open hospitality. We're hospitable to whatever is occurring including all that we would normally take to being ourselves. That may sound a bit strange: *"I'm going to be hospitable to myself."* Who is the one offering this hospitality? This is awareness itself. It is by being simply hospitable to everything that we awaken the actuality of existence: existence which cannot be defined or grasped; existence which is beyond existence and non-existence; beyond both existing and non-existing; beyond neither existing nor non-existing. When we hold on to a particular definition of ourselves we lose the infinity of ourselves, for how can the small contain the large? [2] It's only the infinite, the awareness that we are, the presence that we are, that is able to contain everything – it does it all the time.

So, we sit. Usually we sit with our gaze resting in the space in front of us. You can try sitting with your eyes closed as well. The main point is to relax into the spaciousness of presence. There is no fixed technique to follow, for each of us has to find our way of relaxing, releasing our habitual preoccupations and settling into the spaciousness. In Buddhism there are hundreds, indeed thousands and thousands, of methods of meditation. The problem is that each method has been developed by someone for whom it worked. This doesn't necessarily mean that it will work for everyone else. The practice is very tender, very intimate: you are letting go of identification with all that you have taken to be you. We simply observe how we get tied in knots, how we lose ourselves. Observe without judgement. Don't blame yourself or worry about what is occurring. Just see where you slip into thoughts and remain present without attempting to alter the situation. Everything that occurs is impermanent: it will go free by itself, so leave it alone.

Whatever comes, comes, whatever goes. Just stay present with that.

This simple practice is one you can do several times today. It may seem that there's nothing to it, but actually it is a kind of laboratory where you can actually see the very origin of samsara. You relax and open. There is only space. Then interpretations, thoughts, sensations start to arise. They are moving in the space. Then suddenly you're caught up in something for a while. That's where you can see the nature of attachment. Attachment is often said to be the cause of samsara, the cause of our limited experience of birth after birth. It doesn't merely mean attachment in the sense that I'm attached to my watch. The main attachment of is that I'm attached to the process of taking the aspects of the flow of experience to be something I need or don't need.

As we follow a thought we get caught up in it. We become the thought and with this there is a forgetfulness of the openness of our awareness. The practice is to allow the thought to be there in the field of awareness without interference. When we are focussed on one thing, we tend to lose the field, and when we have the field then we are not connected with anything. This openness allows us to see that there is only the mind which is space. This is the source and field of all appearance. If we are going to function in the world while maintaining meditative space, we need relaxed openness and the precision of engaging with and as different forms, moment by moment. Otherwise you always want to be in retreat in some way, in a quiet place where you can maintain things the way you want them. There's not so much benefit in that.

When you get caught in experience, who is the one who gets caught? It's as if there is a forgetfulness of the ground of being, of the openness of our awareness and then our consciousness and its object seem to be two separate entities. For example, I might find myself thinking about the heat of the sun shining on me, *"Oh! it's getting quite hot."* The thought arises in this room on the basis of the sunlight coming in through the window. Within the open field of experience some aspects are being privileged to the forgetfulness of others. There is a de-contextualisation and an over-specificity and over-investment in one or two things that are happening and a forgetfulness of everything else. We are ignoring both the source and the field of experience and therefore are being trapped in the process of identification with a few aspects which are taken to be either subject or object. *"This is happening to me ... I like it ... I don't like it",* and so on, is how our normal sense of our identity tumbles on.

We can be walking down the street while wrapped up in our own thoughts and feelings so we don't see much that's going on. There's lots of different kinds of people, changes in the architecture, there's shadows, there's colours, there's noises but we are lost in our thoughts. Even if we are attending to the world it tends to be a very selective attention where we select and comment, telling the world, *"I like this," "I don't like that," "that's a terrible building, how could they even build that, look at these all beautiful buildings, this is ugly."* Our minds fill with opinions, judgements, and opinions. This creates a particular quality of experience where one thought is following another, creating the illusion of the continuity of object as entity and the subject as entity.

In the practice, when we find ourselves caught up in judgement, we just relax and give it space. We don't have to push it away, because all life is movement, no experience lasts more than a moment. **[3] There is the external movement of our body. When we speak with each other there is the movement of the voice. Sound is movement, the body is movement and the mind is movement as well.** Subject and object are dynamic and ungraspable. We are the openness of presence offering hospitality to the shifting patterns we take to be identity. No particular pattern of movement is the truth or provides all the answers.

Therefore, you don't have to catch anything, or try to hold onto it, for there'll be another and another. It's not as if you're ever going to get just one thought a day and if you don't catch that thought you won't get any more. It's not like that, is it? Experience is endless, endless appearance. We are part of it, and awakening to this fact allows us to participate without being either in control or out of control.

When we're sitting in meditation we tend to get drawn into something because it seems important. An arising thought might generate an understanding which is valuable. This is the point where we have to let go. Openness itself is the key point and it is always available. Whereas these fleeting thoughts become distracting temptations if we imagine they have enduring importance. Due to our selective attention it is as if the content has been separated off from the source or ground from which it is occurring. For example, when you look in the mirror when you're cleaning your teeth, you just see your face. It is unlikely that you will enter into contemplation about the nature of mirrors. You simply observe yourself cleaning your teeth. You take it for granted that this is me in the mirror. The invisibility of the mirror itself means that we don't see the reflection as a reflection. When you look at yourself in the mirror you see yourself in the mirror as yourself. Of course you know it's not you it's a reflection, yet you see you as you because that's the immediate sense that we have. We fall into the reflection, we identify with it – and this is exactly what happens with our thoughts. We fall into the thought and this seals it as something which is inherently true. Yet the thought is just a moment in the ceaseless chain of becoming which is manifesting as the body, the voice and the mind within the field.

In the traditional Buddhist view, when our manifestation is cut off from its own ground we become a sentient being wandering in samsara. We become an individual, somebody who is travelling, going here, there, looking for this, trying to avoid that. However when you rest in the ground of your own being, then manifestation is clearly linked to the field, and the field is clearly linked to openness, the space within which the field of experience occurs. Openness is called the dharmakaya, the field is called the sambhogakaya and manifestation moment by moment is called the nirmanakaya. These three aspects are inseparable, and this is the Buddha. It's not something high and transcendent and far away, it is the actuality of our life. Yet we don't get it because we're getting something else, we're getting caught up in our stuff, in our habits, our interpretations.

Actuality can't reveal itself to you if you're caught up in telling yourself who you are and the world what it is. You have to allow yourself to receive. It's the very richness and fecundity of our own creativity that stops us registering that we are part of what is going on. That is to say we talk and think ourselves into our individual existence but we're just part of what is going on, the illusory display of the heart of the Buddha.

CONNECTED TO OPENNESS, WORKING WITH CIRCUMSTANCE

Each of us can tell the story of our lives: our family was like this, we went to our particular school, we did this, and we did that. In these stories 90% is the same for everyone. We have to go to school, we like some teachers, we don't like other teachers, we have a favourite food, we have a best friend. This is normal; in fact we make our individuality out of what we actually share. Why do we share so much? This is because we inhabit the shared field of experience – we walk, we talk – and this requires an environment and language we share with others. The uniqueness of our individual experience is something we have in common with all other beings. Our existence is pulsatory; it is part of a movement, a dialogue of communication. We are not things, not entities, not a self sealed in a bubble. We are participants in the unfolding movement which is the world. Our own mode of participation is unique and specific to each of us but our individuality manifests in relation to other people. Our individuality is not the sign or product of an unchanging inner essence – rather it is the manifestation of the interplay of our potential with the potential of the situation. It is a field phenomena rather than a 'personal' quality. This is obvious once we start to look rather than assume. In the course of a day we have many different kinds of conversation as we talk to different people. What you can say to one person is not the same as what you can say to another person, and of course the manner of **?[saying]?** also varies greatly.

We tell of an event in different ways, so what is the truth of the event? Memories and their recounting are situationally evoked rather than 'objectively' true. Someone asks how we are and we say, *"Aah I'm fine,"* yet with another person we say, *"Ooh, it's a bit like this and that."* Why do we say more or less? It is because the person we address will seem to us to be a big door or a little door. If they look like a little door to us, we will not want to reveal much of ourselves, for it seems there is not enough room to let more of us pass through. Yet maybe to someone else they look like a big door! This is the dynamic nature of the unfolding of our becoming; we are becoming ourselves in relation with others. Yet our being itself is unchanging, for being is not the personality. Rather being is the quality of mirror-like emptiness, the openness and clarity which reveals the ceaseless movement of becoming.

This view indicates that it is both fine and inevitable that we are unreliable. It is gorgeous to be unpredictable for we are not machines. However, being unreliable and unpredictable is not the same as being self-indulgent because then you'd be reliably self-indulgent, you'd just be doing your own stuff. Rather it's to see that we are co-emerging with the environment. The environment changes and we change and this co-emergence is mutual interaction. Unpredictability is not created by whimsy – it is the actuality of the interactive field. The infinity of our being opens us to see that what we call 'other people' is inseparable from ourselves. Self and other are movements in the fields of experience. The movement of our body and the shape of the stairs as we walk down them are not two different things. I am not the master, as in 'I am walking down the stairs'. Rather the stairs and our body are in a conversation as I was suggesting earlier. I think you will find that this is true with everything you encounter. If we go to a café to get a cup of tea our body, voice and mind are all manifesting patterns that fit with what we encounter. If we are not able to do that, it is a sign that we are lost in a limitation.

From the Buddhist point of view, this mutual influencing is compassion itself. The more you see how you are is part of the world and let go of holding yourself apart in some separate domain of your own thought, there is less and less barrier to being open to other people. With this empathic attunement you are able to tune in to and be as close to their profile as possible, and this reception of their actual presentation in the moment allows your response to express both the immediacy of the other and your own actual situational capacity. There is no map or template that can show us the 'right' way to be, for 'right' is not a moral judgement but the quality of 'fit'.

Every situation we are part of invites us to taste the plasticity of our identity, our capacity to be moulded and shaped by events since we too are but a series of events. Conversation evokes our body, our voice and our mind to move. Flexibility is part of communication, for you cannot be fully connected with other people and be rigid – it is impossible.

We know that when we get a bit scared, frightened or worried, we become more fixed and rigid. We might want to avoid others for our pre-occupation has rendered us unavailable. Availability is flexibility because it calls forth a fresh response. In this state you have the freedom to access and reveal the whole range of your potential. Thus in dzogchen we offer ourselves into the flow of becoming rather than holding ourselves apart.

Being alive can be quite a complicated business for there are many, many different demands that we have to face, many uncertainties, many unpredictabilities. This uncertainty easily produces anxiety and anxiety easily turns us in the direction of wanting to impose control. Control can be very useful for a while in some areas of life but a lot of the time and in many situations it is not, for it evokes a sense of personal agency that blocks our easy participation. Meditation practice is the presence, which offers responsivity to and within the situation. It is not something that we prepared earlier. This requires relaxing our reliance on knowledge, patterns, and habits. We discard our recipe books and pay more attention to the rich potential of the ingredients we and the situation are composed of. We can do many things on automatic pilot, and often do them simply because we know how to do them. Habits are quick and in some ways efficient. They can make us feel competent. The problem is that often they don't fit the actual situation. So in order to comfort myself by doing more of what I know how to do I end up enacting a subtle or gross violence on the other – and this increases my sense of duality.

This tendency to over-activity is increasing in all public walks of life in Britain. Whether it's medicine, teaching, or anything that is connected with the state, there is more and more regulation coming in. This is driven by a fantasy that 'bad' things just shouldn't happen. A risk assessment is made, structures are set in place, and then if something bad has happens it's obviously because people have not followed the rules. Social work departments can be paralysed by this kind of thinking, school teachers are imprisoned inside narrow notions of the syllabus and so on. Fear is probably not an ally of competence, and if staff are not supported and trusted to be themselves while staying in role they are likely to lose their motivation.

Of course, the anxiety arising from a mistake can easily lead to the imposition of anxious controlling as the best way to keep people efficient and non-harmful. However, mistakes are part of life and are probably best dealt with with calm clarity and a sense of proportion. Nurturing in times of difficulty is vital because when we nurture people we give them resources. The more resources we have the broader the repertoire of possible responses we have, and with the confidence this generates we can allow ourselves to be present in the actual situation and respond into it. This has two main advantages. Firstly, we fit ourselves into the situation and actually meet people where they are, and this is compassion. Secondly, we experience the freshness of our being, and this is wisdom. If you merely have to obey orders and implement something which has been decided by some people somewhere else, you are being denied your creative responsivity, the flowering of your singularity within the web of interconnectivity.

Central planning may be useful with commodities but not with people. Human beings are particular, they are unique. Each one needs to be responded to in their unique individuality. If you don't offer that how can you help people? The standardisation of people is the attempt to make them machines. Human beings have been doing this to other human beings for a very long time. It used to be in the form of slavery but nowadays it manifests as the need for efficiency and its consequent demand for conformity to a program.

Dzogchen proposes that the best way to bring about richness and fulfilment in life is to work with the unique specificity of your own and others situation. This brings genuine contact between people and also highlights the many ways in which this can be sabotaged. The deepest sabotage is not to be our own openness. The next level is the avoidance of the richness of our potential. The surface level is our tendency to hide ourselves in identification with pre-existing structures, generating a sense of belonging which is actually a forgetfulness of being. We can find belonging in a sport, a family, a religion – but the relief these offer is often short-lived.

We have to find our way from loneliness – which seeks a rescuing other – to relaxed aloneness which is open to all.

Nothing you can say about yourself can sum you up. If you tell a friend about how you've been in the summer or what you might do at Christmas, you create a little structure, a little shape. It's a gesture of friendliness but is it the truth about your life? Does it really show who you are? I would suggest not. In that way when we communicate, there is linking, connecting, co-emerging, joint production of value – but not the establishing of an enduring truth. This offers us the freedom to not take ourselves too seriously. We cannot establish what we are, only describe how we are, the current patterning of our manifesting. Moreover how we are is contingent, we arise in communication with the circumstances of the wider field.

So in dzogchen we are not trying to align ourselves with some perfect form, we are not attempting to manifest in a particular, pre-determined pattern. Rather we work with circumstances, experiencing what it is to be alive at this precise moment. If you are in touch with your life, with all the turbulences, the expansions and contractions of your own existence, you realise that you are a dynamic potential of patterning. As part of the non-dual field of experience, our patterns arise in relation to those of the field. Hence we collaborate with the world rather than attempting to dominate it. Flexibility, changeability is inevitable, therefore why would we get very upset when other people are unreliable? This view tends to make us a little softer, more tolerant, and less judgemental as we relax our assumptions and expectations of ourselves and others. We often get disappointed and let down by other people because they don't do what they said they would do, but when we look at ourselves we also find we're not very reliable.

So, maybe prediction is simply a reassuring fantasy, a way of keeping our head above the water: *"My life's fine, and five years from now I'm going to do this, I'll be ok."* However if I think I don't know what is going to happen, then it's upsetting, it's alarming. We can't tolerate the uncertainty and so we reassure ourselves with fantasies – fantasies which help us to avoid the actual nature of our situation. Dzogchen points in the opposite direction: relax, open, and integrate with all circumstances without relying on conceptual elaboration. Anxiety, fear, and not knowing are all part of life rather than limits to it. This is a much more reliable refuge than trying to achieve total control.

THE EMPTY AND OPEN INDETERMINACY OF 'I AM'

The water in a cup could be contaminated by adding something to it, and then it would no longer be pure water. Something can be spoiled in its simplicity by coming in contact with something else, that's obvious. But what could contaminate nothing? How would you put something in relation to nothing? Actually something and nothing are not in opposition. Ice cream and doughnuts are in opposition because they are different things; you can put them on a plate and you can look at them and you can say this looks like a doughnut and that looks like ice-cream. There are different kinds of cars, clothes, houses and so on. What about nothing? How would you hold nothing in one hand and something in the other hand and compare them? Nothing dissolves the game of compare and contrast.

Logically you might think that they are opposites, but because nothing cannot be established, cannot be found, it deconstructs the binary oppositions out of which we construct the narratives of our lives. Thus we have male/female, young/old, good/bad, England/not England, tea/coffee and all the rest of the mutually exclusive signs and categories. Comparing and contrasting brings 'things' close enough together so that you can see sameness and difference. For example, if you go into a clothes shop you can look at two different coats. One is really gorgeous but wow it's a lot of money, whilst the other is not quite so nice and it's £100 cheaper. You have to make your own decision about whether you want the quality or the money and that depends on your immediate budget, where you might wear the coat and all the other pertinent factors.

This kind of comparison depends on reification; we need to first establish that there are two separate entities. We see shapes and colours, we hear sounds – the raw has to be interpreted before it is cognitively meaningful. To do this we rely on our thoughts and feelings which are transient – and the moments of perception they comment on are also transient. Subject and object arise and pass – the continuity of our sense of self seems to be built up of an accumulation of memories, assumptions, plans and so on. Yet our mind itself is different. It is not a thing among things – it is the experiencer, the clarity which reveals the ever-changing field of experience. This is not our usual way of identifying the experiencer. For example, if I ask 'Who am I? What am I as the experiencer?' I might say that I like being here with you and I've got a bit of a cold and I'm a bit tired. The basic experience is that I'm here and that is coloured by me being a bit tired and having a bit of a cold. Thus the subject, me as I take myself to be, has a certain situational shape and that influences the kind of experiences I have. But who is the one who has the cold? *"I am!"* That's a statement. Ok, so who is the one who says 'I have the cold?' *"I am the one who says, 'I am the one who says I am the one who has the cold'"* – but who is that one? We have an infinite regress here because the answer to each of these questions is formulated by employing another statement. All of these statements have the same form, 'I am' – I am the one who is this, that and the other. Who is the one who says 'I am?' *"Please Miss, it's 'me', I am, I know the answer, 'I am me'."* Oh good boy, you are clever! So clever as to be completely stupid! For this is a process of self-seduction. The question is not truly being asked because we already have the answer: *"The one who looks is me."* Who is looking? *"Me."* Are you sure? *"Yes, of course I'm sure."* And so we are blinded by the easy option, the ready-made answer.

This is our main problem, that we are on a well-oiled track which hides the door to truly, directly seeing our nature. Paradoxically the factors which hide us from ourselves are precisely the tools which we rely on to make sense of ourselves and our world. Our knowledge, assumptions, fantasies – the rich variety of our mental creativity is exactly the display of the mind which hides the mind.

For example, those of you who live here in Brighton can name the streets, can indicate that if you go down that street there's a really nice café. You are introducing the visitor to Brighton, yes, but actually it is to 'your Brighton'. You are putting your Brighton onto the potential of this town. If the newcomer was to wander around the streets they might find another Brighton, but you've been living here a long time so you know Brighton, and so you direct people according to your personal map. We do exactly the same with ourselves. We put forward our version of ourselves as if we were describing something truly existing, when in fact what we're doing is creating a temporary constellation. These are quite different. So, for example, I can say 'I am a man'. It's kind of difficult to know precisely what it is to be a man. I used to be in a men's group and would sit in a circle and discuss what it means to be a man. We would talk and talk and there was no end to the discussion, no final agreed description. This is because 'man' is an empty signifier; like a sausage skin you can stuff it with anything. It's like asking what is love? You can talk for thousand years about what love is because you can put almost any content into the signifier. Who am I? This is the best sausage skin of all. Any idea you have can be applied here: 'I'm hot', 'I'm cold', 'I'm young', 'I'm old' and so on. Whatever is arising and passing will momentarily fill the sausage skin and appear to be true and right. Before lunch you say 'I'm hungry' and after lunch you say 'I'm sleepy'. You're always something, but something that is on the point of vanishing.

How is it that 'I am' can be filled with so many seeming truths? Because it is nothing. 'I' is how we refer to our presence. It is not an entity, not a thing or a substance. The openness or emptiness of 'I' is the quick way to see the openness and emptiness of the mind. The mind, our mind, our awareness, our un-mediated presence here and now is like a mirror. A mirror can fill with any reflection because it doesn't have any content of its own. If we look at the painting on the wall behind me, it has a content. When you look at it again and again you see the same pattern of colours, it is announcing itself as something in particular – but our mind is not like that.

Our mind, the basis of our experience, is the openness which reveals our becoming, our manifesting as a ceaseless flow of change. We, the presenting subject, change according to circumstances all the time. It is our very non-defined quality, our beyond definition quality, which allows us to manifest in responsiveness to other situations. Self-knowledge as an accumulation of information about oneself is a red herring and a cul-de-sac. To truly know yourself is to know that you are unknowable, ungraspable yet always present. Our truth is not established by knowledge; it is already present as the actuality of our being. When you are at home in and as yourself, you don't know how you are going to be, how you will become in the next five minutes. Nobody can predict how they are going to be, for being is open and ungraspable, and becoming, manifesting, is always a complex momentary event.

The more at home we are in our actual self rather than in our self-narrative, the more freed we are to respond. Then our response is situationally evoked and its basis is the openness of indeterminacy. It's not a lost indeterminacy as in a psychological depersonalisation where a person doesn't feel like themselves, or can't recognise themselves. This is not about a cognitive feedback loop that reassures me 'I'm still me' because I can recognise that this pattern is 'me'. Usually we have a template of how we normally are, the habitual feeling of being me, and this becomes the guarantor that I am myself. If there's any variation away from this felt sense and its associated memories, we feel, *"Oh, I don't feel so well today,"* or *"Oh, I feel really excited, I haven't felt like this for a while,"* and we notice that we are veering away from what has become the standardised version of ourselves. These movements then generate hopes and fears.

In dzogchen we relax out of this familiar matrix of identity for there is no end to the work of making micro adjustments of the temporary content of the flow of our experience. The more we're trying to rectify ourselves, to bring ourselves back into alignment with our template, we find ourselves struggling against the fact of impermanence, the actual dynamic nature of existence. In the field of experience there is no enduring structure to align with. All such seeming structures are installed through our own interpretation.

For example, when our body is balanced we are aligned with the force of gravity. We then feel centred, our skeleton supports our weight, our muscles can relax, and our breath is easy as the diaphragm is free to move. This balance occurs due to our harmony with our environment – when we walk we have to find our balance in each movement. Balance is not a 'thing' that we have but a sensibility, the optimal way of opening in all directions. The fact that we 'find' our balance through sensing it means that our sense can lead us astray – as ballet students find when they observe their actual posture in the mirror and see that internally it feels different.

In that example at least you have something that can be clearly observed – but when it comes to mental and emotional experience, balance is much more difficult. We become used to our habitual attitudes and that 'normality' gives them the feel of being balanced even when we are fused in attitudes and behaviours that are well off kilter. Being lost in familiar places is difficult to recognise as the familiarity hides the lostness.

The relative balance of left and right that allows us to feel centred is different from the profound balance of resting in the simplicity of the mind itself. Experiences of objects and ones subjectivity needs constant re-balancing, yet the actual experiencer, the mind itself, is not an entity and is beyond relativisation and is always relaxed and balanced whatever is happening. We can look at this directly, for we are here, experiencing something, then something else, and so on. A stream of experience is occurring.

Who is the experiencer? Each of us is the experiencer.

What is the direct taste of that experiencer? What is registering for the experiencer seems to have two aspects, what we take to be the object and what we take to be the subject.

This is what we stay with in meditation, not going to the subject side, not going to the object side, but staying with our own presence itself, the clarity which reveals the co-emergence of the subject and the object. So, we're sitting here, you can hear at least some of the words I'm saying, if you're not drifting off completely, and you have your own thoughts and feelings. From the 'object' side, words are coming out of my mouth and going to your ear, something is coming to you, some object, and you have your subjective reaction.

You experience my voice, is this true?

You experience your thoughts, is that true?

Is it the same experiencer for my voice and your thoughts?

When you attend directly to your experience in this way you see that what I'm saying and your thoughts about what I'm saying are both experiences for you. Now this 'you' who is open in all directions is not composed of the ingredients of your self-narrative – it is the experiencer of that self-narrative without being caught up in it or defined by it. The content of what I'm saying and the tone of my voice and so on, is the object side presentation. The subject side is your response to that with feelings and thoughts. You are experiencing both, but you *feel* like the subject side. So there is a double move, in that sense you are existing on two planes simultaneously. You are both the empty experiencer which is simply revealing the subject and object interplay and you are also the particular thoughts and feelings that you have, and which seem to constitute who you are.

Most of the time we are so caught up in identification with our thoughts and feelings that this more open, empty sense of the experiencer is disregarded or rather made invisible by being taken for granted. It's always there, and it is open, empty, ungraspable – yet because we fixate on the manifest, it is as if the un-manifest is not present at all.

The experiencer is the ground of our existence. It is our awareness, our presence. In Tibetan it is called rigpa. It is not something mystical or fantastical, but the ordinary everyday luminous presence that is the basis of all our experiences. It's not our personality and it's not generated out of our history or our thoughts. It's the revealer of everything including the interpretations by which 'we' respond to the rest of the field. When we look around the room we see people's faces and from the look on their faces we can imagine a little of how they might be feeling. But we will never know. My experience of me seems so much more intimate than my experience of you. I'm having the full me-ness of me and just some sense of you. I'm getting a lot more me than you. It is this which gives us the sense 'it all starts with me'. I have to work hard to try to work out what's happening for you, but the me-ness of me comes first, it seems to be a given. This is how duality reveals itself. In taking myself to be this individual subjectivity, with all the work that entails, I focus on the details and ignore the intrinsic clarity which illuminates the non-dual field.

This is a bias, the prejudice of over emphasis on the content of our own 'personal' experience. Due to this we live our lives as if life is a problem to be solved and so we have to think very hard, *"What am I going to do?" "How am I going to relate to this person?" "What's the whole deal?"* We are busy, busy, busy all day long thinking, planning, making adjustments trying to get it right. All this activity blinds us to the fact that how you are is just as much a part of my experience as how I am. It's different from my experience of 'myself', but then if I take a bite of an apple and then I take a bite of an orange, they are different and we'd say these are different kinds of experience. The experience of me being me and my experience of looking at you are different experiences. But maybe they are different in the way that an apple is different from an orange. The habitual interpretations embedded in our everyday use of language makes it difficult to see what we are up to. The terms 'I', 'me', 'myself' seem to be so self-evident in their meaning that we are taken in by their illusion of finality.

This view suggests that there isn't an essential personal truth or core inside ourselves. Rather, our subjectivity is part of the stream of experience. But the experience of subjectivity is taken to be the hallmark of the experience, and then there is confusion as the transient is taken to define the 'self' as something enduring. It is normal for us to feel that I am here inside my head looking out at the world: *"I am having my experience of the world."* Yet actually the world presents as experience and I present as experience. These two streams of experience are criss-crossing all the time. They are not two separate things but are like little pulsations of water within a big river. They are moving within the wider movement.

It is by disinvesting our subjectivity of the burden of being the totality of 'who we are' that we start to experience the space of our being. So rather than feeling that *"it's all up to me, I've got to think, I've got to go back inside me, and I'll tell you when I'm clear, just don't disturb me,"* we can let go of the transient constructs and stop building our illusory individual isolated self out of them. Conflicts often arise from the sense that *"you being you is robbing me of me being me, so leave me alone!"* This is very strange! For in this view, myself is now something I have to protect like a little egg and carefully carry around with me for it's very fragile. Yet the fact is that me being me is me being me with you. So how can I, on my own, sort out how I am if the self that I'm trying to sort out is the self that I am with you? *"Listen, I think we have to have a trial separation. I'm going to go away and when I'm clear about who I am, I'll come back and see you."* In this way 'you' and 'I' remain separate and the 'we-ness' of life is ignored. We can also retreat inside of ourselves in the search for clarity – yet this simply further separates 'I' from 'me'.

Thus in my interactions with the world, I experience myself and I experience the environment. The self-experience or the subjective-experience is an experience, it is not the experiencer. But it is the experience of an experience and implicitly claims to be the experiencer. This is truly tricky territory. When you formulate an experience as, for example, 'I am tired', it seems that the experiencer is talking, and by means of that talking is defining themselves. Yet by making the next statement with a similar grammatical structure and a different semantic content, this 'I' is redefining itself. Such vagaries of identification point directly to the illusory status of 'I' as denoting a self-substance. Observing this directly for oneself is extremely useful.

The root of all these transient moments of identity is our basic being which is beyond totalisation – you can't sum yourself up. This is the basic freedom of all human beings, and it is why totalitarian states are so dreadful, so terrifying. There are still many countries in the world where human beings are given a number, they are summed up in a simplifying definition, they are seen as terrorists or the enemy. When that occurs the availability of other people's minds to see the infinity of the potential of that person collapses into a very narrow, dogmatic reading of the person, which is then taken to be a true account of who they 'really' are.

We also do this, though in more subtle ways. We reify other people, treating them as knowable entities, and we also see ourselves as existing as things. We objectify others and we objectify ourselves. We judge others and we judge ourselves. This limiting, narrowing, imprisoning structure has infected our own mind. Its rigidity and predictive force gives us a sense of power yet it is itself just movement. We can probably all remember coming home from school one day and saying to our mum, *"Oh I hate Johnny, I'm not going to play with him anymore." "Why not – I thought he was your best friend?" "Ahh, well he did that to me..........."* When you are a kid such events are really terrible and seem so completely real and final. *"Oh don't take it so seriously." "No, I'm never going to be his friend again."* Something has happened that has generated a definite knowledge that 'he's horrible'. Some movement has happened between you and your friend and suddenly it's as if there's a tear, there's an event which you can't integrate, which you can't incorporate into the flow of experience and so there is division, splitting. We know this nowadays in terms of Post Traumatic Stress Disorder where there is a trauma or powerful event, which cannot be integrated into the continuum of the person's psychological life. And so there is a lesion, a tear that feeds into repetitions and so on: *"The world has changed, I cannot put up with this."*

In order to free ourselves from the many forms of limitation we encounter in meditation practice, we listen to the solidity of the way in which these thought formations arise. We're not trying to stop the thoughts coming or trying to push them away, nor are we falling into them. Rather see that they are enticing, sticky, full of an energy that makes us want to throw ourselves onto them. This is like the story from The Odyssey where the Sirens are singing on the rocks and whoever hears these marvellous women singing will want to go directly towards them but then their boats are smashed to pieces on the rocks.

What is this incredible glue that binds us into temporary situations, both 'internal' and 'external' and makes them seem completely true? Why is something which is arising due to causes and conditions, and is clearly contingent and contextual, taken to exemplify an essence? Once the sense of an essence catches us there is a clarity which is the clarity of stupidity. I remember when I was about 11, I saved up some money and sent away for a transistor radio that you had to partly build for yourself. I asked my dad to help me and he looked at it and then he said, *"This is made in Japan."* I said, *"Ok."* And he said, *"Ah, I fought the Japanese in Burma and I won't have anything Japanese in the house."* I said, *"Dad, the war's over."* And he said, *"I don't want anything Japanese in this house, I don't like the Japanese."* We didn't know any Japanese people, we were living in Scotland and there were not many of them there, but he felt that, in his mind *"I know what the Japanese are – they are this and this and this, and I will never forget."*

He had his experience of the world and there was some truth, some painful basis for his belief but it became a huge global identification which can be layered again and again in new situations. We know that there are many prejudices about racial and religious groups and so on, that go on generation after generation. It is exactly this sort of structure which we experience in meditation. We get a chance to see directly our over-investment in certain ideas as being absolutely true. If you just stay present with the thought, the thought will go. Thoughts, feelings and sensations are always passing. They are impermanent but when we think that 'this is a terrible thought and so I want it out', or that 'this is a wonderful thought and so I need to have more thoughts like it', then the glue is working and we are stuck on the treadmill, working hard but getting nowhere.

This activity of yes and no, editing and adjusting, although it appears to be overtly a good thing to do, becomes the basis of not being able to be at home with who you actually are. Energy, which is by its very nature is connectivity, is directed towards the endless task of self-maintenance. The energy of openness is mis-apprehended as being 'our energy' and directed towards the activities of adjusting, shaping, and defining. This is so familiar that we easily take it to be just how it is, yet who is doing it? Who is the thinker of the thought? Who is the experiencer? These questions are subtle and the answer is unhidden yet allusive so we readily return to our habitual pre-occupations: *"Ah, never mind that, let's get the content of the experience right and when all the experiences are lined up in a row and they're all very nice and they're all wearing clean underpants, then you'll know that life's completely sorted."* And it never happens. By focussing on correcting the shape of our thoughts and feelings, our life quickly passes as we try our best with an impossible task.

Actually we live at the crossroads: if you stay with how you are, even if it seems terrible, that situation will vanish and you will find yourself to be where you actually are. But if you decide not to be where you are because you feel that there is a better place to be, then the energy that goes into doing that displaces you from where you are and sets you on a never ending task of improvement. So paradoxically doing less gives more, while doing more keeps you feeling the alienation of lack and hunger. The activity of trying to improve the content while ignoring the experiential field, within which the content is occurring, places us in the world of endless construction of our ideal identity. This is something which at best we only ever briefly taste for a short period of time, for the perfect thought is replaced by another and then another thought comes and another thought comes.

Our identity is not something which can be sorted because it is part of the web of connectivity: if you have friends, or if you know people, or if you are political or if you have children, if you worry, then these are signs that you are concerned. Other people affect you; other people impact your life! So how could you be stable? Being alive means being unstable. Unstable doesn't mean being out of control, it means dynamic, it means moving as part of the world.

OPENNESS AND BECOMING – EXPLORING KADAG AND LHUNDRUB

With this orientation we can now look at two key aspects of the dzogchen view and practice. These are Kadag, the natural purity of the mind, and Lhundrub, spontaneous display or manifestation. Primordial purity indicates that the mind is empty like a mirror. My subjectivity, what I take to be 'I', 'me', 'myself', is part of the moving content of my mind. It is like a reflection in the mirror, it's not the mirror itself. If I confuse the reflection with the mirror itself I'm going to have a problem. The mirror is reliably a mirror because it never shows itself directly. It shows itself through the manifesting of reflections. The clarity of the mind, our presence, our capacity to know rather than knowledge itself, is always open, empty and available. Whereas reflections are much less predictable because they arise in situations, that is, they are an aspect of communication, of identity, of showing, not of being.

Whatever comes in front of the mirror brings about a different reflection. Similarly our experience is situational, influenced by the weather, by the kind of food we eat, by our health, the menstrual cycle, by whether we're getting on well at work, and so on. All sorts of things influence how we are in our experience of the world. This unfolding never stops, it is constantly moving.

Now, if you place an object in front of a mirror and leave it there it may appear that the reflection is stable, is something reliably there, is something which can be returned to again and again. But the reflection as object requires the subject in order to reveal itself – and their intercourse is the flow of experience. The question then is, where will I find stability? Only in the state of the mirror, for awareness itself is stable in its inseparability from space. The experiences which arise are not stable. So if you think that your subjectivity is stabilisable, is something you can make fixed and predictable, that you can gain enduring self-knowledge, then you take the wrong road at the crossroads, and condemned yourself to trying to make movement stop. But movement is always moving the mind is always moving.

It's not the movement of the mind that is the problem. It's our difficulty in allowing the mind to move as it moves. And there is another paradox here: the more tightly you try to control the mind, the more jumpy it becomes, and the more space you give to the mind, the more its flow is harmonious. Trusting the actuality of existence, believing all will be ok, allows the diaphragm to relax, anxiety to diminish, and then the free flow of self and other plays without disruption. This is what is referred to as Lhundrup, spontaneous manifestation which is direct and effortless. The open purity and simplicity of our mind reveals itself as the ever-changing field of complex illusory manifestation.

As we look around the room, everything is here immediately – this is our experience. Wherever we go, there is a world. We don't get half a world, we get this world, the fullness of this moment of experience. Our concepts of other places arise within the field of experience which is me in this room. Each moment is complete and 'perfect' as it is – this is just this, then this, then this.

So, you can look at this room here in two ways. One way is to come into your skin. You can do this now: feel your own skin, feel your own body. *"I'm here, this is 'me' and I'm looking out at the world. You're there and I'm here – we are not the same."* You can look around at all these people sitting over there: *"I'm sitting here, you're sitting there. This is where I am, this is 'me' and this is 'you' – I am me and you are you."* It feels very separate doesn't it? Another way is to relax and release our interpretations, to allow the actuality of the simultaneous presenting of 'subject' and 'object'. They present to our presence which is immediate, infinite, intimate – but not personal, and certainly not a personal possession or quality. Thus there is the experience of your body in that your body is revealed as certain sensations in the feet, the legs, the torso and so on, and this is arising at the same time as the perception of everything around you. These are two areas of perception and they are fundamentally the same. Similarly, we see people and we hear sounds. The visual perception and the sound are not the same in their forms of manifesting but they are both experiences devoid of substance.

I am my experience of me just as you are your experience of you. The experience is infinite, the hospitable host of all the myriad transient experiences which arise – some of which we take to/use to constitute ourselves and some of which we take to/use to constitute our world and all that is in it. This is radically different from our normal way of thinking because it indicates that my home base is not this material form, the fleshy castle that I inhabit. I am in the world, with the world, the world and I have the same status as appearances in the flow of experience. We are the eyes of the world, we are the way the world experiences itself, as display rather than as substance. This is the mandala of all the Buddhas.

Actually we live in this field of lucid clarity all the time; we are an inalienable part of it. The body is clarity and the experience around us is clarity. The clarity of experience is instant. The emptiness of the mind and the fullness of the mind are inseparable, non-dual, without contradiction. We are the playful richness of the mind's display. Our body for us is special, but it's special within the world, it's not special apart from the world. We are moving in the world the way fish are swimming in the sea. We don't move towards the world, we don't have a separate domain, 'my private self', 'my internal world' out of which I go towards you. My movement towards you is always my movement with you within the infinite indivisible field of experience.

If I'm in my own head, in my thoughts, then of course I can construct a thousand forms of alienation and imagine games of manipulating and controlling. Yet all of these are experiences revealed in the mirror of the experiencer. They are not separate 'things' but aspects of experience. The feeling of being 'within myself', being apart, is an experience non-dually, not actually separate from the ceaseless displaying field of experience. In the simplicity of direct presence, I am revealed to myself within the same field of experience as you are revealed to me. This is the non-duality of self and other, and hence how I am is part of how you are. There is no need for the paranoid feeling that I have to ring-fence a private domain to keep out the foreigners, the strangers, in order to protect the purity of my own vision. We don't need to each establish an Aryan personal people's party – membership, only myself: *"I am the chairman and the life president, keep out."* It's amazing how easy it is for us as individuals or small groups with a dogmatic sense of sameness to succumb to that belief and then imagine that everybody else is a potential contaminator of the purity of yourself.

The pristine purity that we all have and are is the purity of awareness, not the purity of personality. The purity of awareness can never be destroyed but the purity of the personality is an illusion because we are co-emerging with the world. Identity is dialogue, not individual essence.

PRACTICE

Let's do some practice. We sit with our eyes open, gazing into the space about two arms length in front of us. We are not staring at the distant wall but just letting our gaze relax into the space. This means that our gaze is open and panoramic so we have a sense of this large space. Just relax into the out breath and be present with whatever is occurring. Sometimes this is predominantly object-phenomena, and sometimes subject-phenomena – experience how both are movements without essence and in this there is no real difference between them.

With this kind of practice we sit for quite short periods of time at first, five minutes, then ten minutes and so on, because it is subtle and we are used to something more crude. We have a strong habit to identify with the subjective form as being ourselves and of course as soon as you do that, because subject and object are born together, you can get caught up in the object flow as well, and they mutually reinforce.

So relax into open presence, which reveals both aspects as the movement of the mind, as the energy of the mind. We are not trying to do anything at all but simply to be with how things are. If we are given a task where we can mobilise ourselves, whether it's weeding the garden or doing the dishes, even if we don't want to do it, we can do it and can get a sense of personal empowerment through the activity. It's the same with thinking: the personality, the spiral of self-reference, has sucked into itself such a lot of importance that it feels as if it is the centre of the world. However in this practice the personality, our individual sense of self is de-centred and allowed to take its actual place as a series of momentary events. It's not that there is no self, clearly we have a self, but the self is an energetic formation which is moving and changing. It's not the centre. It's part of the pulsation of our display and it arises in communication. In the practice we relax and release the pull of our habitual over-identification with a form of energy as if it were the source of activity.

WISDOM AND COMPASSION

A lot of our emotions are generated by people rather than things, so how can we relate to the people who become fixtures of our lives. Situations of familiarity are where we are most likely to develop an interpretive story about the other person, some sense of the patterns and predictabilities of the other person's behaviour and with that the arising of irritation if they change their pattern.

Truly seeing someone, receiving them as they are, is not the same as knowing about them. Being with someone is an allowing of their existence, as it is now, to be as it is without judgement. Yet as we gather information about someone we build up a map that seems to describe them and then when they 'stray' from that, as they inevitably do, we become irritated and may feel betrayed. It was their reliability that was keeping us safe – as if how we had taken them to be was providing us with a secure foundation for our life. In this way we privilege the map in our head over the other persons current actuality. We are saying, *"I know how you should be and therefore if you want me to be happy with you, you should be the you that I know you to be, rather than the you that you currently are. I know you better than you know yourself."* It is we who have created this essentialised view of the other. But this essence is an abstraction while the actual person is a flow of co-emergent patterning.

We do this in order to try to establish the stability of our identity. The fact is that both you and I 'emerge' as 'ourselves' moment-by-moment according to events. Yet this can be ignored if we focus on the images and narratives that we have developed about self and other. If I see you and see myself in terms of my pre-constructed maps and descriptions then this reliance on abstractions helps me to feel safe and stable and predictable in the face of the actuality of ceaseless change. We gain a sense of continuity which is reassuring but limiting, for a kind of sclerosis occurs, a sealing over, a rigidity which blinds us to the potential of the non-dual field.

However, if we trust the world as it directly reveals itself to us, then instead of interpreting it according to maps and fantasies and memories, we work with how it is. If we can work with how it is then the other person will be accepted as they are. It is a good though perhaps unsettling experience to be accepted as one is; it's not all that common in life. We accumulate a lot of knowledge about people and items in the course of our lives. The question is, what does the knowledge pertain to, what function do we employ it for?

Resting in our knowledge about someone is a violence to the actuality of their current presentation. We actually cannot know how they are until they disclose this and this disclosure is relational; it is influenced by how we are in that situation. Some of what we know about the person may be relevant to this new moment – but which aspects? That will be determined by the moment and not by our plan or intention. Knowing about people and knowing them in the sense of being with them are very different. The former mode is cognitive while the latter is immediate, the receptivity of awareness which reveals the complicated, unpredictable richness of the situation and is more authentic than trying to organise on the basis of predictions and maps.

'Being' itself doesn't change because it is open, empty of any defining content of its own. 'Becoming', which is our experience of being in the world with others moment-by-moment is the arising of thoughts, feelings, perceptions, memories, expectations, etc. in specific transient patterns. 'Becoming' is contextually evolving – so how could we have accurate information about another person as they actually are in this moment? How could we have accurate understanding predictive of ourselves? Only by aligning ourselves with a pre-established template and by privileging this over the openness of presence.

This view would indicate that a lot of our mental activity is redundant, that we do a lot of planning and sorting things out which is not actually useful or necessary. Our mind can be empty and contented, and it can be full and contented; the contentedness of the mind is not dependent on the content of the mind. Our mind itself, our awareness, our presence is intrinsically contented, at peace, satisfied – this is the great completion, *dzog pa chen po* (Tib.).

All of us have huge creativity; to be alive, especially as a human being, is to be endlessly creative. Our creativity reveals the open potential of the world, of the field of experience. It is our own limitation which fixes 'things' in their 'place', defining them as 'this' or 'that' as if the definition related to a truly existing essence.

When we meet the world and ourselves through the veil, the screen of our knowledge, what we see is the veil and not the actuality. Our knowledge doesn't improve our sight, in fact it makes us blind while we think we are seeing better. This is the nature of ignorance according to the Buddhist view.

From this point of view compassion is linked with not knowing rather than with knowledge. Compassion is to open ourselves to receive the other as they are – and this is both their openness and their precise configuration at this moment. Our receptivity is part of the pulsation of co-emergence, and from it our response arises as a gesture of contact, of connectivity. It is the naked openness of our presence which offers this compassionate or attuned connectivity. We dispense with the protection and cladding that makes us feel safe, yet we are safe since open presence is invulnerable. We are more vibrant, more alive and this invites others into their vibrant aliveness.

When we bring our knowledge about another person into the present moment, we might consider how big, how strong, how stable is this moment is. Can it support a feather or a tonne of assumption? It is normal human practice to bring a lot of ballast into each moment in the hope of stabilising it and making it understandable. The gravity this brings may be reassuring to us and support our sense of personal agency yet we are also encumbered and burdened by it and lose touch with the lightness of our open presence. We have to trust that all is well and open to the situation, however it is. You meet a friend for a coffee and the conversation goes wherever it goes, because to-ing and fro-ing in an unpredictable is what a conversation is. In these moments you have a good time, a good conversation, you were really there. This is being alive, it's not esoteric or magical or transcendent, it's just, *"Oh! I could have more of that. I could have that all the time."*

Having trusted this, why do I let it be something rare and special in my life rather than being the flavour of everyday life? Why is it that I abandon being fresh, alive and connected? What do I think is better than this? What is so frightening about being connected? That's a very central question to look into: where am I better off than being here now with you?

Part of the function of meditation practice is simply sitting with whatever's here. This is all there is, this is it, as it is. Funny sounds arise in the room, people move about, memories come, sensations in the body – it's a bit higgledy-piggledy. Shouldn't we have some spring-cleaning, a bit of order? No! This is how it is, the disorderly unpredictability of the emergent field. We're still alive. Life is like this, however 'this' is. There is no designer, no pre-existing plan. Patterns emerge and interact. If we relax then there is space for contact free of the conflict that arises from defensiveness.

Actually not quite knowing is a very friendly space. If we say someone is a know-all, it's not really a compliment for it usually means they're pretty closed. It's difficult to relate to them because they're always hitting you with the answer. Whereas not knowing is friendly and inviting. Keats is famous for his notion of negative capability, the capacity to not know what is going on, to not have to make sense of things, to allow the unfolding of possibilities. In order to make sense of what is happening we tend to lose contact with ourselves – we give ourselves over to the domain of concepts. Whereas, if you stay in your senses, you remain part of the immediacy of the situation.

This immediacy is the inseparability of primordial purity and spontaneous emergence. The purity of the mind is its intrinsic lack of a fixed content. Whatever content is arising, including the interplay of subject and object, can be accepted as ok, because it's not going to cause any harm. The purity of the openness of awareness is indestructible. It is not an entity among entities. Therefore, we don't have to protect ourselves against the world. Self and world are transient experiences devoid of substantial essence. Thus naked engagement, trusting, spontaneity, improvisation, is the simple way in which we can be vital and alive and connected with other people, open to change in all directions.

Wisdom is to recognise the fundamental openness of our situation in which you can't grasp any fixed content as to who or where you are. When we look back over the years we've been so many people, we've had so many emotions, moods and hopes and fears...all gone. I can't define who I am, but I'm here. This being-here-ness is the being here-ness of an openness which is ungraspable and simultaneously of a potential which can manifest in infinite ways according to the particularities of each situation.

This is the non-duality of primordial purity and spontaneous manifestation, or wisdom and compassion, and this is the heart of the practice. The function of meditation is to relax unnecessary effort and thereby allow our controlling tendencies to go free by themselves. Releasing our habit of employing the patterns that we are familiar with we are free to find ourselves anew in the new situation. Of course that can feel a bit scary: *"How will I know what to do?"* Our anxiety promotes the sense that we need to know what will happen so that we can prepare. Yet actually we simply have to trust the practice, open and relax, and the creativity of the ground will flow through us.

The mind itself is open. Open means free of foreclosure, no shape, no colour, no form. The mind is not a thing yet how can I be somebody who doesn't have a shape? The mind, my mind, is not the content of the mind, not the patterning of thoughts, feelings, tendencies etc. which constitute our personality. The mind is our presence not the transient experiences of our subjectivity. Our body has a shape but it's a shape that changes but the mind itself has no shape or colour.

You can investigate this for yourself. When a thought arises, it may seem to have a shape, a colour and an intensity. Emotions have an impact, then they're gone. Actually whatever has shape and form is moving and changing; the only thing that doesn't move or change is our being, and it has no shape. This is weird! Our existence is very, very strange. We are not what we think we are. We are what we are, but because we don't recognise what we are, we create what we think we are. But we are not what we think we are, we are what we are and this is a given, it is there without any effort on the part of our subjectivity. To find this natural freedom all we have to do is to stop asking thought to do work it can't do.

Thought can do many, many things but thinking cannot give you a stable personal identity and thinking cannot tell you who other people are. It can help you remember somebody's name but it can't define the person, because human beings are beyond definition. Whatever you think about yourself, however you define yourself, this is not who or what you actually are. We are, we just are, we are present prior to and throughout all the myriad experiences which occur.

WHATEVER COMES, COMES; WHATEVER GOES, GOES

In this meditation tradition the basic principle is ... whatever comes, comes, whatever goes, goes. While you are sitting the key point is to not interfere with the flow of experience, not try to improve it or make it fit your template. All kinds of thoughts and feelings arise yet we're not clinging onto any of them, nor are we trying to push them away. Simply be the openness which is the mind itself and allow the energy of the mind to manifest freely however it is.

Sometimes the mind feels very sad and depressed. If that happens it may seem like a heavy mood that's pervading you, like morning mist that fills a valley. Everything is opaque and you've no idea what's going on. Don't worry, don't try to do anything, just sit with the one who knows nothing: *"I'm lost and confused, I feel hopeless."* Ok, that's a feeling, that's a mood. Who is the one who is experiencing this? The storyteller is here, yet so is the immediacy of the presence which is revealing the movement which is the storyteller.

Without changing the story simply be present with the unfolding of the story – however it comes. However, this infinite hospitality will not be available if you have a predetermined notion of how your meditation should be. Whatever comes let it come, even if it is harsh, judgemental, toxic, dreary. Meditation is not about getting a better kind of thought, it's about seeing, really seeing that thoughts are empty and leave no trace. You only need to try to grasp a good thought if you can keep it. What's the point of working very, very hard to get good thoughts in your mind if the buggers keep vanishing? When you look in your mind thoughts are always vanishing, even if they are very lovely thoughts, they're always going to be going.

Don't worry about the content of the thought. In fact, when you get self-hating thoughts, when you get hopeless thoughts, crazy thoughts, destructive, cruel thoughts or any kind of thought, feeling, sensation in the mind, don't fall into seeing it as being inherently meaningful, as something telling you the truth about your situation. Just observe without involvement: whatever comes, comes, whatever goes, goes. Let it come and go – and be the unchanging presence.

In this way we're not like a nightclub with a bouncer on the door, we're not trying to keep the bad guys out. We're living in a house which has no front wall and no back wall, and so the good guys come in and they go out, and the bad guys come in and they go out. There are only side walls on the house and then they start to fall down and everything's space. So, coming and going, coming and going, that's the heart of the practice.

In the Tibetan tradition the mind of the Buddha is said to be like the sky. It's like space, it's infinite. Storms arise in the sky – thunder and lightning – then next day it clears. There are no scratches in the sky, just beautiful sunshine and rainbows, it looks gorgeous. Then it changes and clouds come again. Then the clouds go. This is the sky. The sky shows many, many different forms yet the sky is still the sky. We say, *"I don't like the clouds."* We say, *"I don't want to have a mind like this."* We say, *"This is no good, this isn't the real meditation, this can't be it because I know what it should be like.''* With this attitude our narrow prejudice is already filling the space of possibility.

I imagine I'm not alone in the fact that when I was a teenager I often told lies about myself, pretending I was more sorted than I was, for it felt too confusing and shameful to say, *"I have to admit that I don't know how to do this and I don't know what that is.''* This was a terrible state to be in, full of anxiety. Moreover, in pretending, you miss direct contact with others and miss out on their normalising reassurance. It often takes us a while to start to offer ourselves, warts and all – *"This is how I am.''* Meditation takes this truthfulness to a deeper more open level, revealing the richness of our potential as we start to see that all the possible forms of samsara and nirvana are nothing other than our own mind at play. The infinity of my mind opens me to the infinity of other people's minds, so that however other people are I can find space for them in my mind, in my heart, with compassion because I'm not entering into judgement about what is occurring, simply seeing it as it is and working directly with that.

With meditation we relax judgement, relax the will to power, the need to control. We allow the mind to be as it is and remain open as we enter into daily life. This is how it is and this is what we start from, not how I would like it to be, how it should be.

Our starting point is always this moment, this event – not ideas about it or plans for it. With this approach we can truly see that the thoughts that constitute me are a potential for communication rather than a definition of who I am. This releases us from the fear that if other people knew what I thought or how I felt they wouldn't like me. The maps we have developed are allowed to be part of the territory and non-duality is pervasive.

From the point of view of dzogchen, meditation and ordinary life are not two separate domains. It's not that you go on a meditation retreat and create some particular structure of clarity and then bring that back into daily life, where due to the friction of events the clarity gradually fades like a melting ice cube. Rather sitting and moving are interpenetrating as we open to being with how things are. This is the willingness of the Buddha to enter every situation.

Teachings given at Brighthelm Centre, Brighton, UK, 2nd December 2012.
Revised by James Low.

Wisdom and compassion

The field of buddhism is very vast and many of the ways of understanding it offers are to do with the illusory nature of our existence. That doesn't mean that it's all an illusion and so nothing matters. Wisdom is inseparable from compassion, which is to feel the immediacy of the link we have to everything which is occurring. Compassion is not an effortful practice. It's not an artificial practice in which we struggle to become a better kind of person. Rather, by experiencing the inseparability of ourselves and others, we see directly that we are always in a movement of interaction and that what we call a 'self' is not cocooned in a bubble.

We are not isolated individuals. Our potential is revealed through our participation with other people and it's the very absence of a precisely determined, or an over-determined, sense of self which allows us to offer this free flow of compassion. The more tightly we define ourselves, the less freedom we have to respond to and participate in the world around us. Of course, when we are small, we get many different kinds of definition given to us and out of that we construct our personality, the sense of the continuity of ourselves based on the familiarity that we have with certain patterns that we repeat again and again. That can be helpful and reassuring if the patterns of our familiarity are relaxed, open, ethical and so on but often we also have internalised patterns that are full of doubt, anxiety and even self-hatred, in which we have become alienated from ourselves in terms of our potential. Very often these patterns were given to us many years ago and when we look around, we can see that there are many people who don't have these same beliefs about how life is. Nonetheless, we cling to these patterns and identify with them as if they are who we are.

The function of meditation is to open a space in which we can see the contingent nature of the building blocks out of which we construct our familiar sense of self. It's not that we are attempting to radically transform our personality. It is more about not taking it so seriously. If we are kind to ourselves, if we hold ourselves lightly, then we can start to hold other people lightly, which means we don't get pulled into their story lines. Having more room to manoeuvre, we can start to participate in the rising crest of the wave of potential. That is to say, new formations are always coming into being but a lot of the newness, the freshness, the unformed-ness of the emerging moment is hidden from us because of the projections of our habitual interpretation.

Our expectations of how things will be lead us to actively look for any signs that confirm our expectation and as a parallel move, to edit out the relevance of information that would put our expectations into question. Buddhist practice is very concerned with the immediacy of experience. Of course, there are many, many aspects of the tradition which describe particular kinds of constructs: of the nature of enlightenment, of buddhist pure lands and so on. These are methods of helping us prise our awareness and our attention from the foreclosure of our everyday expectations.

That is the key point: all the building blocks of our identity are transient. There is no substance to them. That doesn't mean that they are meaningless. It means that moment by moment, we live in an emergent gestural field, that we are moving in a world which is moving. There is no stability.

The fantasy of stability becomes persecutory because we start to think we should be 'sorted'. The years go by and we think we should have worked out who we are and what life is all about and how we should be with other people. We give ourselves to particular readings or identifications of situations. We inhabit that bubble for a while and then the bubble pops – and along comes another – and another bubble – and another bubble. We have bubbles of hope and we have bubbles of disappointment. You can be hopeful for many years and then you can be depressed for many years and then you can be something else for many years. Each is like a particular room. It has a colour. It has furniture. It has a mood and you inhabit that mood and you think, *"Well, this is it. Can't get out of it. No doors. No windows."* You make the best of it. Sometimes it feels good. Sometimes it doesn't feel so good. The key thing there is not the nature of the room you're in but the fact that you are experiencing rooms.

We tend to be very object-fixated. We try to make sense of ourselves by talking about ourselves. Either we're thinking about our situation or we're describing things about ourselves to other people. That creates a triangulation because you have the immediacy of your experience; you have the qualities of what you take it to be; and you have your interpretation of it. The interpretation is a culturally derived set of story lines. Whatever stories we tell about ourselves, we can be sure some other people are telling fairly similar stories about themselves because we have a lot of similarities as human beings.

What is ignored in that is the very nature of the experiencer. There is a presence which is continuous and it is continuous because it has no content. This is not how we normally think about ourselves. Normally we experience ourselves as an engaged consciousness. We know the things we like and don't like and we bring that furniture in to the room of our experience. That is to say, we are already filled with ourselves when we meet the world. We meet the world out of our particular shaping or construct but if we look back over the years, this furniture, or our set of structures, has undergone quite a lot of modification. The beliefs that we had when we were fifteen are probably not the beliefs that we have now. The kinds of things that we do now, the clothes we wear, the people we talk to, the things we talk about, will have changed many times in the course of our lives. So what constitutes 'me' and feels like 'me' is a content of experience. It is not the experiencer itself.

When I talk of my 'self' I'm talking about what is inside me. At the moment I am holding a glass and I can say that the glass has water in it. The glass can be filled with many other things. The potential of the glass is the fact that as an empty glass, it offers hospitality to many other contents. This lack of definition allows the glass to be useful. If somebody had put petrol in it, for example, every time you went near it to take a drink, you'd think, *"Whoa! That smells bad!"* because the trace of petrol lasts a long time. So, the more the glass is carrying its history, the fewer possibilities we would have with it. It's a similar situation for ourselves.

IDENTITY: THE ILLUSORY SENSE OF SELF

These traces of our past events are called *vasana* in Sanskrit, subtle traces that linger from previous events or karmic traces. Whatever we want to call them – habitual patterns or unresolved neurotic schemas – they bring particular orientations or taints to the freshness of each new moment. Because a certain flavour is hovering around the glass, there are many things that you wouldn't want to put in the glass. It wouldn't make sense to put a fine wine into a glass that smells of petrol. In that way, the more we identify with the patterns derived from the accidents of our history – the fact that we went to a particular school, had particular kinds of teachers who encouraged or didn't encourage us – the more we maintain the shaping influence of the past. The somewhat random trajectory of our life which can often seem orderly in retrospect, but at the moment when you're in it, you haven't really got a clue about what's going on. We're just blown hither and thither by the random nature of events.

The traces of all of these impinging moments give us particular kinds of anxieties, particular kinds of avoidance, particular kinds of desires. The busyness of pursuing these particular patterns distracts us from asking, *"Who is the one who's experiencing this? Who is the actual subject?"* That is to say, *"Who am I?"* Moreover, what is the nature of our awareness since the world only exists for us because we are aware. If we don't register events they are not there for us. For example, you can be out walking with a friend and they say, *"Oh, Look! There's a woodpecker on that branch."* You look and suddenly you see that there's a bird. You had seen it but not seen it. When the bird is pointed out to you, you incorporate it into your world. Prior to your friend's comment the bird was in the field of your potential experience yet invisible because you weren't attending to it. That is to say, the particularity of our world is what we actually attend to. We're all very familiar with that. When we go clothes shopping our eye is taken to certain garments, certain colours and shapes. Many things you see look nice but you couldn't imagine wearing them. That has to do with the particular topology you have of your body, the contouring and shaping of your sense of self based on your own history. We can't dissolve that into 'year zero' and begin again.

The function of meditation is to have some space within which these particular shapes are allowed as they are without being over-invested as being the truth about ourselves. If we are over-identified with the traces of our history we are very vulnerable. Any construct can be bumped into by new events and then we may feel gutted, disorientated, torn apart... because in fact all constructs are fragile.

Everything which exists is held dynamically in place by the meeting of many different factors. There is not one single entity which 'exists' in and of itself. We know this about ourselves. We have a body. Inside our body there are vulnerable organs prone to blood-clotting. There may be cancerous formations. There may be wear and tear on the spinal column. There are multiple ways in which this beloved body can gradually fade and collapse as well as many sudden ways it can suddenly go 'pop.' So although we talk of 'my body' and it feels so familiar to us, it's not a possession that we can necessarily take good care of – because, how will we take good care of it? On these cold mornings is it good to go out jogging or not? Some people say that red wine is good for us, others say the opposite. Likewise with coffee. Actually, we don't know. Some people have a long life even though they live in a crazy way and other people have a short life although they eat very healthily. That might indicate that something else is going on. In that sense, we are moving in a field of interactive vectors, of pulsations which generate our existence. My existence is something I experience rather than something that I have. However the language that we use in talking about our self, is to talk of it as if it were a possession. There are plenty of nice people who have very sick bodies. To draw correlations between ethics and physical health can be experienced as very punitive. Perhaps it is better seen as our luck or fortune. In Buddhism this is spoken of in terms of karma or activity: how our body is in this life is an indication of our behaviour in previous lives. We participate in an emergent field over which we have some influence.

'Influence' is an important word because it's about fluidity. It's about a movement into an evolving field. We don't have control; we're not actually in charge. We are not out of control either, but neither are we in control. This is the middle way, which is being part of what is going on. We are always in the world and however the world is, it is influencing us. We participate, and as we do so we are both influencing events and being influenced by them.

What we take to be self and what we take to be other, are two moments which are always occurring at the same time. You cannot 'just be by yourself' because even if you close your eyes and put your fingers in your ears and cut yourself off, you still have to keep breathing. If you block your breath, you'll die. This is a basic fact. We are part of the world. The world comes into us with the in-breath and we go out in to the world with the outbreath. This is going on all the time. So although we talk about '*I, me, myself*', it's a bit phony. It's not really how it is. Our being is dependent on access to the environment. To have trouble breathing can be frightening and seeing somebody struggling for breath is horrible. They are being cut off from what they need and what they need is something which is other than them. They need the breath of the world to come into them.

We need the sounds of the world to come into our ears. We need the light of the world to come into our eyes. This is what replenishes us. Our movement into the world, through the world, is a movement of responsiveness. In buddhism this is taken to be a basic given. There is no inherent self-nature in a person. There is no fixed internal definition that tells us who we are since our identity is contingent. It is adventitious. It comes to us through the interactions that have been there right from the moment of conception. The development of the foetus in the womb could be a source of joy or of anxiety. The baby could be coming out into a warm, prepared, receptive environment or somewhere quite scary and difficult. All kinds of things happen to us. When you're small, you have no power at all. You're completely at the mercy of what's going on in the field. Gradually we build up more sense of separation and identity and we want to be self-defining. We struggle with our parents and siblings to 'get our space' and do things our own way but mostly we're constrained by what's going around. The world is always offering us particular kinds of deals and we have to engage with these.

This is a way of saying that identity is participative. It's determined by our potential which is arising in the moment. Each specific instance of our potential is never our entire potential since each aspect is constellated in each situation and is textured by the particular shaping of the environment at this particular moment. Doors open and doors close. Sometimes when a door is wide open in front of us, we can't move towards it. Sometimes when there's no door at all, we run straight into the wall! We may be full of enthusiasm but there's no way forward. I'm sure we've all experienced these kinds of situations.

When life goes well, it tends to be because there is harmony between what is arising for us and as us, and what is in the world. What can we do to promote that? By not having established a tight notion of what our 'proper shape' is. In other words, flexibility is health. Being flexible means, *"I will become what is fitting for me to become."* But, *"What about me as me?"* Fixed notions of ourselves interfere with our capacity to be in connection in the world. The foundational Buddhist reflections on old age, sickness, impermanence and death are not practised to terrify us but to let us see how identity is formed in relation to events.

CONSCIOUSNESS

Mental consciousness is the means by which we construct patterns of identification and develop assumptions, intentions and plans. This kind of mental clarity allows us to have an intention towards how we're going to proceed. However our mental consciousness can be a very sophisticated liar. We all have a little Public Relations Department inside us so that when things go badly our little spin doctor steps forward, *"Oh well, it wasn't too bad really because at the end of the day the show must go on."* We've got to hang in there but this involves a lot of editing, a lot of adjusting. This is the nature of consciousness. It's a very busy phenomenon. It is the organisation of our mental structure, of all the different thoughts, feelings and sensations that need to be sorted out into patterns and evaluated as helpful or unhelpful and so on. This is continuous work, going all the time.

It's not surprising that we get very tired. Some unexpected new event comes along and, *"Whew! I've had it up to here. I just don't need any more."* We are a sort of middle management; we're not the big boss; we're not the CEO; we're trying to get the people underneath us to do things but every time we delegate, the buggers do the wrong thing! You delegate a task to your memory but as you get older your memory lets you down and you forget. It all gets a little bit scary. 'It's all up to me' is the paranoid position of an individualised sense of self-identity when in fact our consciousness is constituted by a stream of thoughts, feelings and sensations. Some of these thoughts may seem directly relevant. They feel not only 'like me' but 'helpful to me'. Others can feel 'like me' because they are familiar but they are not very helpful and some other thoughts are just plain weird! All kinds of strange stuff comes to us: in sleeping dreams, in daydreams, in sudden thoughts that shoot across our mind. It's all too much to make sense of.

That is why traditional buddhist texts say that there is no end to samsara. The field of experience is too complicated, too complex, to sort out. It keeps changing. Consciousness, which has a function of organising our participation, is essentially a dynamic, interactive movement. It is a function of engagement but it's not a stable identity. So the question, *'How can I know who I am?'* is actually a false question since you cannot know who you are. You can be yourself. You can be yourself as an emergent subjectivity, but you are never actually a thing, an object that can be known. Interacting with circumstances, we are present as ourselves however that might be.

Being and knowing are not the same and especially knowing about things is not the same as a kind of 'pure knowing'. For example, you go out and see some snowdrops – and they're very sweet – but then you see a robin. Oh, a double whammy, snowdrops and a robin! Oh! The heart melts! It's very nice. You're looking at this gorgeous little event. In a sense you know it and so there's nothing to think about. You just look at the snowdrops. It's a sort of wonder, an awe. It's a knowing but not knowing *about*. That causes a little door to open and we have a sense of being fresh. We're replenished. We return to ourselves through these simple moments of beauty. Blackbirds singing in the evening. It's evocative, maybe of memories of childhood or other happy times but it's also evocative of a deeper and lighter sense of ourselves. We are evoked into, '*Oh! Oh!*'

That's the arena of meditation, to move from knowing *about* things towards trusting the direct meaning given to us in the spontaneous revelation of the world when we open to it. It's much easier for most of us to open to a snowdrop than to open to the sound of a tyre screeching. We retract from that. We don't want that in our field even though it is just a transient event, like the perception of the snowdrop. That's where we see that the openness of awareness is easily closed down by the particularisation of egoic judgement, when we say *"This is good and I want more of it. This is bad and I want less of it. I don't want it near me."* How is the emergent event is in its simplicity is being distorted by my self-referential interpretations of it.

Our habit of trying to get the good things and trying to avoid the bad things is considered again and again in buddhist texts. In my book *SIMPLY BEING* there are many encouragements not to try to push away bad thoughts and hanging on to good thoughts in meditation. It is as if bad thoughts are like squatters breaking into our house. We know they are going to spoil how we want it to be. By opting to prolong good thoughts we're back with gardening: flowers and weeds. Get rid of the weeds; feed the flowers. Busy, busy, always busy because seeds are blowing in the wind into your garden even while you're asleep. Some little weed is starting to dig itself in. When we meditate we encounter all these thoughts sprouting.

Meditation involves two aspects: one is to relax into the open spaciousness of awareness itself and the other is to become aware of the incredible pull of our habit of identifying with thoughts. These thoughts seem meaningful to us.

In the field of psychotherapy it is very common to encounter people who have become reliant on negative views about themselves. They are convinced that they have something wrong with their physical form, or that they are unlovable, or that their life is meaningless and the best thing they can do is kill themselves. If your own life is not too bad you may wonder why somebody would hang on to a belief like that. They come to therapy for a couple of months and you hope and expect they will get some progress now that you have given them a description of their patterns. Another two months go by, the description of the problem still seems valid however nothing much is changing. Why do they hang on to a belief which is so awful, that restricts them and keeps them in a frightened inhibited place? That is because being frightened and inhibited feels like home. That is the domain which that person's particular structure has adapted to and therefore its familiarity has become more powerful than the bitter taste of its content. *"This is just how I am."* Why would the negative, the destructive, the awful, become home? Because anything can be home. Human beings can identify with anything no matter how seemingly awful.

We can see a softer version of the same structure in our meditation practice. We want to relax into open awareness but we fall into thoughts again and again because thoughts seem so useful. We merge with the thought. The thought seems incredibly important. It seems meaningful to go off in a daydream about something. You're sitting, you want focus your mind, relax and be open – but you're gone! Why? *"It seemed a good idea at the time."* Maybe we could all have these words carved on our gravestone! It is important to see this because there can be a danger that we use meditation to beat ourselves up if we feel we are not making much progress. Or that we give up on it and think it's not working. The attachment that has us merging with our thoughts is the root structure of samsara. This is why we're here, because of the nature of attachment. Attachment in this sense is not a conscious kind of attachment like me (subject) being attached to something (object).

This more problematic kind of attachment is the immediate merging of our consciousness with what is arising for it. Consciousness only emerges as a formation in relation to an object. The actuality of our world is non-dual. There is no wall between subject and object, between the mind and the content of the mind. We can't set up a border post with a barrier that announces, *"Hey! You can't come in here"* or *"You, you're very welcome."* There are no Customs Officers checking what thoughts can come in and what can't. Thoughts, feelings and sensations are immediately here so we can't prepare in advance to control them. They occur before we knew what was happening. If you feel persecuted by your thoughts and fight to control them, then meditation is going to be very difficult for you. We need to relax out of our assumptions and attend to thoughts as they are. Only by this does it become obvious that they have no inherent existence. The reifying ego-self cannot outwit the thoughts that it itself reifies.

If you self-identify as a drinker then struggling not to drink is very hard. Why? Because you're a drinker and until that core definition of being a drinker stops, then if there's a bottle, you're going to open it. If you stop being a drinker, you can look at the bottle and think, *"Hmm, I'm not fussed. Someone else can have it."* Some space has opened up. Nothing has happened to the bottle. The object hasn't changed. The object is the object but the hook between the object and the drinker has dropped. It's the same for smokers. If you're a smoker, the packet calls to you. If you're not a smoker, the packet doesn't say anything at all. In fact, it says what it says on the label, *'This will kill you.'* But if you're a smoker, it doesn't say that at all. It says, *"Oh, that will be nice!"* That's how it happens. That's what we have to see.

It's exactly the same structure with thoughts, feelings and sensations. As long as our primary self-definition is rooted in an individual particularising consciousness, that consciousness will merge with thoughts, feelings and sensations. We will always be caught up in this interaction. Therefore, the heart of the practice is to relax out of consciousness into awareness.

DISTINGUISHING AWARENESS AND CONSCIOUSNESS

Awareness and consciousness are not the same. Awareness has no form, or shape. It doesn't come from anywhere and it doesn't go anywhere. It is uncatchable. That's why you cannot know awareness. It's not an object for the mind, but you can *be* aware. You can relax into a state of awareness within which consciousness will be moving around. Consciousness as the individual personal subject and the experiences of consciousness as your perceptions of the world – these will be moving together and you can see them to be the energy of your experience but not as the ground of your experience. The ground of your experience is the inseparability of awareness and space. That is to say, awareness is uncatchable, ungraspable. It's not a thing, yet it's always present. That's why it can be filled with whatever is occurring and whatever is occurring is devoid of self-existence.

Consciousness, on the other hand, is always taking on particular shapes in particular moments. Suddenly you feel thirsty, suddenly you want to go for a walk, suddenly you remember, *"Oh, tomorrow it's Monday and on Monday I have to go to the dentist."* A moment before you might have been relaxing then suddenly the thought comes, *"Oh, did I turn off the gas?"* The body tenses, you start to get a bit preoccupied. That's consciousness at work. A thought gives consciousness a poke and consciousness runs after the thought. It's an interplay of energy. It's like a pas-de-deux. Two dancers are moving together. They are no longer two separate dancers because the choreography has linked the movement of their bodies as a communication. The consciousness that says, *"I remember what I have to do on Monday"* is two things. It's an object in the sense of being a flow of thought patterns arising in the mind, and it's also the subject in being aware that this is what you have to do on Monday. Whatever is happening, whether seemingly subject or object, is simply a transient patterning of the ungraspable energy of the mind. It is this which is misconstrued as being our existence in a world of existents.

Experience has no experiencer. Experience is the unborn clarity of awareness itself. In the traditional example awareness is said to be like a mirror. A mirror shows what is there. What is there in terms of our existence is the ceaseless movement of thinker and thought, feeler and feeling, sensor and sensation. Sometimes awareness shows what looks like a subject, sometimes what looks like an object. They chase each other like a kitten chasing its tail. This tumbling is the energy of our experience and is the way in which as patterns of energy we participate in the world with others.

When it works well this pulsation of energy is very stimulating. It is the external form of our internal active and passive movement of being the thinker *and* the thought. This energetic formation of dance and dancers needs a stage. The stage, both the external stage and the internal stage, is awareness. Awareness, because it has no form or colour or content, is the field in which all our experience is arising. It's hidden from us, not because it's secret, or high, or holy, or special; not because we are unworthy or damaged or obscured, but just because we are caught up in all this falsely reified stuff. We are so busy looking at interactions and being part of interactions, that we don't see the field within which it's happening. We take the space for granted. We take being alive for granted. What does it mean to be alive? What is this freshness of existence? The fact that experience is revealing itself moment by moment by moment.

In the dzogchen teachings we talk of three modes or three linked fields. There is the open field, which is awareness itself, which is empty and unborn. This means that it has no substance to it; it's inconceivable. You can't really describe it.

Within this, instantly, is the spontaneous revelation of the entire field of experience. Each of us sitting here has a unique world being revealed to us – our particular take. Whatever seat you've chosen to sit in, gives you through your sense organs a particular revelation of this room. Nobody else will have the same: neither perceptually nor interpretatively. Each of us is the centre of the world in this specific way. There are similarities but these are similarities established through language and concepts. The openness is this field, vibrant and changing.

Within this luminosity is the third field, which is our gestural presence in which we speak, we listen, we move, we stretch, we hear, we have thoughts and feelings. It is a responsive field. The open field of awareness is unchanging. The richness of the field of spontaneous display, called *lhundrub* (Tib. *lHun Grub*) in Tibetan is immediate, always changing. Within it we have the particularity of our fresh emergence, moment by moment. Each emergent patterning is specific, responsive and ungraspable yet because we're not in touch with this open arena which is our ground, we don't see the light, playful, illusory nature of what is displaying itself.

Forgetfulness of the open ground and its radiance and its responsiveness gives rise to our busy thinking by which we have to make sense of what's going on. This busy-ness is the preoccupation by which we avoid seeing the ground of our existence. It's as straightforward as that.

BEING IN THE WORLD WITH OTHERS

IDENTITY

Imagine two sentient beings in the sea. One of them is waving their hands and shouting. If you had a rope with a big hook at the end you could throw that for them to grab and then you could pull them safely to shore. However if the other sentient being is a fish and you threw a rope with a hook at the end, it would not be so helpful because dry land is the wrong place for a fish to be. As human beings we don't do all that well in the sea; we may manage a few hours. So it is important to see what is the right environment for us and for all the sentient beings we encounter. What sort of environment does each of us need in order to flourish?

On the level of openness, the environment that supports practice is a quiet one where we are not disturbed by other people. So think about how much time you could put aside for sitting meditation practice. It doesn't have to be a huge amount of time but if you don't go into a room, close the door, sit and relax completely, meditation is going to be difficult to enter.

Modern life has us in a fairly constant low level of arousal. Many people have mobile phones with them which can interrupt their behaviour at any time. We have many demands on us and we are primed to take them seriously and to respond. This state of readiness gets in the way of relaxation. For practitioners in traditional Tibet, it was very different. It's a big, big country with not many people. There was no television, no radio, no comics, no novels, no cinema. An occasional storyteller might come to your village but most of the time there's nothing much going on. You might have a shrine room in your house or you could go to a cave and quietly meditate. Just the sound of the wind or occasional birds calling. We're not living in a world like that at all, so applying the traditional approach in our situation is problematic. In order to survive in our world we have to engage with it as it is, and the toxicity in the environment cause forth a toxicity in ourselves. We need to survive toxic states of arousal suitable to our environment without being intoxicated by the toxins.

Most of us are not very aware of the toxicity of our arousal because it has become necessary in terms of harmonising with our environment. Perverse environments require perverse behaviours. It is normal on the London Underground to stand very close to other people and ignore each other. This unusual behaviour has become normalised. Human beings are social and communicative. It is against our nature not to say something to someone we are standing close to. We use language to mediate social distance but in the Underground, we don't use language to do that. People ease themselves into a dissociative state, blocking out all the people around. People who can't do that may start to get anxious and have panic attacks when they go on the Underground. Dissociation becomes vital. You can't say to the people around you that you're feeling anxious and unwell since they are all disassociated and avoidant of contact. That is the price of survival, of getting to your work on time, if you live in London. It's toxic, it's poisonous, it's wrong but it is necessary.

Our ego-self lacks the capacity to remain relaxed and open in stressful situations. It is dialogic and reactive. However, awareness is intrinsically open. It does not have to try to relax. To access this, we simply dis-identify with our habitual patterns of identification and involvement. Awareness is not our 'true self'; It is not an aspect of our personality. Rather, our personality and our self-referencing egos are frozen energy, habitual patterns of unawareness that all experience is non-dual with the open empty ground. Our ground, our basis, our source, is naked open and available. As such, it needs no protection. It is the delusional ego that is vulnerable. The ego is easily hurt due to its fragility and lack of inherent existence. Yet it cannot see this and imagines that the cause of it suffering is the unreliability and selfishness of the other. It is this misperception that fuels the desire for control and dominance, as if this would bring security. What it actually brings is hyper-vigilance, uncertainty and loneliness.

As I sit here looking around the room, I see different faces. I am here, and between me and you is a space. If that space were not there, I wouldn't be able to see you. We see each other access the space of separation. This gives us the chance to manoeuvre ourselves to get closer or further away from others. We can mediate our interpersonal distance in this way. This is how the ego is kept aroused in active engagement with the environment. Awareness is different. It is open and intimate yet unengaged, like a mirror. With a mirror the reflection comes into the mirror. It's immediate, direct and unmediated by any conceptual apparatus. This is the same with the basic openness of awareness; it neither has nor needs any protection because it is indestructible. Awareness is like space; it doesn't have a material basis.

AWARENESS

Awareness itself is indestructible. In Sanskrit it is referred to as *vajra*, meaning indestructible, diamond, adamantine. There's a story that the first *vajra* formation came with the Hindu god, Indra, who meditated for a very long time and completely calmed his anger so that no matter what provocation was offered to him, he didn't respond. Thus he became imperturbable, unruffled and was said to be *vajra*. This story is helpful for meditators because it's a good litmus test of the stability of your meditation. If you're in the domain of reactivity, you're in the domain of consciousness.

When you are very relaxed and spacious you can see experiences arising and passing yet with reactive involvement in the various forms that occur. The field of experiences is arising and we are present within it as an interactive pattern of experience. The pure presence of awareness is not a graspable activity. It is empty of self-defining content and so is invulnerable. This is very important. When present in uncontrived openness you don't have to edit your experience. Whatever comes, whether seemingly good or bad, if we are alive in unborn openness, these forms are clearly inherently empty of defining content and their 'existence' is merely a name put by transient mental activity.

Wisdom means to see the emptiness of every occurrence while compassion is hospitality to everything that occurs. If you experience a steam of negative thoughts, self-hating thoughts or cruel thoughts you can welcome them by offering them the space of emptiness. They are just thoughts. They are not going to harm your open empty essence. They are transient illusory forms that fill the space and then vanish. If they are allowed to just come and go while you remain relaxed and open, they will leave no trace just as reflections leave no trace in the mirror. As you know, if you make a mark on a piece of paper with a pen, or a pencil or a paintbrush, there is a trace and the trace stays on the paper. In fact it can be quite difficult to get it out of the paper without disturbing the paper. You might remember being back in school and rubbing out your mistakes with a rubber. You rub and you rub and now you've made a hole on the page! That's what happens isn't it? So when you try to rub bad bits out of yourself, the self that you're trying to erase the bad bits from is also getting marked.

Awareness itself is not marked. Consciousness is marked. It is very important to note this difference because on the level of consciousness we need to be very, very tender with ourselves since we mark so easily.

We carry the marks of past events and they hold the patterns that we bring forward. Too much pain is not good. It makes us anxious and fearful and turn away from life. When you find yourself getting caught up in your thought patterns, don't enter into judgment and the thought will vanish. Everything that occurs will vanish since all the contents of the mind are transient.

Transient occurrences are not a reliable basis for establishing a fixed identity but neither are they dangerous if we allow them to be in that transient flow. If you let all movement pass through then there is no trace. It is when you resist what is happening that you get a reaction. It's like rolling with a punch. When you catch a cricket ball or a rugby ball, you catch it by moving with the ball because if you block it in a static catch then you'll feel the full force. That is very painful and you're likely to drop the ball. If you allow that movement it passes through.

If you relax in unborn openness and offer spacious hospitality to all occurrence you will not be harmed because in that non-dual state there is no one to be harmed. However this does not function on the level of egoic participation in the world. As a person in the world, if you give a lot of space to others you may well get exploited. If you open up your space, someone else may come and inhabit it. If you don't set any limits, you may get taken for a ride. All parents face having to set limits for their children. Most parents recognise that it is not good for them and it's not good for the child if they don't set limits. Limits are helpful because reified energetic forms have an impact when they encounter other reified forms. This impact is the basis of karmic accumulation.

When integrating the meditative state with being in the world after meditation you have to to maintain the non-duality of the open field and the arisings. Openness is unguarded, unprotected, tolerant of whatever is occurring, for all occurrences are equal in that they are simply movements in the field. If the meditative state is lost then self and other will seem to be real and inherently different. In this case, you have to be mindful of the pull towards reactivity. Mindfulness of transience loosens the grip of reification and so arousal declines so that the inherent emptiness of the mind is revealed.

The mirror and the reflection are inseparable. The mirror doesn't need to interfere with the reflection in order to be safe. Naked unborn awareness is itself open as is all that is revealed in that openness. Openness is not something you can catch. When you look at a mirror you cannot catch the mirror; what you seem to catch are the reflections. The presence of the reflection lets you come to the conclusion that it is a mirror. If you look at the wall, you don't get a reflection of your face. You look at the curtains and you don't get a reflection. You see the wall, you see the curtains, but you cannot see the mirror itself. The mirror reveals itself through its function of showing reflections. The mirror-ness of the mirror is ungraspable because it is empty of self-content. Our mind also is empty of self-content and it is because of this that I can show an endless stream of thoughts, feelings, memories and so on. The mirror is shown by its reflection.

The nature of awareness is shown by what it reveals. The content of the mind is not showing what the mind itself is like. The reflection in a mirror doesn't show what the mirror itself is like. Our mind offers unlimited yet non-defining content. A mirror can show many different non-defining reflections. Each time it shows a reflection we think, '*That is a bus!*', or '*That is a person!*' or

'*Gosh, my nose is a bit odd!*' Likewise a content arises in our mind and we think, *"He's got one of these new mobiles I want",* or *"I'd like a handbag like hers"* or *"Oops, I wish I hadn't said that."* In that moment there's a sense that how I show myself reveals myself as I am: that I can be defined by the current content of my experience.

This is such an essential point for meditation. The self that is shown in a social interaction – through a slip of the tongue, an inadvertent disclosure of a secret or whatever – is the ego-self. An energy formation, a temporary pattern, a construct. It is not our true nature. It is not who we are, but when we take these transient images to be ourselves as if we were something, the very intensity of that grasping creates an over-identification and then it is as if we are a knowable entity.

So the key point is that '*I am open. I, the source, the ground nature of who I am, the ground of my being, is not a thing.*' That's quite remarkable – to not be 'a thing' yet to manifest in the field of manifestations, just as the empty mirror allows many reflections appear.

BEING WITH OTHERS

In terms of our being in the world with others, we have to remember how supported we are by our Dharma study and practice. We need to maintain relative truth compassion of helping those wandering in samsara. If we increase our capacity for intuitive spontaneity we need to maintain our relaxed openness while being careful in our interactions with others since other people get hurt easily due to their dualistic frame of reference. We don't want to abuse them or create trouble for them. We have to attune to others as they are in their habitual patterning. Life is better for others and for ourselves when we show finesse, when we can fine-tune how we manifest. If we are self-preoccupied it may be difficult to feel in touch with others.

However if we remain relaxed and in contact, we can co-emerge with this specific presenting state of the other. With this, our freshness in the moment invites them to be fresh, too. We don't need to know what to say in advance but if we're fully present here and now, the words will come. This is the gift of uninterrupted spontaneity of the non-dual field. Subject and object are not too different planets. By opening to the face of the other, we will come into being in a way that fits the other. That is something quite remarkable.

This level, is referred to as *lhundrub* (Tib. *lHun Grub*). *Lhun* means 'a heap' and *Drub* means accomplished, hence 'accomplished in a heap' all at once. It means the whole is spontaneously here. For example, in this room everyone is here as they are, some slumping, some alert, some distracted, bored, some looking a bit tired... All kinds of pulsations going on. This is what we're sharing and inside this some gestures are possible and some aren't.

Will we lose ourselves by tuning into others? This is a central question because as long as we have an individualised sense of self with our own particularities, then there are going to be things that we feel we need to have and things we feel we need to not have in order to feel okay. The idea of the idea of ourself as a noble entity can blind us to the patterns all around us. If we start from the position that I am real and you are real and the differences between us are real and defining, then this dualising of the field of emergence is likely to lead to a fixation on the eight worldly concerns. These are: hope for pleasure and fear of pain; hope for gain and fear of loss; hope for praise and fear of blame; hope for good reputation and fear of bad reputation. These attitudes are pervasive in human cultures, and so not only do we have to release ourselves from our own tendencies but we have to practise equanimity in the face of the provocations arising from the attitudes and behaviours of others.

By releasing ourselves from fusion with group identities, we can still fulfil our social roles and obligations – but in the manner of a dream. We have to see that our behaviour does not define us since there is no fixed self to define. And the same applies to other: no reifying, no judging. Simply ungraspable patterns meeting and parting. All of us belong to the emergent field. This truth is quite challenging because we have received a lot of messages about being true to ourselves, being our own person, dancing to our own drum. It can seem obvious that life is a matter of, *"Be yourself, do it your way..."* Of course there are costs to that but, *"at least I've been true to myself."* This is very, very far from a buddhist understanding.

Being with other people is not about how we can pull them into our way of thinking and get them to go along with what we want to do. Such tedious management skills become all-pervasive and are essentially a politics of brutality based on a contempt and a lack of respect for others. We follow the middle way, seeking to benefit all without bias and without exception. The focus is not on what they want or what we want but on the practise of relaxed openness, which frees us to respond as required by the actual patterning of the emergent situation. By staying relaxed and open we find ourselves abiding in the integrity of the ground openness, the field of clarity and our non-self-referential responsivity within the field.

What is fundamentally important is to stay connected in the world, because we have only these three things: openness, the field of our experience; and how we integrate into it. That is all we have. Moment by moment through our lives, that is all that is ever going on, whether you're in school, in your work, in bed with your lover, wherever you are, you've just got your presence in a situation. To feel open, to feel no need to protect oneself, is a delicious feeling. That quality of aliveness can become more constant in our lives by not protecting ourselves against the world.

PROTECTION

Who is the one who is vulnerable and needs protection? Awareness, the intrinsic illuminative power of the mind, doesn't need protection. Although all the shapes that we experience are inseparable from emptiness and lack all self-substance, our deluding ego-self claims certain patterns as its own and regards all the remaining patterns as 'other'. The patterns I claim to be 'my shape' certainly need protection since it is the very nature of such patterns to be impermanent. 'My shape' does not belong to me and it is not inherent in my sense of self. Rather, it is composed by selecting elements already in the field of experience and then claiming exclusive rights to them. But of course, such claims have little power – if you shoot me, my pattern will start to decompose. Our shape is always a shape already in the world.

People worry about identity theft and cybercrime. Well of course, if you transact with your bank across the internet, why wouldn't people access that information and steal from you? You've put it out there. Why would you trust that 'out there' is okay? The idea that you can have a private space in a public sphere does not hold up. All private spaces are niched within the open public unknowable space – the space of the earth free of the contingent discourse of lawyers. The ego-self is a similarly merely conventional imposition upon the unknowable open space of the dharmadhatu – the space within which all phenomena appear. Isolating, defining, ring-fencing, owning – these are all moves occurring within the deluding discourse of duality. All that is taken to be separate, existent, ownable, is in fact inseparable from the unborn open ground source. If this is seen, then all the names, the hierarchies of value, the attributions of specialness, are revealed as merely the ego's playtime. All that seems to be established is inherently unestablishable. All entities are merely names put by the mind.

Relaxing one's identification with specific forms as being 'oneself' allows us to access the ever-fresh potential out of which each moment arises. Then we see that we have the infinite protection of being grounded in the indestructible source, of being inseparable from the potential of the radiant field, and of being the responsive connectivity that is love itself.

In acknowledging and experiencing the unique specificity of our world – the actual contouring of our life moment by moment – we can feel the growing edge of how we are with the world. The actual pulsating interface is not conceptual; it is direct for we are co-emergent with the environment. This points to the importance of relaxing out of our reliance on concepts and opening ourselves to the freshly revealing richness of the world as revealed through our senses.

THE HEART OF WISDOM IS EMPTINESS

From the mahayana point of view, the heart of wisdom is emptiness. Mahayana means 'great vehicle' and this term is used because it describes an approach to dharma that is inclusive. It means that all sentient beings are included in our practice, no matter what kind of practice we do. We are not trying to get enlightenment or liberation just for ourselves but for all sentient beings of whatever kind.

If you get something just for yourself you may gain this marvelous possession but you also have a little bit of worry. For example, when I was coming here by car we passed through some wealthy-looking suburbs. As the suburbs began to look more and more wealthy the fences got higher and higher and more and more the houses had alarm systems. If you've got something, you can lose it. In the same way, if you get enlightened but there are still all these miserable creatures wandering around causing trouble, then who wants that? So, unless you are prepared to live in a kind of buddha gated community, keeping out the rabble, it's best to take everyone with you when you get enlightened. That's the general view of the mahayana. This is both altruistic and pragmatic.

The generosity of spirit or compassion or love or altruism is grounded in the idea that there is enough to go around. The openness of awareness is not in opposition to the specificity and precision of our manifesting in our environment moment by moment. Resting in our ever-open ground, we manifest without taking the patterns of our manifesting to be our self, our true identity, who we are. All our arising forms signal not that we are discrete entities, but that we are ever-shifting patternings of unborn potential in play with other such patternings. This is the emergent field free of duality within itself and non-dual with the ground.

When we live in a world where the resources that we need to maintain our sense of self are perceived to be finite, then we're immediately in competition for ownership; the more *you* get then the less there is available for *me* to get. Yet when we see that the basic field of experience is infinite, we see that there is enough for everyone.

The concept of emptiness may seem rather daunting or abstract whereas in fact it is extremely practical. We have already been looking at the impermanence of phenomena and we no longer are how many of the identities we have been in our lives. Identities that we once held, that we were completely committed to, somehow have washed out of us. They have vanished from our repertoire. They may be physical things, like climbing trees or wanting to go out on your scooter. They may be ideas we were once committed to yet now are indifferent towards. They no longer have 'pulling power' for us. Everything, which comes into existence, passes out of existence. There are no enduring phenomena in the world. Houses are built and fall down. Economies grow and shrink. People grow from children into being powerful adults and then, if we are fortunate, we become old and frail until eventually we die. No matter how much we may cling to something, to anything, we have no ability to make it last forever.

Our attachments are always contextual and how we experience both ourselves and our content are ever-shifting. The things that we relate to tend to be a means to an end. We make use of something at a certain period in our life – and then not. The toys of our childhood have lost their magic. In our present circumstances, our body, voice and mind are adapting to the emergent environment. When we are preparing food in the kitchen there are certain knives that we use for chopping vegetables, but we wouldn't put out these knives on the table to eat with, because they're too sharp or too big. They have their place. They're taken up and they're put down. Taken up and put down. This tends to be the somewhat pragmatic relationship we have with the world: we make use of things and we make use of people. We probably don't feel very comfortable acknowledging or saying that we make use of the people we meet, but it is quite true. 'Use of' is not the same as exploiting. Is there anyone here in this room who would like to be use-less? If we're not going to be use-less, then we're use-full and if we're use-full, then that means other people can make use of us. If they don't make use of us, we feel a bit 'spare'.

Perhaps that should give us a sense that the world is one of mutual engagement. It is wonderful if we have some value and our value is revealed by other people partaking of it. If no one partakes of what we have, then it remains hidden. We can't reveal ourselves to ourselves and so it is through interaction with other people that aspects of ourselves are given an invitation to manifest. Without the invitation of others, without them needing to make use of us, we wouldn't have that opportunity.

Some people here may have had the experience of becoming grandparents. That has advantages and disadvantages but it does mean that qualities which have been quiescent for some years, can be reactivated and get a new lease of life. All that parenting knowledge which had become redundant due to the children leaving home, is allowed to express itself in a way which can be useful. So there is a sense of aspects of ourselves being called into play.

'*I*' APPEARS TO HAVE SELF-SUBSTANCE THAT CONTINUES THROUGH TIME

Is there any continuing 'self-substance,' which is always there? From the buddhist point of view, no – there is not. According to the abhidharma tradition, there are three things which continue through time and there is one thing, which *appears* to continue through time.

The three things which continue through time are: enlightenment, the moment of enlightenment and the sky. The thing which *appears* to continue through time is the inherent existence of ourselves because we think, *"Well, I'm still alive. I was alive some years ago and I'm still here now."* Who is the one who is still here? 'I am!' This 'I' is a conceptual presentation. What is continuing is our capacity to use the first person singular. However the content of the first person singular has changed. '*I'm still here*', but not as the 'me' that I was. That's a bit weird isn't it? So...the 'me' that I was before, I no longer 'am', but 'I'm still here.' Now, of course, when we talk of 'me' we tend to be talking of the more objective narrative notion of ourself. 'I', the first person singular, is the naked bit of us that moves out into the world. 'I' – and then we can announce whatever we like after that. '*Here's something you should know about me*' is presenting an image of ourselves as a character. The information we offer conceals just as much as it reveals. 'I' and 'me' link together because 'I' can always identify or misidentify with 'me'. That is to say, we can deny ourselves. We can pretend that we are other than how we are. Why? Because we want to stay ahead of the game. How? How, because 'I' is empty of self, of inherent existence.

It is the emptiness of the empty signifier that is the first person singular that allows 'me' to say whatever I like about how 'I' am. *"I am this. I am that. I am the other."* On the table in front of me is a recording machine. By the look of it, it costs a lot of money. Therefore, whoever is the owner of this will presumably be quite protective of it. I might notice a nail sticking out of my chair and since this recording machine is made of metal, and since I don't have a hammer, I could make use of that object to bash down the nail. It has some hammer-like potential. The owner of the recording machine would counsel against doing this, insisting on a very tight construal of the article, *'It is for recording sound and for no other purpose.'* Many objects are like that. They have one specialised function and although with our creative imagination we could turn them to other purposes, that would be unwise because we would be running against the definition of what it is, or rather, of what we *say* it is. These separate objects we identify in the world seem to be what we take them to be – in describing them we are confident that we know what we're talking about.

However the first person singular is a different story. 'I' is always empty and all its attributes remain attributes and do not remove the intrinsic emptiness of the signified. To be understood you actually only need three words. *"I am hungry." "I am tired." "I am sleepy."* Three would be enough. Or if you're a child, you can use just two; *"I go."* 'I' by itself doesn't do anything or go anywhere. 'I' has no content. It needs something linked to it to give it content.

That is it's wonderful potential. It doesn't foreclose or over-determine the sphere within which it operate. It's like an amazing universal tool which can immediately link in with whatever environment it meets. It is the emptiness of the first person singular that makes it useful.

This sound recording device in front of me is very useful for its defined purpose. It has a very particular technology behind it which means that it has a very restricted remit of what it can be used for. 'I' can be used for anything. 'I' is empty of fixed, internal content. 'I' is 'open', an openness which allows it to be filled with the 'not I' which becomes 'I' by being linked with 'I'.

Emptiness, in terms of each person indicates that there is nothing fixed about us – not in our body, not in our voice and not in our mind. What our mind fills with will depend on particular circumstances. We may be doing something that requires great care and attention so we focus our mind in a way which allows our body to be very precise in its actions. At other times we just let our mind wander hither and thither. Neither the body, nor the voice, nor the mind, has a fixed content. The constituents of our self change and yet we appear to continue.

I as the empty signifier can generate a false sense of continuity, hence I can say, *"I am still me."* That is a delusion, an illusion. We are deluded by the illusion that just because we say something is the same, it is the same. *"I have been in Macclesfield before."* In what way is the Macclesfield that I have previously visited the same Macclesfield as I am in today? At the entrance to the city there are signs that say, 'Macclesfield', 'Welcome to Macclesfield'. You come to the boundary of the town. Before you cross the boundary, you're in non-Macclesfield. You take a step across that boundary and now you're in Macclesfield. This shows the arbitrary nature of the name 'Macclesfield'.

By relying on the abstraction, on the name, it is as if the abstraction is identical with the phenomenon but phenomena are always changing and the abstraction seems to be continuous because it is preserved in the refrigerator of the mind. It's in the freezer. The word flows out of our mouth and it goes back into our mind. Every time the term 'Macclesfield' is used, 'Macclesfield' sounds the same. You might say, *"I hate living in Macclesfield"*, you might say, *"I love living in Macclesfield"*, or you might even say, *"I used to hate living in Macclesfield but now I love living in Macclesfield"*, or vice versa. There are endless permutations you can make around this. Yet each time you say it, it is as if the other person will know what you mean when you say 'Macclesfield'. Which of course they don't and they can't, because they don't live in the same Macclesfield as you do. Your Macclesfield is what is revealed to you of the potential of Macclesfield as an unstable co-emergence with your embodied participation.

I can only directly access my own experience. I can, of course, access narratives others give of their experience. The first is unmediated, the second is mediated. The point is that I alone have my particular experience. This can be very lonely since nobody else has my actual experience. That is a fact. Therefore, we need to communicate. We can't take it for granted that other people know what we're talking about. The realm of language and the realm of direct experience are not the same. The direct is essentially inexpressible. It is unique and stands alone. The indirect realm of linguistic composition is expressing concepts which provide the illusion of shared experience. Yet shared signifiers do not equate with shared experience. Language lets us treat knowledge of something as a commodity. Yet the 'something' we know about is not self-existing. We create what we talk about in the very active talking. The 'object' is revealed through the 'subject' and is always mediated. Profound, direct experience is free of both subject and object.

In school we probably study a lot of subjects and have to memorise a lot to get through various exams. Is it fair to say that a lot of that information has not been enormously useful to us in our life? What we were learning, however, was how to be in a group of people, how to take our place, how to take our turn. This is the key point: the 'stuff-ness" that we learn is not what it's all about. It's about how we find our way into connectivity: that we need to interact with other people to work out what we are on about.

It is quite difficult to examine ourselves. If we have a problem and are wondering what to do we often have an urge to talk about it to a friend because in talking about it we lay it out and express our doubts; even if our friend does not ask a question, just the look on their face somehow helps us to unpack the problem in a more open way than we could have done on our own. Even how we tell a story about ourself will depend on our circumstances at any given time.

Working as a therapist, I see some people over quite long periods of time during which they may tell me many times about the 'same' event. Each time they tell it, it's slightly different. Communication is the revealing of nuances in the service of making the bond of shared experience. This 'shared experience' is actually the sharing of narratives about the idea of what occurred. Experience has to be objectified if it is to be shared. However such objectification creates representations which disguise the actual experience. Since there is nothing really 'to get', we make use of other people to find out who we are, because we are who we reveal ourselves to be. As individuals were born through the process of objectification. If we can't reveal ourselves, it can be very hard for us to function in a world of images.

Early buddhism examined the structure of phenomena and identified that in being compounded, they were impermanent: buildings, places, people, experience. They appear, remain for a while and vanish. What we are looking at now is generated by our residing inside our assumptions, judgments, memories, plans and predictions. The mental apparatus that we have, our capacity to construe, construct and interpret has us tracking entities and events across the three times. We move to the past. We move to the future. We're momentarily in this conceptual present. The actual present is always fresh, fresh and ungraspable. It is untouched by concepts.

It is likely that very little of our lives has been situated within this open availability. We tend to mediate all that occurs through our conceptual discourse – telling stories about life as if it was composed of a stream of existents. Reified event following reified event brings a sense of reality and stability to our lives. Yet the realm of the unconceptualised is always available. Conceptualised and unconceptualised might seem to be mutually excluding categories, yet concepts emerge within the space of the non-conceptual, like rainbows in the sky. If we can see this, then the concepts that were our friends and have become our obstructors as we seek clarity are now revealed as the radiance of our non-conceptual unborn awareness.

At lunch, I went for a short walk along the banks of the nearby canal and I was remembering how as a child, I used to play along the banks of a canal in Glasgow – but that canal is not this canal here in Macclesfield. I am back in a place which I haven't been to for a long time, which I have no desire to visit, and even if I went, I couldn't be there because that canal, in that form, no longer exists. The experience of this moment by the Macclesfield canal triggered a 'hook' whereby I absented myself from where I was, to be somewhere where I couldn't be, and yet I was.

I'm sure that's a familiar experience for many of us – that we slip away from this moment into the future and into the past. It's not that it's wrong to do this – because we do need to make plans and arrangements – however, whatever is occurring, whether it's a memory or a plan, is now. Planning or reflection needn't remove us from now. It can be the way in which the now is showing itself. That is to say, you can be present with your memory, or you can fall into your memory. When you fall into your memory it takes you off on a little riff going here and there, until something happens and then we're back here again. But that journey was kind of nowhere, a sort of cyberspace. It didn't truly exist; we can't get a handle on it. So, how can we stay present?

HERE AND NOW. THERE AND THEN.

In fact the openness of 'now' is the very basis for it being filled with thoughts of elsewhere, which are actually only now. Does that make sense? If you look at a photograph from last summer you go into memories of last summer, but the photo you're looking at is in front of you now. The memories are happening for you now but it is as if you have gone somehow into that realm of last summer. You haven't gone anywhere! All your life occurs in here and now. It has no other site of occurrence. Yet within the hear and now, the there and then occurs, and it is as if that occurrence was real and not the illusion that it actually is.

This is important for meditators because it means that two aspects are present simultaneously: the openness of the present awareness; and the arising thought which is denying its open empty nature by pretending to be something else.

It's like a child pretending to be Batman. They got their little costume for their birthday and now they go about in it saying, *"I'm Batman"* or *"I'm Spiderman."* They probably want to have a duvet cover that's got Spiderman on it as well and the matching pillow – the whole kit. *"This is me and this is my world."* They are Spiderman but they're not Spiderman. They are – and they're not. There is no real division.

In the same way, when we get lost in meditation we haven't gone away anywhere else. This is important because if you see the truth of this it means that there is nothing to be corrected. You don't need to do anything to improve or make reparation for what has happened because nothing wrong or bad has actually occurred. You are here, just here and now. This moment of here and now is filled with the illusion of there and then. Here and now is not destroyed or tainted by this illusory there and then. Just as a mirror is not tainted by the reflections which fill it so the openness of your awareness is always present in the here and now even when the images arising seemed to evoke there and then. The power of the illusory arising lies not in the arising but in our belief in it, in our letting ourselves be taken in by it. To take an illusion to be real is to be deluded.

Under the power of this delusion, you might conclude, *"Oh, I can't meditate at all. This is all just a waste of time. I don't know what I'm doing."* Then having been distracted in the meditation you enter another level of distraction by beating yourself up about having been distracted by an illusion. You can fill the whole of your life looping thoughts in this way: thought chasing thought. Where is this occurring? Here and now. Where is here? The space of awareness. Where is now? The space of awareness. There is nothing outside now. This is all there is. Every memory that we have, we only can access, now.

Can you remember your first day in primary school? Remember what that was like going up to the playground? You'll have some memories and some feelings and you are having these memories and feelings *now*. However that 'there' and 'then' appeared to be, it can only ever actually be 'here' and 'now'. Likewise whatever futures we can imagine, they are also only 'here' and 'now'.

The dzogchen tradition talks about the one *tigle*. *Tigle* means a sphere or a ball. It's visualised as a ball of rainbow-coloured light. It represents the infinity of existence. Now, this moment, is like an infinite ball which includes everything. It includes all the past, all the future, all that is here and all that is there. We could have a conversation about New York or Paris. All of these words, memories, plans, hopes, would be – here and now. You have never been anywhere other than here and now. 'Here and now', just like 'I', just like the mirror, is empty, because anywhere can be 'here'. We're here and then later today, we won't be here. We'll be in another place, which we will call 'here'.

This evening someone may ask you what you are going to do now. *"Well, it's two o'clock in the afternoon so let's go out for a walk." "No, it's not. It's seven o'clock at night and it is dark outside."* 'Now' is whenever now is. 'Here' is wherever here is. 'I' am whoever I am. The mirror is showing whatever it's showing. Despite this hospitality we become selfish, stupid, and blind by not recognising and honouring the openness of here and now. We take openness for granted, ignore it and fall asleep in our stories. This is very sad because actually it's quite amazing that the only place you can ever be is here and now!

The semantic content, the interpretative content, which we take to be the truth of each and every situation, is a non-intrinsic import, a transient filling. All such momentary fillers of the space of possibilities are themselves unreliable in the way that they seemed to point to something reliable. *'We're here in Macclesfield together.'* This is where we are. Some of us may go to a restaurant tonight and then we be 'here' in that restaurant. Both will be in Macclesfield but they'll be different 'here's in Macclesfield. Likewise there will be different moments of 'now'.

The freshness of 'here and now', the very basis for the arising of these different experiences is ignored because we are caught up in our stories, the staleness of talking about something. The fresh is right in front of our nose but we don't see it because we've locked onto our storyline: *'I'm like this, that or whatever.'* We fill the space of here and now with a story which obscures for us the freshness and connectedness of here and now. The actual here and now is us as we are in this moment, co-emergent and ungraspable. It's us; but in my storyline it's 'me'. In the story inside my head I'm looking out at you all in the room. However if I relax and release myself from that interpretation then 'we' are here.

The actual basis of our existence is non-dual: there is no barrier between self and other, good and bad, right and wrong, heaven and hell. Each of these binary oppositions only has meaning in the intercourse between its polarities. Only by knowing what the concept of bad is referring to in a specific context can you work out what might be conveyed by good. In buddhist terminology all polarities are co-emergent. They have to arise together to create the field in which discriminations are possible. In that way they are mutually dependent with no real barrier between them. Emptiness of self allows us to see everything that we experience as illusory movement, dynamic and unborn.

Even our tendency to tell stories about what is going on is itself an empty self-dissolving activity. If I have the thought, *"Ah, Macclesfield – there used to be a lot of silk production here."* I have now installed a thought about Macclesfield: *'Macclesfield: the end of the silk route.'* It takes maybe four seconds to set up that thought. Four seconds gone. Now what? Our whole life is, *'Now what? Now what?'* This is impermanence. We cannot establish anything through construction because it just washes away. *"What will I do then, if everything is empty and open and ungraspable. I'm drowning."*

Well, the fish doesn't drown in the sea. You drown because you conceptualise yourself as somebody who has to hold themselves together and make sense of what's going on. If experience is inherently self-validating then it has no need of effort to make sense of it. *"But if there is no sense to be made of anything, what am I going to do?"* The one who is worrying about that, is itself simply thought in flow. There is no inherent self-nature to either subject or object.

The practice arising from this view is to release identification with the thoughts, feelings and sensations that are the ingredients out of which we construct our familiar sense of self. We're not pushing them away but we're not gathering them together either to build a construction. In the meditation, thoughts come and go by themselves. We don't have to push them away or hang on to them or fall into them. They're just there and they're gone. There is no mental arising, which stays for a long time.

Moods can seem quite insidious and subtle, are like morning mist in a valley. They change in their texture. You may wake up in the morning feeling a bit depressed but if you just lie in the bed and open yourself – staying with the depression as it presents itself without over-conceptualising it – you will find that it presents many different flavours. However if you move away from the immediate experience and focus on the thoughts that tell your that you are depressed then you are wedding yourself into a concept which will mop up the gravy of each moment like a sponge and subsume it into your definition of yourself as being depressed. This will blind you to the changes in your mood. By being touched and moved through contact with others I am taken out of myself. I find myself in a new form. Whereas if I seal myself in my self-definition, the other cannot refresh me.

Essentially this is how emptiness is our basic freedom. It's not something abstract or vague, theoretical or esoteric. It is simply the non-duality of the experiential field. We're in this here and now together. The revelation of the here and now is the only actual. An anxious teenager may hide in their bedroom but the world is still going on. If they carry on doing that for some years, by the time they come out of their bedroom, they will be four years older with the same level of social skills that they had when they were sixteen. They haven't protected themselves. They've actually made themselves more vulnerable. The only way to learn – which is painful for most of us – is to participate. If you participate, you make mistakes and get embarrassed, but open and empty and self-liberating. So observe the dynamic nature of your experience. Nothing is fixed. Nothing is set in stone. Just allow experience to arise and pass.

TWO MOODS THAT CAN BE A PROBLEM FOR MEDITATORS

The dzogchen tradition refers to two main moods of energy which can be problematic for meditators. One is *gö-pa* (Tib. *rGod-Pa*) and the other is *ching-wa* (Tib. *Bying-Ba*). *Gö-pa* is a dispersed wild energy, perhaps a bit manic, and surrendering into that energy may feel exciting. You may want to go and get drunk, or spend lots of money, get carried away by lots of thoughts... *Ching-wa* means 'to sink' and feel a bit like a tired swimmer who can't go on any more and just wants to give up and sink under the waves. You can't summon up the will to keep going. Both the wild energy and the sinking energy are experiences inside the ocean of the mind so just trust their inherent emptiness and be present with them without merging.

The energy of the experiencer is participating in a field that is arising from the open spaciousness which is the basis of both experiencer and experienced. So relax and open, relax and open; just be with however it is. *Whatever comes, comes. Whatever goes, goes.* If you feel completely awful just sit present with 'awful', not falling into it, not pushing it away but allowing it space to be the current content of your experience. It will definitely pass.

The experiencer has no fixed content. In this state you are open and empty and self-liberating. You are in the state of the mirror and the mirror neither adopts nor rejects any experience which occurs. Every now and then you are likely to fall into a particular ripple of experience and when that happens, don't try to push it away. Don't blame yourself, just very gently pull your awareness back to being present with what is arising. Always remember that the reflection is in the mirror but the mirror isn't contaminated.

THE NATURE OF COMPASSION

Our mind has three aspects. The first is the field of openness, in which there are no separate phenomena. The field of openness revealed by awareness is devoid of any content. It has no shape, colour or form and yet it is the basis for the second aspect, the field of radiance. This is the field of luminosity, the clarity of bright experience offering nothing to grasp at. Within this there is the field of our illusory participation, as we emerge as apparitional forms dissolving the delusion of duality. The inseparability of these three is a self-rectifying balance. The ego-self on the other hand is prone to imbalance. If we lean too heavily towards the aspect of being a separated individual whose ground is an internal personal essence, then this isolation makes us overburdened. If we lose any sense of the particularity, of the unique specificity of our own situation, then we can also lose our balance by going to the other extreme; we can become very vague, spaced-out and 'all over the place', not able to hold our lives together.

The integrity of openness and the field of experience and our own particular arising, is precisely just this moment by moment. Resting in this the emergence of how we are is as a site of delicacy, grace and poise, an inclusive responsive co-emergence with others. We are neither internally preoccupied and functionally cut off from others nor so open and porous that we are invaded and pulled into reactivity by whatever is going on. Instead we manifest as a ceaseless pulsation moving between the polarities of active and passive.

The function of meditation is to help us experience the flow of experience and see that everything is dynamic. Stasis does not exist; it is a concept which we superimpose on movement because movement seems to be so overwhelming when an individual self tries to make sense of it. Samsara is a state of confusion, repetition, compulsion and the endless reiteration of the same old patterns. Samsara is maintained by trying to exert control through interpreting and finding meaning in events, through trying to make sense of what is going on. Samsara is endlessly busy with a task that can never be completed.

The difference between the busyness of samsara and the calm state of nirvana is essentially whether or not we are relaxing in openness and experiencing the given-ness of intrinsic presencing, the basic facticity of 'just this', 'just this', 'just this'. It is as it is; and within this you respond and move. Seamlessly, yet just prior to the gestures of participation there is the basic truth of what is arising – that it is empty of inherent self-nature. There is no substance to it and yet it is undeniably here.

When you start to get a cold, it's undeniable. There are signs and symptoms. You have to keep blowing your nose and keep a tissue handy. It's not that we can magic things away by saying, *"Well, it's all illusion, it's not there."* What occurs is a pattern. Having a cold has a particular sequence. It lasts a few days and then it usually gets better or it may deepen into something else. It is a dynamic unfolding. Before you get a cold, you're in one state. That state is not your true state because since you've been small, you've probably had all sorts of colds and scratches and illnesses of various kinds. The embodied ego self is not a stable home base, because even when you're physically healthy, sometimes you may be more tired, sometimes you may be more upbeat and so on. There isn't a 'real me'. There isn't 'my true self' as a form which can be established. What we experience are multiple forms through which we arise. Each of these forms is a situational relational identity that we seem to 'be' momentarily. Yet none of these has enduring existence.

How can we offer hospitality to our life as it is? How can we open to yet not merge with all our transient apparitions. This is the real question. Usually we're trying to correct ourselves, to modify ourselves, to make adjustments because we have some game plan, some map, some image of how our life should be. We want to reduce interpersonal stress by transforming maladaptive procedures into adaptive procedures. Most psychotherapy is concerned with such issues. In our dzogchen practice however the key point is abiding in our integrity with openness rather than alignment with a map. So, instead of trying harder, contorting ourselves to fit into a particular image, we can stay relaxed with how events actually are and then work with that. Because actually, this is all we have. The maps neither exist nor describe real existents. They are abstract concepts which have whatever truth concepts have.

The basis of our practice is again and again to ease ourselves out of our habitual identities so that openness, revelation and participation are seamless. Maintaining this integral view of non-duality, how shall we become sites of kindness and compassion? Generally speaking, in Buddhism, compassion is the intention and practice of supporting universal happiness free of pain and suffering. This compassion is *focussed on the ultimate welfare of sentient beings.* We wish all beings the unchanging happiness which arises from them recognising that they are buddhas. Buddhas are not human beings. What does this mean? Our identity as human beings is not definitive. This view of who we are arises from our obscurations and karma. When the obscurations fall away, we see that we are not who we thought we were.

The mind is infinite, it does not have limits. When you actually see how awareness is, it doesn't have a top or bottom. It doesn't have sides. It doesn't have a beginning or an end. It doesn't come from anywhere, stay anywhere or go anywhere. This is something you can investigate for yourself. As you examine each of these statements in turn, you see that your thoughts can describe other thoughts but they cannot represent awareness. Awareness is not an entity and is beyond conceptualisation. Consciousness seeks an object and also can consider itself as an object. Consciousness needs an object in order to manifest, it needs to get its teeth into something. Yet whatever presents itself is an evanescent moment. It arises and passes. We keep on looking but each conclusion we suppose to be final, vanishes. The mind cannot catch itself.

With this we start to be aware of our actual nature which is luminous, vital, alive. We are the presence of ungraspable openness. Neither our ground nor our presence is a substantial entity. We are 'just this', the immediacy of participation in the ever-open field of luminosity.

WE, AS PEOPLE, DIE BUT AWARENESS DOES NOT

When we take our body to be an entity, something we have or we are, then we are not open to our unborn ground. The basis of our emergence as ever-shifting co-emergent patterning is ungraspable openness. We are not a thing. The body is a site of dynamic communication. It manifests as a relational formation. As such, it is shaped by and with events and after some time its patterning ceases to support the manifestation of awareness. And this is what we call 'death'.

The body as process is susceptible to outside dangers and internal diseases. There are many ways in which the dynamic function can come to an end. Every gesture that we make with our body is finite. It has a beginning, a middle and an end. Every speech act is finite, finite and contextual. But the mind itself is infinite. As the Buddha said, *"All beginning things are ending*

191

things." Everything which has a beginning will have an end. Therefore, everything which is finite will go towards dissolution but the mind itself, awareness, has neither beginning nor end.

This is why awareness is the true refuge. We take refuge in the nature of our own mind. We do not hang on to a concept of our real nature, which would be dualistic, but rather we enter into the practice again and again. We find our way into relaxing through the layers of stickiness of our habitual identification with thoughts, feelings and sensations until we fully open to infinite awareness. Infinite awareness indicates that it has no beginning and no end. This has huge implications for how we understand death. The forms of the energy of awareness – our physical forms, our memories, thoughts, intentions and so on – are always changing while we are alive. Death is when this internal patterning of emergence ceases to emerge in a way that supports our dualistic consciousness. We, as people, die but awareness does not. Openness is the ground of awareness and awareness is like the sun shining in the sky of openness. Awareness is not consciousness. Consciousness is reificatory knowing focused on the particularities of experience. Awareness is non-reificatory.

WHAT IS HAPPINESS?

Thus, when we say, *"May all beings be happy"*, it is a brief way of saying *"May all beings rest in the ground of their own being."* We are not saying, *"May they get lots of nice experiences all the time."* Nice experiences will necessarily be ephemeral.

In English we have a saying, *'You can't have your cake and eat it.'* If you keep something nice for later, it might get spoilt but if you eat it now, you won't have it later. This is the nature of time. It just is like that. You can't hang on to things in this world because they change. People want to have a secure place to put their money. They put it in property. Prices go up and down. They put it in equities. Prices go up and down. They trade in foreign currencies. Values go up and down. Nobody can predict what's going to happen. It's a moveable feast. There is nothing secure in the world of manifestation.

Therefore, to wish happiness to all beings is not to wish them some-*thing.* Of course on a relative level we hope that people have a safe place to sleep, are protected from violence, have food, kindness and so on but each of these situations is vulnerable to events. If you've got a house, problems arise with it. Either you do repairs yourself or you get in a builder. If you get in a builder, you may as well sign a blank cheque! Every problem starts as some good idea. You buy a car; somebody scrapes your car. How could that happen? Driving along, a stone flies up and chips the windscreen. If you've got a car, you get problems. If you've got a house, you get problems. If you've got a body, you get problems. Problems go with the territory because all phenomena are impermanent. We have built-in obsolescence and everything around us is crumbling away all the time. That is why real happiness comes from awakening to the contentment or satisfaction of residing in the natural condition of awareness.

The mahayana tradition describes two aspects of profound universal compassion, or bodhicitta: compassion which is like planning to go on a journey and the compassion of actually going on a journey. The intention *'May all beings be happy'* is a beautiful thought that can open our heart and make us feel connected with all beings, but then we have to go on the actual journey. We have to act in a way which will bring about that happiness.

In the tantric tradition it is believed that visualisation practices open up a luminous world that includes all beings, bringing actual direct immediate benefit for others. The practice itself within the view of non-duality brings an actual change to the condition of beings. However, because beings repeatedly choose patterns of lostness, these practices have to be done again and again.

COMPASSION AND EMPTY OF ESSENCE

We are used to the difference between fantasy and reality, where reality is provable and fantasy is like a daydream. The term 'illusion' points to a different approach to experience. An illusion is an appearance which has no actual existence. It arises due to causes and can be seen yet it has no substance, as with a rainbow or a mirage. From the view of emptiness, all that we encounter, including ourselves, is like an illusion.

For example this recording machine in front of me has no essence. It is operating on the basis of the interaction of many factors. There's a supply of electricity coming into it and there are many metal and electronic components inside. Through their collaboration, they function in a way that will lead to the recording of sound. The machine operates through juxtaposition and interaction. If the pieces are put together in the right way and the flow of power coming into the machine allows these connected pieces to operate, then the recording function is performed. However if you open the machine, you won't find some little essential piece which is doing all the work, just as inside us there isn't a homunculus, a kind of mini-man or mini-woman, who is our real essence. Our body has no essence in it. Some people say that the heart is the essence but if you remove the liver or the lungs we're not going to do very well either. Our bodies have many vital organs and function through the communication of these vital organs. The body is a communication system just like the recording machine. There is no essence. Each of these vital elements functions yet there is no essence driving them and they produce no fixed existent.

When we look at sentient beings, we tend to conceptualise them. We imagine that thinking about them will somehow bring us closer to who they are. The naming of a person is a bit like inserting the keystone in an arch. It locks the arch. When builders are making an arch they put some wood in the centre as they build up the arch. When they drop in the keystone this locks it and they can remove the wood. You know someone's name so you apply their name to them and it is as if we now know them. Our habitual picture of that person, a picture built up over time and on the basis of diverse situations, can be summoned forth by evoking their name. It's as if their name represents some essential form. Yet of course, 'our name' is contingent, given to us by our parents at birth or changed by us later on in life. Although there is no essence to a person, when we take a person to be an entity it can seem as if we're being kind and thoughtful by remembering the details of their individual life. What we take as a given about them is what we remember of their life. This is only a minute slice of all the things that have happened in their life and so when we sum people up according to our experience of them, then the image that we create is not going to be true to the complexity of their interactive life. Human beings are unfoldings; they are moving and changing with events. When people engage with each other two complex dynamic systems are engaging with each other, generating new patterns of communication. When we bring our over-conceptualising knowledge into a situation like this and to try predict how it's likely to develop, this interference will interrupt the free-flow of the possibilities of the situation.

For example, if one member of a family has a problem, let's say an addiction, then the others start to think, *"Oh, they are behaving in that way because they are in the grip of such and such an addiction. There's not much we can do about that."* The fixity of reading of the situation, which they return to again and again, and which is held by other members in the family system, starts to insert a perverse choreography in which everybody is adapting to the identified patient. *"We all have to put up with Johnny because you know that's just what Johnny's like..."* Then the pendulum swings: *"For God's sake! Is this ever going to change? I can't bear it anymore."* The problem is, *'I can't bear it anymore.'* Since we have decided that we know what 'it' is, there is a frozen reading or interpretation of the situation. Actually what you have is somebody revealing themselves moment by moment in particular ways. If you can respond fluidly to how they present themselves, unmediated by this grand story about who they are or what they need, then there is the possibility of a true meeting with some authenticity.

The more you believe that you know who and what another person is, the more you're constrained whereas compassion free of over-fixation can open up a space for spontaneous contact with other people. By not getting caught up in a dramatised reading of a situation, which over-determines what moves we can make, there is the possibility of authentic and genuine responsivity in the moment. Knowing that what we say in the moment applies just to the moment helps us not to consolidate our sense of the other, but to stay open to their potential even when they are disregarding it to themselves. To sum other people up is to do them a violence.

If you're responding in the moment it is important to have a sense of where that response is coming from. If you have a stored-up notion of the other person, even if you think you're not activating it, it is going to be activated and what you're going to do is whack the other person with an impulsive, rather than a spontaneous, response. Impulses are not spontaneous. They are always preformed. *"Here is something I prepared earlier",* as TV chefs often say. Impulses are story lines that have been run before. They come out of the freezer, into the microwave and into your mouth. This is not fresh food. It's just something I happen to have handy, so we whack the other person with that. It's not a very useful way to respond.

SPACE AND SPONTANEITY

Spontaneity means being relaxed and open. This is particularly difficult in family dynamics because we have built up such huge memory banks about who we take the other members to be. Like chess players, we are often planning and fantasising several moves ahead: *"If I do this they probably will do that and then I will have to do..."* In betraying the freshness of contactful emergence we deprive the other person of the chance to encounter the space of fresh potential.

Of course predictability can reduce anxiety and other people may prefer that to a fresh and open encounter. Confirmation of knowable and enduring identities may be the culture of the family or the wider group. *"Only if I am sure that you are one of us will I feel safe with you."* This narrow self-protective stance is an impediment to the practice of opening to the open. Whenever mutuality breaks down, we are constrained in preformed choreographed scripts.

OUR ORIGINAL NATURE IS OUR BUDDHA NATURE

Our original nature is our buddha nature yet at the moment we live without clarity regarding our true nature. We maintain our belief that we have an enduring self and this acts as an obscuration, a cover-up, a veneer of habitual intoxication. We are intoxicated by ideas, judgments, evaluations, memories, intentions and so on – by the whole maelstrom of mental activity. While we are invested in that level of turbulence we experience a lot of stimulus and so we are endlessly busy, acting and being acted on. Because we are so busy 'hoeing our garden' we are not aware of the potential of the soil. In fact our buddha nature is hidden from us by our very efforts to stop ourselves being bad people. That's terribly sad.

One of the functions of meditating and relaxing into the unborn open dimension of the mind, is to access the fundamental goodness of our being. The primordial buddha of this lineage is called Kuntuzangpo. *Kuntu* means 'always' or 'always already', and *Zangpo* means 'good'. This is our basis and fundamentally we have not strayed from this basis, despite all the activities we have engaged in.

There is a basic goodness or a basic health which is fundamental to all of us; difficulties are adventitious. They arrive. They have a beginning. They are not intrinsic. They function in our lives and have to be dealt with some way or another. Yet they have no real existence and do not arise from our true nature. It can be helpful to examine our negative core beliefs in order to discover the actual nature of such beliefs. Perhaps we hate ourselves, distrust ourselves, think that we are a bad person, or greedy or lazy. *"That's just like me. I always get it wrong. That's just my luck. I'll never be able to fit in."*

When we take up these beliefs as definitions of who we are, it is as if they are essential truths which sum us up. However when we notice how they arise and pass and have no stability of their own, we start to doubt that such transient structures could truly define us. Then we start to notice how they are like echoes of what others have said about us. We have built up images of ourselves and taken these to be the truth. Meditation is the means to avoid such limiting conceptual constructs. We learn to relax, open and allow the stream of thoughts, feelings, memories, and so on to show us directly their illusory nature. We have been trapped within the dream of existence and now we have the means to waken up.

AN ENDLESS CONVERSATION

By neither merging with nor trying to avoid our own experience, we can let it reveal itself. We start to see that what has seemed essential about us is actually contingent. All we need is to learn proper punctuation: *"I'm a complete waste of space,* **when I get lost.***"* Once you begin inserting commas in the place of full stops, you start to see that you are caught up in an endless conversation. You make one proposition about yourself and then you supply other evidence to support it, and then you identify more evidence and more evidence... When you see what you are up to you start to articulate all the positions of yourself, your self-states or self-aspects or sub-personalities. All these positionings, core beliefs, voices, are part of a conversation that goes on and on, the infinite conversation that is the engine of samsara.

When we attend to this conversation, we understand that we can never reach a final definition of ourself. Everything that I say about myself may be true contextually while in terms of the wider picture it may be untrue. It is both true and false. It may be true about the moment but it is not true about a core identity. Once we start to understand this then we start to access true freedom. This is freedom from final definition, from summation. We all have limitations and our limitations mean that we will let other people down. We will not be able to provide other people with all that they want. However, this fact points only to transient circumstances; it is not the truth of our actuality. To believe in it is to thicken the veils of obscuration. The practice is quite simple – do less assuming, speculating and judging and relax and see how your mind actually is when it is not interfered with.

MAHAYANA COMPASSION IS TO ONESELF AND TO OTHERS

If you over-privilege yourself, it's not good. To see the co-emergence of self and environment is the liberation of duality. Our environment includes everyone: everyone in this room, everyone in Macclesfield, in England, in the world, all the worms in the soil, the birds in the sky, the ducks in the canal. All sentient beings are within the open field of presence. Nobody is a stranger to us for we share the same basis.

The mahayana tradition offers us a narrative to support adopting this position: we have had many previous lives and in every life we have had a mother. These mothers have taken care of us, fed us, clothed us, done difficult things in order to keep us safe. Whenever we meet another sentient being, we meet them from the place of debt and obligation since they have been our mother in a previous life. They have done this kindness for us and now it is our chance to repay them.

That is a very powerful vision to adopt. It really serves to undermine any notion of putting oneself first. In fact, the task of my life is to pay off my debts, and so every time I do a good thing, I don't go 'one-up' – I go from 'one down' to 'neutral'. 'Neutral' is the middle way. It's equanimity. This is a very beautiful kind of practice. The ways in which these mahayana practices have developed over time are so exquisite. They are so finely attuned and balanced and are so good for the heart. They are truly good food.

DZOGCHEN COMPASSION IS OUR BASIC GOODNESS

In the dzogchen tradition, however, there is less reliance on supportive narratives and more direct trust that our basic purity and goodness will give rise to ethical conduct. The dzogchen view is that we are the emergence of the ever-pure basis or ground. Its purity is our purity since it is our actual source. All seemingly limiting factors are merely non-inherent contingent patternings of transient experience. All interpretations of experience are illusory. The sole truth is non-dual open emptiness.

The infinite ground source has no limit. Therefore all that occurs is occurring within this infinity. There is no source other than this. There are no imports because there's nowhere to import anything from. This is the all-inclusive expanse of awareness. Whatever is occurring is the illusory radiant manifestation of the dharmakaya, the intrinsic mode. The more we trust this the more we see the light, radiant, luminous quality of all experience, including our experience of ourselves. However these experiences may appear, they are intrinsically pure and unborn.

We are all sitting here in this room, seemingly in the same room yet the room is revealed to each of us in different ways according to our particular patterning. The particularity of how we arise is often compared to light going into a crystal. A natural rock crystal will have different planes inside it. These could be referred to as impurities yet they help to reveal the richness of the potential for refraction. As the light goes in, it hits a particular plane which reveals the colours present within clear light. The intensity of the colours in the refracted light depends on the brightness of the light. When we are thickened and dulled with beliefs in inherent existence very little bright light comes in, and so we seem to encounter fixed, solid objects.

Each of us is like a crystal and the potential of any situation shines like light through us which we refract as our unique 'take' on that situation. When this crystalline potential is unobscured, refraction occurs prior to conceptualising, so that we manifest as an aspect of the integrated responsiveness of the field.

As we come to trust this intuitive spontaneous responsivity we rely less and less on conceptual planning. We are not reviewing the past or projecting into the future. We are part of the emergent field of experience and this inclusivity brings a simple fit to our presence, moment by moment. Then we can see clearly that isolation and hesitation are products of conceptualisation. Non-dual participation is free of anxious control. Paradoxically, by allowing the self-arising and self-vanishing of the many moments of experience there is more instant clarity leading to effective participation. Habitual preoccupations cloud the freshness of the sky of emergent moments and lead to impulses based on the past. This self-referential concern distorts the arising activity so that it manifests as a pre-patterned reaction rather than as a fresh response.

So the heart of the healing contact which is compassion is to trust that being relaxed, open and connected allows a finesse of engagement that is fundamental and ethical. Ethics then feed relaxation because you start to find that you're on the point; you're on the beat. You are emerging with the field. That's how musicians would start to jam isn't it? They hear each other playing and they get a sense of what's possible and then they're in a groove and it takes off. Nobody's leading, nobody's deciding, but somehow the 'field' is the organising factor rather than the individual.

POWER USED WELL

One of the big problems in religious structures is patriarchy and hierarchy because the basic rule of power positions is 'never apologise and never explain'. I think it is important that dharma practitioners apologise a lot and to learn to explain, in the sense of a clear description rather than a justification. To say, *"I was cycling home from work in a hurry and I was went through a red light without stopping. I did not see you crossing the road. I did not mean to hit you and I am sorry that I did."* That's factual and neutral. You're not abasing yourself by saying something like *"Oh my god! I'm so sorry. I'm so stupid. I'm always making mistakes."* This will not help the person you hit, and neither will blaming them: *"Well, you should not have worn a black coat on a dark night and then walked so slowly across the road..."*

The issue of power has to be worked with again and again until we are clear about our agency. As long as I believe that 'I' am the doer of the deed, the source of the activity, the stable basis of everything I do, then I will remain unaware of the open, empty ground of my manifestation. The personal pronoun 'I' is actually a sign without referent; it does not point towards an inner self. 'I' is pointing to the site of this activity and this site is the unborn openness of the mind. My power is the power of the source, it is not a personal possession. Every aspect of who I take myself to be and what I believe that I do is the emergent patterning of the potential of the ground. When I consider myself to be this particular person this is a conclusion that indicates a primacy of the 'self', of 'I, me, myself' as a separate entity with inherent existence. This is a false understanding an erroneous belief that is standard and normal within our world as structured by a belief in duality.

This is why it is vital to relax and observe how your mind is. When your mind reveals its own open emptiness to you it is obvious that there is no hidden ego-self as doer or core identity. With this clarity we can relax even more and not interfere with the intuitive spontaneity of responsivity – which is our actual participation in this ever-changing, ungraspable field of experience. My power is not mine; it is the expression of the source arising in the service of the field of radiance of the source.

Fundamentally, I am not a person and so do not need power over others. But as long as I believe in the delusion of separate egoic existence I will seek the kind of profit that goes with having power so that after each moment of being powerful, I will 'scrape the cream off the top of the milk' and use it to build a power edifice from whose heights I look down on other people. As we go through the years we all develop a bit more expertise at some things and we can use that to feel that we 'know what's what'. That is the wrong direction of knowledge. Knowledge in the service of the moment – like an array of ingredients to be taken up as required for cooking a particular recipe – is useful. But knowledge as a protection, knowledge as a way of proving that

'I'm right and you're wrong' or that *'I'm a good person'* or whatever, becomes very opaque and dangerous.

Knowledge can provide useful tools when it is freed from its tendency to serve power structures and positions. From the point of view of dzogchen, every time you take up a position, you enter sclerosis. You enter into developing a carapace, a rigidity, a lack of movement. Then, having established a position you have to protect it.

Other people, strange to say, have minds of their own! Other people will make of us what they will, and all one can say is, *"Good luck to them."* We can't control other people's minds. You might stand on your head. You might bend over backwards. You might do 'the right thing' again and again but the other person continues to have a 'mind of their own'. How can that be? Because they don't see the world the way we do. Neither I nor 'others' truly exist. Moment by moment we shift in posture, gesture, expression. We are not fixed and we have no fixed core self. It is not that we have a mind of our own, but rather that habitual tendencies generate the delusion of an enduring self. We are unborn emergence, never parting from the source. This permits true co-emergence, ceaseless co-patterning without the distortion of self-reference. Aspects of potential form transient self-arising and self-vanishing patterns which can be opened to as responsive presence or which can be reified as aspects of myself.

This is the intrinsic freedom of the ground, our ground. We can open to it and rest within it, as it, or we can claim to be apart from it as a stand-alone entity, an individual. Having met the lineage teachings this choice is revealed to us. How we proceed is up to us.

We don't need knowledge or information about other people in order to be connected with them. The contact that we have arises within a connection which is prior to cognition. We are always already connected. It is our cognitions which allow us or don't allow us to live with that. We manifest as sentient beings. As sentient beings, we all share a lot but let's just take human beings: two arms, two legs, two eyes and so on... In Shakespeare's play THE MERCHANT OF VENICE Shylock asks, *"If you prick us, do we not bleed? If you tickle us, do we not laugh? if you poison us, do we not die?"* Antonio has put him in a category (Jew) that does not merit being treated decently like other categories (Christian). *"Hath not a Jew eyes? Hath not a Jew hands, organs, dimensions, senses, affections, passions? Fed with the same food, hurt with the same weapons, subject to the same diseases, healed by the same means, warmed and cooled by the same winter and summer, as a Christian is?"*

Putting people in categories is such a powerful thing to do to an individual or a group. We can see it happening all over the world. All sorts of dreadful things are being done by people to people because people who are incredibly similar say to other people, *"Oi! You're not one of us! You are in a different category"* These 'cuttings' that we make occur on so many bases: gender, age, religion, nationality, appearance, sexual orientation... Due to this, aspects of the integral field of experience are cut off, excluded, rejected and even annihilated. When individual identity is privileged over intrinsic belonging within the ever-open field, then opacity and projection become the ego-stabilising functions.

Under the power of unawareness we take ourselves to be individuals. With our selective attention we notice which thoughts seem to confirm who we are and so we want to hang on to these thoughts. We also notice thoughts that seem to undermine our sense of who we are or who we want to be. We try to exclude these. This splitting and projection, editing and manipulation, goes on all the time. However, simultaneously and without effort everything arises from 'the ground'. Everything is movement in space and therefore any division which gets introduced is not inherent in the ground but arises due to intoxication with conceptualisation.

We have to be aware of just how powerful the toxic power of concepts can be when they dominate our experience. Recent conflicts around the world show how all lived and shared experiences are vulnerable to being wiped out on the basis of our intoxication with a concept. *"We know who you are. You fit into such and such a group. We don't want you here."* The intensity of that thought formation, albeit blind, stupid and blunt, is incredibly powerful as it takes us back an infantile clarity where our feelings seem to tell us the truth about what is going on. The good and bad qualities we see in situations tend to be identified on the basis of their impact on us which is taken to be the truth of how they are.

If we can stay with the freshness of the impact, we might see that *"I am having a response to this moment of how you are for me."* However if I flip into my narrative of *"I don't like you because you are..."*. then the other gets more and more defined on my terms. Regardless of their actual presentation our interaction can come to a point where there's nothing they can say or do to step out of my accumulated narrative definition.

Meditation is a very practical way of engaging with our tendencies to regress to simplistic formulations about our world. As we experience our capacity to open we find that we can live with more of the actual complexity. This means that we have less need to squeeze other people into the compartments of our conceptualisation. Our violence towards the other arises from the limited ability of the self to make sense of what's going on. When it's all 'too much' then shrinking the variables makes life easier.

Reducing the available labels for the other to just 'you're one of them/you're one of us' is an easy but false simplification.

By relaxing, opening and resting in spaciousness we start to see that truly we're part of the field. The field arises in its integrity as the display of the ground. All divisions are adventitious, having been artificially introduced. They don't belong and they are unnecessary. They are vibrations of excess mental activity. We don't need strong judgements. We don't need definitions. We don't need defining conclusions because if the world is as we've been exploring over this weekend, then we inhabit an unfolding field in which final statements are impossible.

THREE ASPECTS OF IGNORING THAT CREATE SAMSARA

The traditional explanation of the development of samsara describes three aspects of ignoring. The first aspect is a kind of momentary disjunction. The natural integration of the flow of the three modes is interrupted. There's a hiatus. Sometimes it's compared to a drunk person falling down the stairs, *"Oh!"* There's a shock. Instead of relaxing back into the ongoing flow of unborn experience there's a question, *"Oops. What happened there?"* This question is not asked by someone. It is more like a circling eddy in the flow. It gives rise to a dualistic process of conceptualising the situation as a way of clarifying it. Once this starts, we move into the second aspect of ignoring whereby each item of experience is assigned a name or identification. Now the nascent ego consciousness enters a world of interpretation. With this develops an increasingly sophisticated mental apparatus filling the world with more and more names and categories. Of course once you've got a noun, you're going to have adjectives and verbs and adverbs and so on. We now have the complex identification of myriad particular entities, whereas in the flow there are no entities – there are only moments of experience, of appearance and so on which are changing. With the first aspect of ignoring there is a retraction from the whole with a consequent thickening and solidification of experience. The reification of 'I am real and what is around me is real' brings a confidence that everything can be defined and known.

Once that aspect has been established it leads on to asking and answering *"So what is this? And who am I?"* This results in the manufacture of thoughts, concepts and endless narratives.

This leads into the third aspect where we are caught up in activity without quite understanding the delayed consequences of our actions. This is referred to as the ignoring which is the stupidity of not understanding karma. We are getting along with our lives, doing this and that, thinking that each sequence of events is self-contained. However because our lives are energetic, all our actions create patterns of arousal which lead us into experiencing different patterns in the future. As we shape ourselves towards a particular activity, that shaping sets up a particular form which then reverberates as an energetic vibration that will have another manifestation in the future.

These three aspects of ignoring are going on all the time. In the first aspect of ignoring, because there's forgetfulness, we lose touch with the open nature of our mind and its natural radiance displaying the field of experience. In the second aspect of ignoring, the natural radiance of the display of the field of experience which is arising just by itself, is now appropriated into being a sequence of entities which can be moved around according to our definitions. In the third aspect our unique and precise participation in each moment by gesture, posture, tone of voice and so on, is not recognised for what it is because our experience is now mediated through our dualised interpretation.

To free ourselves from these three aspects of ignoring we relax into space again and again. In order to do that we have to confront our habitual desire to be preoccupied by busy activity.

That was the point about the drunk person falling down the stairs and then trying to make sense of what just happened. Only by relaxing into intrinsic value, the fulfilment of the integrity of all aspects of our presence, can we fully release ourselves from the burden of having to make sense of everything. The loss of the intrinsic is the birth of the burden of the reified contingent.

THE TUMBLING OF LIFE IS WITHIN OPENNESS

The root of samsara is agitation and anxiety. Relaxation is the fundamental medicine, the pure restorative. Relaxation allows form to be experienced integral with emptiness. There is nothing to protect. Patterns arise and pass and change. They will always do that. There is no way to stabilise the aspect of manifestation. However we don't need to do this since our presence spans these three aspects: open; part of the field; and just this. 'This' never lasts long. Participation is always moving and changing. The field too is ungraspable.

At night when we go to sleep, we can sit quietly, relax into openness, and gradually fall asleep. In the morning we wake up into the open and then life starts tumbling along. The tumbling of life is within the openness. Life is like a dream and inside that dream many events will happen, none of which can be fixed or accurately predicted. Again and again we relax into the ever-open and this is the integration of the field and the participation. This brings the unravelling of the three modes of ignoring. From the dzogchen point of view unravelling is resting in the natural completion of life, the perfect fulfilment of it is as it is.

THE OPEN WELCOMES ALL

Opening to the space of experience means that pleasure and pain come together. Good and bad. Success and failure. Happiness and sorrow. Loneliness and connection. So many different flavours. If we become picky eaters and mobilise all our

209

intelligence towards being a 'picky eater' then, entitled to be 'a picky eater', we can indeed spend our whole life eating only fish fingers or whatever, but to what gain? Every time we have an experience, we are not alone. If we have a bereavement, or a sorrow, or a betrayal in our life the world is full of people also experiencing that. Experiences come and go – they are not mine and they do not happen to me. 'I, me, myself' are aspects of experience – they are not apart from it. The mahayana view of infinite love, compassion and connectivity is not other than that of the dzogchen view of opening to life as it is. We participate as part of as it is. This is itself non-dual compassion as we abide in a relaxed openness that is always available for contact.

Teachings given in Macclesfield, UK, 22-24 February 2013. Edited by Barbara Terris and revised by James Low in March 2023.

The natural freedom of the mind

Turning towards the light

The story of buddhism began when a young man in North India, called Siddhartha, had some experiences which disturbed his sense of how things were. He had lived a very protected life, having all his needs met immediately and being surrounded by healthy, beautiful people. One day, however, he ventured outside his palace compound and he saw a sick person, an old person a corpse, and a dead person. This was a big shock for him. It caused him to put into question the assumptions that he had about what life was all about: *"If other people can get old and sick and die then this will happen to me too but so far nothing I have experienced has shown me that life has its troubles and sufferings."* Another day he saw a wandering holy man and decided that he too should follow that path because that person was looking for truth. He did this until finally he awakened to his own actual situation.

Right from the start buddhism began with a disruption of assumptions. Had Prince Siddhartha not had these experiences and had not been disturbed by them, his life would have gone by enjoying all worldly pleasures up until he died. He had wealthy parents who created a whole private world for him to grow up in and tried to protect and seal him inside a set of assumptions about life. I doubt that many of us have grown up with parents so wealthy that they could give us a whole private world to live in. We have probably all been faced with a range of experiences that have challenged some of our assumptions. Luckily, we have an editing suite inside our head. We edit the film of our life in order to show a particular kind of continuity of our sense of self. In other words, we are electively blind. We ignore many things that could shock us. We know that climate change is coming, but we don't get upset about it, not really. We know many things but they have no consequences on our actions. If we were to take such knowledge seriously and bring it into ourselves then everything would change. We would have fear; we would be outraged at government decisions. Life is easier with anaesthesia, and this is what buddhism begins with: a young man, Siddhartha, fighting against the culturally-induced anaesthesia of his family situation.

The first step of the path is to wake up to the pervasive nature of suffering. We often do not want to know just how bad our situation is. Looking on the bright side and finding the good in others can help us to be cheerful – but it may come at the cost of avoiding seeing the structural nature of our difficulties. The problems arising with birth, old age, sickness and death are not just a matter of bad luck. Buddha Shakyamuni points out how they arise from unawareness of our actual ground or source. Being unaware of the intrinsic simplicity of our mind, we get caught up in the turbulence of thoughts and emotions. We grasp at transient phenomena as if the intensity of our wishes could make them permanent and real. We become addicted to the cultural beliefs we imbibe and rely on our received concepts as guarantors of truth.

Becoming conscious of the suffering that our beliefs generate, we can start to enquire into what is reliable and what is not. The first turning point is to trust the dharma teachings and practices rather than our own conceptual interpretations. If we want to open to enlightenment then it helps if we can see that the Buddha is enlightened while we, at this moment, are not. Our own bright potential, our buddha nature, is obscured by our deluded beliefs and egocentric orientation. Therefore, we need to study the teachings and reflectively apply them to our own experience so that they can illuminate the structure of our confusion. We reflect on the impermanence of each moment of experience and commit ourselves to stabilising our attention by learning to focus on our breath without being distracted.

SHAMATHA OR SHINÉ MEDITATION

The function of this is to detoxify the addictive quality of thinking, feeling and sensing. Somebody who smokes regularly will have the experience of opening the cigarette packet, putting the cigarette in his mouth and lighting it without even being conscious of doing this. It is so automatic. Something is happening but it is as if nothing is happening because the person is so used to that happening. This merging into the experience so that one is blind to what one is doing is something we may also recognise in others as well as in ourselves. Many things can capture our time and our energy without us hardly being aware of it happening. Whenever a thought comes up in the meditation, we try to allow it to just be there, as if it were in our peripheral vision. The thought is a possibility: we could be part of it and through that make it part of us, or it can be allowed just to go away.

What we often find when we begin to meditate is that even when we try to focus on the flow of the breath, we get lost. We suddenly become aware that our mind has wandered off somewhere else. This should be quite alarming since we refer to 'my mind' but I have no control over it and whatever thoughts it thinks. Controlling the body is easier than controlling the mind. Resisting the temptation to identify with passing thoughts, feelings and sensations is difficult. It happens without our awareness. Thoughts don't arrive with an invitation to join them or not. We don't choose, we just find that we have wandered into distraction.

There are two important things in this. One is that we need to increase our clarity. That means increasing our calm so that we can see things before they quite arrive. In the past when a castle was preparing to be attacked, everyone would go out and cut down all the bushes and trees around so that they could see where their enemies were coming from. The equivalent for us meditators is to simplify our lives, not live with too much excitation where little secret thoughts might hide under cover of the over-busy movement of the mind.

The second is that I need to examine the fantasy that I am in charge of my life, that I am the boss. The fact is that I cannot even manage not to get lost in my daydreams. If I get lost, who is losing me? I become aware of being lost after the fact of being lost. To see myself as the agent, as the one who makes things happen in my life, is a deluding narrative. If I accept that life is happening to me, rather than that I am making it happen, then there are two questions: 'What is life?' and 'What is me?' Once we start to attend we find that life is a process of experience, of transient patternings of energy. Because of the patterning a sense of repetition appears, which allows us to take the patternings as enduring. However the pattern itself is repeating: it's not something that is there all the time.

Who is the one who is here? I develop attention; I am attentive and yet I'm not, because I got lost. I may have the sense that I can stand apart from the world and make choices but when I start to meditate I see I have no choice. I have already bought the thought without examining it. That's not something you would do when you buy things in the shops. You would probably read the packaging to find out if the product was fresh and good for you. My mind is an excellent thought factory producing the highest quality of thinking, or so I believe. But when I meditate, I find some weird constructions. Something has gone wrong in the quality control department of my mind factory!

Meditation is done not only to achieve a calmer mind but to open up the possibility of seeing what we are up to, of observing the actual process whereby we move from a degree of clarity to a degree of enmeshed confusion. The thing about calm is that it allows more subtle expressions to be recognised early. If you go to the countryside and stand or sit where it's quiet and still, then you start to hear small insects which you wouldn't hear if they were in a garden in the city. In the city we get used to a lot of background noise and in order to deal with that we dull our senses so as not to be disturbed. One of the functions of meditation is to re-sensitise ourselves so that we pick up the very subtle traces of past thoughts and the very subtle beginnings of future thoughts. This allows us to separate off thoughts' temptation that they can offer us true meaning if we just follow them. Why is it tempting? Because all of us are looking for meaning in life; all of us have a sense of lack, a sense that something is missing. What is missing? It could be anything.

Yesterday on the bus coming here from the airport there was a mother with two small children. The children had been sharing a small container of juice. The process of sharing this was not very easily managed but once it was emptied the container was nothing at all. The boy discovered that he could blow down the straw and make the container big and small, big and small like a balloon. His little sister's hand kept going out to grab it. When the juice was finished she had no further interest in it but now…, now I need that. Lack suddenly was disclosed to her and the more pleasure her brother had in blowing this up and down, the greater her lack and need became. When we look around in life we see many such situations. Lack is a free-floating signifier that can lock on to anything which arises. If only I get that object then I would be completed, especially if someone else has it. I feel that something is missing in me and that I have now identified what it is.

In the Western tradition the idea of this is represented by Plato in THE SYMPOSIUM, where he expresses the idea that originally human beings were both male and female but were punished for some reasons by being divided into two parts, one male and one female. That is why now we may find ourselves looking for our missing half. Incompletion arises as a punishment. The Christian view is exactly the same. Once we were living in the realm of God, but we were cast out of the Garden of Eden and keep longing to return. On the basis of that, religions sell all kinds of interesting goods. Rock bands sell tee-shirts and hats and many such souvenirs; church is selling exactly the same. From the buddhist point of view, we ask the question, 'What is it that is missing?' Is it an object which is out there? Is it some qualities of the subject? If I had more compassion, if I were more generous, if I were more thoughtful, would I then be a complete human being?

From the point of view of meditation in order for me to be complete the only thing I have to find is myself. We might think, "But I already have myself." Of course we already have many ideas about ourselves and can tell many stories about ourselves but as we get older and look back we see we have had a lot of selves and at different stages of life we define ourselves in very different ways. Perhaps what I take myself to be is not me because if it were truly me it wouldn't change. Perhaps what I take to be myself is a situation or a manifestation, a construct co-created with the factors around me. That is to say, we can only be ourselves with the permission of the people around us. If somebody is a teacher then he/she has to have a situation in which he/she teaches. It's unlikely that teachers build their own school by their own hands, that they interview themselves for the job and so on. Whatever we say about ourselves is constructed out of situational factors, not intrinsic factors. So is there any intrinsic truth or basis for our own sense of our existence?

The real goal of meditation is to awaken to the one who is here, not indirectly through telling ourselves stories about who we are, but through being present in the moment of the arising of experience. We do not get intoxicated by experience and neither do we hold ourselves back as cool distant observers. We allow the non-duality of fresh present awareness and the unfolding of the manifold existences that we encounter.

Let's begin with some basic calming of the mind in order to loosen up our attachment. Sit in a comfortable way, letting your spine carry the weight of the body so that the muscles are very free and relaxed. You can sit with your hands on your knees or folded in front of you. For this practice the chin is slightly down, the tongue is resting on the palate behind the front teeth, the eyes are slightly opened gazing down the line of the nose, shoulders are back and dropped, and the breath is moving easily, a little through the mouth but mainly through the nose. Sit in full lotus posture if that is easy for you, but it is not necessary. Then simply track the movement of the breath as you feel it on the nostrils. This is not something to think about, you're just being with your sensory manifestation. Whenever you find your attention wandering off and you get caught up in something, then very gently bring it back into focus.

Another useful function of this simple practice is that it's a kind of diagnostic. It reveals that we have certain faults and failings. So what to do? Maybe I think I could do better; I see room for improvement. Maybe then I should try harder. Maybe I am not in such a good place and it would be better if I were somewhere else. Yes, I should make use of the Holy Dharma in order to get somewhere else! The nyingmapa system has nine yanas, nine vehicles, nine methods for traveling. The mahayana system has five stages and ten paths. As you move through them you probably get a sense of progress, a sense of accomplishment. That's one way of orienting oneself. There is a long way to go, the great heroes are already there, we however are walking pretty slowly and unfortunately death is going to meet us before we arrive at our destination. Better luck next life, hopefully.

The dzogchen system says: *"Oh, so you have problems? Who has problems?"* This is much quicker. When we focus our attention on being present, on being aware, we become aware of distraction. Distraction means being moved from where we are. There is a traction, a pulling, whereby we get distorted: *"Ah, something to do. This is good I like something to do. From this day on I will always do my best to resist distraction. Even if I am not going on a big journey I can still be a hero. So I'm going to struggle with distraction. If I want to defeat my enemy, I have to find my enemy. I'll look at my mind, and whenever there's a dangerous thought I'll get my gun out and shoot it!"* But before you can pull the trigger it's gone. This feeling that seems to catch us, that we're going to be in a struggle, is gone. It's very difficult then to be a hero!

Thoughts, feelings and sensations go free by themselves. This is the deep basis of all dzogchen paths, and it's a strange path because it's a path to being here. It doesn't involve going anywhere else. What goes somewhere else is the illusory journey of thoughts and feelings and sensations. Our awareness never moves. Everything else is moving. Experience is always moving, but without awareness there is no experience. Movement and stillness are inseparable. Movement is not the enemy. The problem is the forgetfulness of stillness in the moment of movement. The nature of the mind is space. Clouds move in the sky but the sky is not marked by the clouds. Clouds are merely one of the ways that sky shows its potential – white clouds, dark clouds, storms, rainbows, clear blue open space...

What then do I have to do? I don't have to do anything. How do I do that? That's how we get lost, trying to do something that can't be done.

All that we have to do really is to observe ourselves in the process of being ourselves; to look, rather than to act, because when we see, the need for action is less and less. We see that we are dynamic, that we are born and die again and again and again, that what I take myself to be is exactly a taking, a theft out of the undivided field of experience. I see that I roll a little circle around certain aspects of myself and say that this is what I am but then in the next moment I say that I am something else, and then something else...

The most reliable thing about us is our unreliability. This is the impermanent nature of the mind. So you can see there is a crossroad here. You may decide, *"Ah, I'm going to be reliable. I'm not going to be like one of these lost people wandering in samsara. I will know what I think, and I say what I think and I will be clear."* But this is impossible; impossible because the mind is open. We refer to 'my' mind as if it were 'my' possession, but we appear within our mind. The ego is niched in the mind. Yet we act and behave as if the mind were niched inside the ego. This is what is called a category confusion.

'I' will never be solved because 'I' arises in relation to others. So how could 'I' ever know how 'I' should be? I can know how it might be useful to behave in a certain situation but I can't know in advance what the situation is going to be. That is to say, we are more when we are less. The less able we are to define who we are, the more we can allow our potential to arise as required into the situation. This is the functional meaning of non-duality. It means that by not holding yourself apart as something separate, by being a participant, the spontaneity of movement will arise as part of the field and will be intrinsically harmonious.

If, however, you start from a position of separation, that there is 'you' and there is 'me', and I have to work out what to do in advance, then a whole sequence of adjustments is required. I may say something with a particular intention but then you may react to it in a way that I didn't expect. So now I have to say, *"Well I know I said that but I didn't really mean that, what I meant was..."* There is no end to this and so nothing we say is complete or clean.

Dzogpa chenpo means 'the great accomplishment', meaning that from the very beginning everything has been whole; every part is a participating part, not a part held apart. By trusting the wholeness of the situation, less pre-planned activity is required. We find ourselves moving in connectivity.

The focus of dzogchen practice is to open to the awareness which is already present and to allow the freshness of the arising of manifestation through the body, speech and mind. Gradually we have less and less interference from the habitual formations that we have acquired and adopted.

Most teachings I have received are within the nyingma tradition, which has lineages in two forms: an open lineage and a treasure lineage. The open lineage comes from Buddha Sakyamuni and from other early buddhas and has been passed on from generation to generation. The treasure lineage comes from Padmasambhava who taught in Tibet during the 8th and 9th centuries. These teachings were hidden, some in the earth, some in water, some in the sky. They were later revealed by so-called 'tertons' who were the reincarnations of his early students in Tibet. The accounts say that he was not born in a human way but manifested in the form of an eight year old boy on a big lotus in the middle of a lake. He had little beads of sweat on his face, fresh like early morning dewdrops. Completely fresh and not interfered with in any way.

The outer lineages are transmitted to you by someone, a teacher, and there is the inner direct lineage of your own awareness. The function of the outer lineage is to awaken the inner lineage. The function of the teacher is to be a site of recognition of yourself.

They are many things in buddhism that you can learn. There are hundreds of thousands of books, hundred of thousands of different meditation practices and so on. You can learn about them. But knowing *about* something is not the same as inhabiting it. To inhabit something is to make it your own, by massaging it into yourself so that you become the living embodiment of it. Knowing *about* things is like stitching patches onto yourself since, in fact, what they do is displace you from yourself because everything is coming back to you through something you have heard or read.

That is why it is very important to learn how to transform what appears as objective knowledge into subjective experience. The central question is how do I find myself? I am here, I am hidden from myself by myself and because I am hiding myself from myself who will I ask to stop doing this? In the tradition we speak of the Guru. Guru essentially means yourself. The guru is not somebody else. The guru is the generosity of the world manifesting as the way of returning you to you. The guru can be visualised as Padmasambhava, or in his/her physical form, or as Tara or in any of the tantric forms. In the dzogchen tradition we usually visualise as forms of light.

In the tantric system we work with idealisation: the guru is perfect; I am not perfect. By praying to the guru with great faith I come into connection with the teacher. We might then visualise rays of lights coming from the teacher purifying all the limitations and imperfections of body, speech and mind until I am full of light. The guru in front of you is in a form of light and comes to the top of your head and dissolves into a ball of light, which comes into your heart. Then your body, which is now full of light, dissolves into that ball of light. The only thing which exists is one ball of red, white and blue light which becomes smaller and smaller and smaller until it vanishes in space. In this spacious open state, you are inseparable from the mind of the guru. Gradually thoughts, feelings, sensations arise again. However now everything you see is the form of the guru, appearance and emptiness; everything you hear is mantra, sound and emptiness; all thoughts and mental experience is the mind of the guru. You continue in that understanding.

When a thought arises in the mind, such as *"Why is our president so useless?"* is this really the mind of the guru? Why would an enlightened mind of all the buddhas give rise to such a thought? When I would put such a question to CR Lama he would say, *"When you meet the Buddha ask him, don't ask me."* Then you see how we make a judgement and then we judge the judgement. Thought is chasing thought, round and round and round.

This is the mind of the buddha but it is not what we have read on the packet. When we visited buddhist temples we saw shiny statues of the Buddha, clean butter lamps, everything beautiful and bright. If people were talking it was about important serious things and not the sort of nonsense that goes on in my mind! It's a bit like going to a famous restaurant which has a very good chef but unfortunately on the night I go the chef is away and the apprentice is cooking. I didn't get the real buddha mind; I got the apprentice's mind. Maybe that's why I have all these silly thoughts. If I was really enlightened, my mind would be shining rainbows, filled with beautiful thoughts and spreading love to all beings. If I told my holy guru that I only have thoughts like this he would say, *"I'm glad you are able to tell the Buddha who he is. Now you know what the Buddha is like."*

However we don't know what the Buddha is like. This is the difficulty of being with things just as they are: we already have so many thoughts about how they *should* be. We have our map; then we visit the territory but, hey, the territory doesn't fit the map. Now we have two choices: either to change the map or to ignore the territory. When we are attached to our map, we close the eyes and enter dreamland.

Everything is the mind of the buddha. *"You mean when the planes are bombing hospitals and innocent civilians, this is the mind*

222

of the buddha? Surely the buddha is good and that is bad." Thinking like this is not meditation practice; it is being an amateur lawyer. If it is this, it can't be that. This is good, this is bad; they are not the same.

This is the way duality manifests, firstly subject and object and then good and bad, mine and yours, sacred-profane, enlightened-not enlightened. All these many dualities manifest. We say this is good, we say that is bad. When army troops return to their homeland they are often treated as heroes, honoured and fêted and given medals. However the defeated populace remembers them as rapists and killers. Who is good? Who is bad? On the basis of opinions we kill people. All the wars in the world are created by opinions. We take an idea, blow on it three times and think we have turned it into the truth.

Judgement is something we have to exercise with care, especially in the practice of meditation. We have to see the difference between two aspects. One, we can call discernment, which means the accurate perception of what is there. Discernment has a relational quality. It's very nice to go to the perfume area of a big department store where they wave little perfumed strips under your nose. The different strands in the perfume start to reveal themselves. With the first one the nose is fresh and you smell many things. When you get further down with the bottles, the echoes of the first smells are starting to wend their way into each fresh new perfume and you end up comparing and contrasting your experiences rather than being open to them.

These ordinary life experiences are very helpful because they show how easy it is for us to slip into building structures of interpretation which may appear to be illuminating, but are actually obscuring. If we want the freshness of the situation we need to have a clean nose. We clear the palate between each course of a meal but how do we do this with the mind? Thoughts wed themselves together into patterns very quickly. The key freshener is emptiness. Emptiness means that whatever is being experienced and the experiencer of the experience are not things, are not separate items, but are appearances. Something appears to the eyes, to the ears, to the memory.

Appearance is impactful; it has its quality which is revealed in the moment but there is no internal definition to it. It arises due to causes and circumstances, then its impact diminishes and it vanishes leaving space for something else. *"Oh springtime, the winter is over, happiness."* Then the clouds will come again. Something was there and then it's not. The fact that it's there means it's not nothing at all. There is something which is nothing, as is set out very clearly in the *Heart Sutra*. We have an emotional resonance, a cognitive resonance but there is nothing to grasp. Perhaps you chat with someone and they tell you a sad story. The mood of pathos fills you. Then that too shifts.

Emptiness is the basic space of potential, both the source of what arises and the space within which everything arises. It is the ground, which is inseparable from whatever arises. Thoughts don't leap out of the mind like a fish leaping out of water; thoughts are in the mind.

Experience is the movement of the mind and as such it is impactful and ungraspable. We arise with it but we can't get it, hence the freshness of our existence. In Sanskrit this is referred to as *sahaj*. *Sahaj* is the spontaneous co-emergence of subject and object. In Tibetan it is called *lhan chig kyepa* means there are not two things but there is not one thing; it is the non-dual integrated arising. Appearance is inseparable from emptiness. It doesn't mean that appearance is dissolved into emptiness and becomes empty but that ungraspability shows many different forms of itself.

So what happens when you go into judgement? *"I don't like this tasteless tomato!"* What am I talking about? About my idea of

224

tomatoes. This particular tomato has been recruited into my campaign against tasteless tomatoes. I have the idea of a proper tomato and I have this poor specimen on my plate, this betrayer of tomato-ness! It has cheated me. I approach the tomato through my idea. Do I actually taste the tomato? I tasted it in terms of what I thought it should be. I was not fresh and open to the tomato. I was assessing whether it fitted my tomato template? My map comes first; the world comes after. This is what buddhism means when it refers to judgement: our relation with what is arising is mediated through our mental constructs. In Sanskrit these mental constructs are called samskāras. They are composite in themselves and they are also compositional in that they gather and shape more factors. It's very important to observe how much energy goes into creating our judgements about the world.

I myself have not been appointed Official Government Tomato Inspector, so my distress at having this tomato in front of me changes nothing except my mood. It's the same with a lot of our judgements. We are small powerless people, and though we may become angry or upset about something, nothing changes. Nothing changes except that we have upset ourselves. I am upsetting myself. What does that mean? 'I' – ego self as a set of ideas – is being disturbed by the development of other ideas. Idea is chasing idea: thought is chasing thought. There is always something to complain about. Always.

When we were walking here this morning, somebody came up to beg from a woman who was walking just in front of us. She waved him away and was quite disturbed by his presence. She began to tell us all the faults of this man, that he had a mobile phone and yet was begging, and so on. The moment had passed but she was now thinking that it was not right, that people shouldn't do that. If people behaved properly, life would be better. All this may be true but it's not going to happen.

What we see here is the bed for omnipotent ego formations. *"If I were in charge, I would not make the world that way. How come these incompetent people are in power? Don't they know how to behave?"* This is irrelevant. Nobody cares. But we care. Why? Because we are talking and thinking ourselves into existence. Just as the dog going down the street pisses on the lampposts to mark its territory so we put our judgements on the world to say: I exist. These judgements are actually self-referential, they are confirming to me the validity of my self-position. They are part of the on-going process of the construction of the individual sense of self. And they are activity. If you want it to stop you just have to not do it.

"I need to do it. If I didn't do it who will I be?" Well, you can't know until you stop doing it. *"But I'm already me. You want me to give up my Me Land passport and to become a citizen of Buddha Land? No, I want to have dual citizenship. I want to be 'me' and also be enlightened. Who knows, maybe if I stop being 'me' the Buddha won't give me a passport. What then?"* This is why they always say faith is very important.

The encouragement here is to start observing just how busy you are in generating your particular take on the world. It's not about trying to stop the thought production. The first thing is to see how much busy movement is in our life. The ego is always giving its opinion, running a narrative, creating patterns of importance. From the point of view of the ego this is vital because this is how it confirms its existence. From the point of view of open awareness this is very sad since you are hiding your own actuality from yourself. It is our own activity, which blinds us to the openness of being.

The freshness is the ground of our experience always present, always generous. However when we are caught up in our thought production it becomes invisible to us. The practice is to open to freshness.

THE THREE STATEMENTS OF GARAB DORJE

The transmission of dzogchen teachings into the human world began with Garab Dorje. The first level of transmission was the direct transmission spontaneously arising from the primordial Buddha Samantabhadra to Vajrasattva. He in turn gave the second level of transmission, the symbolic, to Garab Dorje. Then Garab Dorje gave the third level of transmission, the auditory, to Manjushrimitra. This was effected by his enunciating the Three Statements that convey the essence of dzogchen:

1. See your own face – open to the truth of how you are.

2. Do not remain in doubt – stay open without thinking about it.

3. Continue in this way – do not be distracted by concepts. Let them self-liberate as they are.

THE THREE STATEMENTS OF GARAB DORJE begin with what is often translated as 'pointing out instructions' and sometimes described as an introduction. I can point out where the clock is on the wall. A clock is something that can be pointed at, however the mind cannot be pointed out because it is not a thing. So, before we even begin to consider what Garab Dorje said, we have to be clear about the nature of knowledge.

Knowledge is generally based on the accumulation of bits of information. Somebody is deemed to be knowledgeable if they have accumulated a lot of information and can present it in ways that other people can understand. The 20th century European philosopher Wittgenstein wrote about the distinction between telling and showing. Many things can be spoken about and described, but some things can only be shown. The traditional Tibetan example for this is somebody doesn't know what sweetness is. You could use thousands of words to describe sweetness and they can memorise all these words but they still wouldn't know what is sweetness. However, if you take a single spoonful of honey and put it on their tongue they immediately will know what sweetness is. Now that they know what sweetness is, you can ask them to tell you what it is, but they too would find it impossible to tell.

When we talk about pointing out the mind or describing the nature of the mind, it is important that we take what's said in a very light way. The mind cannot be encompassed and told in words so the language used is metaphoric, alluding to things, evoking things, even though they cannot describe precisely what the mind is. The descriptions are an invitation to put yourself in the way of something which is already there. 'To put yourself in the way of your mind' is to get out of the way of yourself, that is to say, to get yourself out of the way. It means relax, open and be with what is here.

The mind is described as being naked, not covered. Although we think we perceive external objects just as they are, we are actually projecting our knowledge on to that appearance. In our ordinary life we rely on such mental activity to make our world function. We are glad when a thought comes that we have to pay a bill: *"Oh, I forgot to do that. I'd better to do it now."* The thought arises as a kind of illumination. It is the light which guides most of our actions, the light of conceptual elaboration. The more thoughts we have, the more sophisticated are our thoughts, the more we can illuminate our life. It is difficult to recognise that this practice of illumination is itself obscuring.

If you go out on a dark night gradually your eyes adapt and there is usually some starlight to give you a sense of what's there. Maybe a friend arrives and tells you, *"Don't worry, I have a torch."* They put on the torch – there is a very bright beam and some of the world is suddenly illuminated, but what is not in the torch's beam is still in darkness. It's the same with conceptual illumination: it doesn't deal with the problem of darkness. It creates a pseudo illumination. As long as the torch battery is working the light will be there. As long as you keep thinking, the light of the cognitive illumination will continue to radiate for you. However, this is a light that arises due to causes and circumstances. It's not self-existing. It can be influenced by all sorts of factors such as your health. In order to find ourselves we need to have an illumination which is not that of concepts.

In paintings of the primordial Buddha Kuntuzangpo he is dark blue in colour. This dark blue indicates the colour of the sky at the very first moment of the dawn. It's just a couple of shades up from black. Out of not knowing, comes light. 'Not knowing' means letting go of our reliance on thoughts. This means that when we get a bit lost in our practice – perhaps not sure what we are doing or why – then we can think about it. We might wonder if we would be better of reciting mantras since at least then we would know what to do. From the dzogchen point of view thinking this way is a very dangerous friend because the intention is to not feel like you. *"If I don't feel like me then who will I feel like?"* Feel like anything. The mind is just empty. Nothing. Stuff is happening but none of it's me. Leave it all alone. When thoughts and feelings arise in the mind they can be experienced but if you try to incorporate them into your sense of self, then it becomes a problem. We arrive with nothing, we play, and we leave with nothing. The playing is playing in emptiness.

The nothingness of the dark gives rise to Buddha Kuntuzangpo, known as Samantabhadra in Sanskrit. It is the radiance of the mind showing itself. It's not an illumination which brings some things into the foreground and leaves other things in the background. It is the soft soft light of early dawn, which lightens everything. I find it very beautiful to be up early on a summer morning, out in the country, seeing the first light. Everything is just as it is in its own place. This is the light of the mind of Samantabhadra. It's not a busy light; it's not doing things and making things. It's a light that we can be. When we open to the dawn, we are part of that experience. When the mind is quiet, and the world is quiet, there is wholeness.

So what is my mind? From the very beginning our mind is here. Without a mind we wouldn't be able to think or walk or move; the mind is the illuminator. It illuminates everything. We turn our head and everything in the room is illuminated just as it is. It's not selective. In the Tibetan tradition it's often compared to a mirror. The mirror shows whatever is placed in front of it. The mirror is not selective. It's not composing any image; it's a simple showing, a showing which didn't invite, doesn't hold on and doesn't push away. It just allows.

A car mirror has shown thousands of images. Each image arises and passes, arises and passes. Each image, each reflection, is in the mirror but they are not stacking up like layers of lasagna. Each image is there and then gone. The image is present and yet empty in the mind, which is also present yet empty. The reflection is in the mirror – it's not added on to the mirror – but you can't take a reflection out of the mirror. Nor can you say the reflection *is* the mirror because the mirror is not defined by whatever particular image is being reflected at that moment. Similarly, our mind is opened and empty. Moment by moment we have sensations, feelings, thoughts, memories, hopes, and fears arising and passing. They are us, they are in us, and then they are gone.

The emptiness of the mind allows the emergence of the patterning of situations. What arises is true experientially but not essentially, just as the reflection in the mirror is there, is undeniable, and yet has no self-substance. There is no essence to the reflection. A traditional example is full moon light. You may see the reflection of the moon in a pond. If the night is calm and the water is unruffled then you can see the moon very clearly. It is as if the moon is in the water. *"It's the moon! Look at the moon!"* It's not the moon, but it appears to be the moon. I look at my face in the mirror and know it's me, it's not you. Something is there but there is no truth, or reality, or substance to it. It is the illusory nature of a phenomenon, which is both the consequence of, and the guarantor of, the emptiness of the mind. If the mind were a solid substance, a piece of clay, a piece of wood or metal, you could make lots of things from it, but not everything. If you took a piece of the wall here, you could draw and paint on it, put many different colours on it and after a while it would just become a mess and any further mark that you made wouldn't make much difference. What you would have is the building up of marks. The wall seems to support accumulation. But a mirror doesn't offer accumulation. As the next arrives, the earlier one has gone. We observe this in our mind, the impermanence of all phenomena revealed through the arising and passing of whatever is happening.

To recap, in looking for our mind we have to look in a way which is different from how we look for other things. If you're looking for an object, you'll surely find an object. Why? Because all objects are created by mind. If you think of your mind as an object then you can imagine that your mind is anything whatsoever. You can imagine that it is the echo of god's love. You can imagine that it is your brain produced by DNA. You can imagine that it is cursed by demons. You can imagine all sorts of things. This is your freedom. Your imagination wants to give you what it is. Mind, however, is not something to be got. How will I get something, which can't be got? We are here, we have a mind, we *are* a mind and we don't need to get what we already have. You are here, your mind is present. How to be your mind? But you *are* your mind.

The real question is how not to be the one who doesn't know how to find their mind. Your mind is hidden by the mind's own mental construction. Thoughts don't hide the mind by standing between me and my mind. If I am looking in a mirror to try to see my reflection how will I find that reflection? If I put my hand in front of my face the reflection of my face will be hidden by the reflection of my hand. Something has been interposed between me and my own mind. *"I have to get it out the way. Whatever it is, it's in the way. I want to find my mind!"*

THE DOG HAS A TAIL

CR Lama once used this example to explain it to me. A dog has a tail. The dog and the tail belong together. The important thing to realise is that the dog wags the tail. If the tail wagged the dog it would look strange! I, the dog, am now trying to find my mind, my tail. I, the dog, can't seem to find my mind/tail. If you are thinking/looking in this way you will never find your mind. Why? Because you are looking in the wrong way. The dog wags the tail; when the mind moves/wags, ten thousands things all appear.

'I' am the movement of my mind. The mind moves 'me'. The mind comes first. It shows the interplay, the eternal dance of subject and object. In our normal way of conceptualising, 'I' am a permanent fixture that has experiences. Experiences come and go but 'I am' is always here. I can remember being five years of age. I can remember my first bicycle. I have had so many experiences since then. This is the view of duality. I am the enjoying subject and I have had experiences out of which I can create more stories. But who is this 'I' that is talking about itself? Everything I say about 'me' is arising and passing.

The impermanent flow, the ever-changing flow, of the unfolding energy of the mind shows itself as subject and object. Every subject exists with object. You don't have a subject without anything going on. Subject and object is a *pas de deux;* it's not a solo. The subject side in the *pas de deux* of dualistic experiences, is me. I'm here but I am the tail of the dog. That's a central thing. Where is the dog? You may think, *"I am going to work everything out. I am going to find my mind."* but the ego is very big and powerful and the mind is a little lost sheep wandering on the hill. This is what makes meditation very difficult – you're starting with false axioms and the axioms determine the progress of your understanding.

When the text says that the mind is naked, what could it be covered by? The perception of subject and object. However, I do rely on the perception of subject and object to help me know what is going on. So this requires a radical shift. Enlightenment is not gained by more thinking or by better thinking. It's not a conceptual creation. It is the direct revelation of how it is. I am going to meditate by letting go of myself. I will do this by allowing all that I take to be myself to be what it actually is – which is part of the flow of experiences. That is to say, 'I' am an experience, not an experiencer. 'I' experience 'myself'. I experience myself talking with you. In that moment I can see that 'I', as energetic formation, is something arising and passing. So who is experiencing myself as an experience? That's what we want to find out.

When we do the meditation, the simplest way is just to sit in a comfortable way and relax into the out-breath. We do it with a gaze slightly open, looking into the space in front of us. That is because we don't want to create the sense of going into ourself; we're just here. What's here is me and everything. Here I am; thoughts, feelings, sensations are all going on. There is an urge to identify with certain aspects of what is arising as me. I may become a little bit aware of some tension in my legs for example, *"Oh my left leg is a bit sore."* This is a construction but it seems to be saying something about me. Let it go. Whatever occurs let it go.

The letting go is not effortful since everything goes by itself anyway. It's the holding on that is effortful. So here we are just sitting on a sunny afternoon; time is going by, nothing is gained, nothing is lost. Where, how and with whom is this occurring? If I don't tell myself a story about who is the experiencer, experience is occurring, therefore there is an experiencer. If you want to find the experiencer, be at the point of experience. For example, a little sensation suddenly arose here on my forehead. Since that is the main thing that is manifesting for me at the moment, then because it's there, awareness is there also. We find the mind at the point of experience, because there is no experience without mind.

Again and again, do not merge into the experience and be part of it. Do not stand apart from it either and try to examine it. Rather, be the very field of awareness within which experience is arising and passing. You then start to see that what you take to be object arises and passes, and what you take to be subject arises and passes. This is the showing, or the display of the energy, of the creativity of the mind.

However, it is not the mind itself. Without the mind it wouldn't appear but no matter how it is, it doesn't define the mind. It's the same as with a mirror. You wouldn't have a reflection without the mirror nevertheless the particular details of the reflection don't define the actual nature of the mirror. We are not blocking the flow of experience, we are not trying to capture any of it; we're just staying present in the very moment of the unfolding of space and time.

Don't push away thoughts that you think are negative; don't try to hang on to thoughts which you think are positive; just relax into the open presence which is your awareness. Allow the energy formation, which is the self-referential ego, to relax into its own ground of spaciousness.

[Practice]

You don't need to do this kind of meditation for long at first. It's not a matter of making effort; it's not a matter of struggling. It's about again and again gently finding yourself where experience is. It's just a matter of practice. Little and often. For some people it's quite easy, for others it's more difficult, but it's neither a race nor a competition. It's about being fully at home in yourself. All the familiar thoughts and feelings and behaviours that you have can continue to arise. There is nothing particular to renounce, nothing to develop except this singular point of identification. For example, if I say, *"I am talking"*, the comment 'I am talking' is like a friendly accompaniment to the fact of talking. They are running together. But if I tilt it slightly by emphasising the first word, '*I* am talking', then that little gap gives me the sense of evaluating what I am doing so that instead of it being a process description, it is a sort of review from 'central command' evaluating how I'm doing and also giving me the chance to have a feeling of importance.

So what we are doing in our practice, is a very subtle rebalancing so that we are as close to our experience as possible, without falling in. Not merged in it, not apart from it, but present with it. The mirror is present with the reflection. The mirror is not doing anything to the reflection, not defending itself against the reflection, or rearranging it, or trying to get rid of it. So if you are sitting and a thought comes such as *"I don't know what I am doing. Whatever it is, it is not meditation"*, just sit with that. Sit not believing it, not disbelieving it, sit where the experience of a manifestation is. The mind is there because the mind is the shower of the experience.

It is not the semantic content of the thought that is important. In our hunger for meaning, we want to get good thoughts that give some value and get rid of bad thoughts which seem to devalue us. Here in our meditation all thoughts have the same status. They are all just reflections. Their main function for us in our meditation is to show us how to be present with our mind.

Ignorance, the beginning of samsara, is the identification with the thought. Who identifies with the thought? The thought of 'I'. Samsara is thought chasing thought, thought building thought. There is nothing wrong with thought. But thought in its self-intoxication has a blindness or ingratitude. Without the mirror there is no reflection. When you look in a mirror, the reflections seem to come out and you never see the mirror; you just see the reflection. The reflections fill up in the mirror in a way that hides the mirror itself.

We all know the story of Cinderella. Poor girl, her mother dies, father remarries with a woman who already has two daughters, big daughters, strong daughters, self-admiring daughters. And the daughter of the father is moved down into the kitchen. All day long she is cleaning, repairing, being the servant. She is the daughter of the house but she is usurped. In the story there is a magical transformation, which allows Cinderella to be returned to her true status. So it is in the story of our lives: awareness is like Cinderella. All day long showing nice images, showing nice images... the images are preening themselves and taking up all the space. We think that the thoughts and feelings and memories are who we are. But this is dependent on the mirror. The tail is dependent on the dog. Without the mind, none of these experiences would arrive but in the moment of forgetfulness of the mirror, thoughts become self-cherishing and self-absorbed.

Samsara is an ungrateful child. The mother is there. The child and the mother are never separated. The child is continuously dependent on the mother but the child says, *"I exist, I'm me, I have always just been myself."* The child doesn't remember coming out of the mother's body. The child says, *"As long as I can remember I've been me."* The mother is thinking, *"Oh, Oh. I have a different memory."*

So, awareness is open to everything but our ego self is constructing this narrative of self-existence and self-validation. It's not that the ego has to be transformed; it simply has to recognise its own ground: the ego is the radiance of the mind and is not the mind itself, although it is a part of what is going on. If a small part clings to be the whole story something is wrong, because it's clinging too much while standing on very narrow ground.

In the practice we relax, and open, again and again, and in that way we merge into the ground. We are the ground, we waken to be the ground, and then we directly experience all that we take to be our subjectivity continuing to move in the space of the mind.

The tantric method of doing this that I described earlier is exactly the same. Meditating on the image of the guru, the yidam, meditation on deity, receiving the four lights of initiation and then dissolving into and through the deity into emptiness. That which appears to be separate is re-grounded in a ground that it has never left.

The buddhism we need is the buddhism that we can use. Dzogchen practice is not the practice to use when you feel tired, exhausted and weary. Tantric practice is better at this time. If you're upset and confused you can put your hands together and pray, *"Big mama, big papa, please save me."* You call the mama Tara, you call the papa Padmasambhava, and this is the best practice because it fits the quality of your energy. You may be feeling feel weak and alone, and you want to hang on to something, so rather than phoning your friend in the middle of the night and giving them a hard time, then pray! Dissolve into the deity! At other times when you are more relaxed and at ease in yourself, you can do the shiné direct sitting practice.

What this means is that you have to respect yourself. You have to find the dignity of your own embodied existence and work with that. If you feel depressed and hopeless for some reason, rather than seeing this as something shameful or difficult, the question is what will you do with this. In the kitchen you realise that you only have some old bread and some onions ... dumplings! You have to know how to cook and cooking depends not only on the recipe book but on your ingredients. You can have twenty recipe books with lovely bright pictures but if you don't have much food in the kitchen, that's going to limit what you can cook.

So be friendly with yourself, be kind towards yourself, respectful of yourself. However you are, think how you would like to collaborate with this patterning of energy. If the body is tired you shouldn't do vigorous exercises. We have to listen to our capacity because if we are against ourselves, if we are driving ourselves, how can we awaken to a state of integration and collaboration? From this point of view, no matter what state we find ourselves in, however we are, we can work with that.

It's a paradox that when we are chasing something we are usually disappointed and when we open to having nothing we find we have everything. Desiring something is not bad or wrong, it's just that it is hyper-focused. Try it now. If you focus your gaze directly in front of you, you get a particular kind of experience. Then if you relax your gaze, a peripheral vision opens and you have a completely different experience. Our wide room is always here but when we have this fixated vision, we don't see it. It hasn't vanished or gone somewhere else. When we let go of the fixation on something, by not wishing for anything in particular, we find that everything becomes available. Having access to everything by being relaxed and open, any sense of lack, any sense that something is missing, starts to dissolve. What could be more than this? What makes 'this' small is comparing 'this' with 'that'. When you have just this, this is this. It is what it is, this is it. Satisfaction and contentment are revealed through being open and empty, accessible to everything. We are not blocking or editing our receptivity. We are available, in so far as we can manifest different aspects of ourselves according to the situation.

In the tradition they refer to this in terms of 'the three kayas', or the three modes of the buddha's existence. The first is the Dharmakaya, which is the mind of the buddha inseparable from open space. Because it is without limit in any direction, everything is already within it and so it has no lack. Then without effort, the clarity of the spaciousness reveals itself. Returning to this image of the mirror, when you look into the mirror to find the mirror-ness of the mirror, you can't find anything. The mirror however shows itself through its clarity of revealing reflections of whatever is placed in front of it.

In the same way, since our mind is empty it has hospitality for everything. Its shining illuminating quality of clarity is the display of the field of experience. It doesn't have to do anything to display this. In the traditional example the mind is like the sun in the sky; it is bright in itself and it sends out rays. These rays fill the sky, which is the clarity, and when they hit the earth, it is in the form of focused light and heat. Within this open clarity of our mind, we find ourselves walking and talking and speaking. This arises situationally. For example, where we are now in a buddhist setting taking part in buddhist teachings, we find ourselves talking to people in ways that we might not talk if we were at work. The setting allows and supports particular kinds of conversations. It's not that we make a decision to talk in this way but that by being in touch with the environment we find that particular words come out of our mouth. Traditionally this field is referred to as the sambhogakaya, the enjoyment or the aesthetic appreciation quality of the clarity of the field. It is often linked to the idea of pure buddhalands, like Buddha Amitabha's western paradise. Our world, right here in this room, right now at this moment, is also a buddha field.

Within that the nirmanakaya, the movement of the energy of the buddha as a compassionate expression, just arises. Something occurs. We find ourselves being part of something in a particular way. Talking is occurring without a talker, movement is occurring without a mover. It's not that there is some little person, some homunculus inside us who is pushing out our words or our movements, but rather when we are self-forgetful, that's when we do 'being ourselves' better. When I don't know that I'm doing me, I do me better. The nirmanakaya radiates out through the shared field of connectivity. When we retreat into anxiety about ourselves, this creates a threshold in front of us that we have to step over to go out into the world. This dualistic splitting generates a feeling of self-consciousness and a process of artificiality. How should I be in order to be okay with other people? What are they thinking about me? Many unanswerable questions are generated by such anxiety. In response to these questions, a very anxious person might formulate rituals and obsessional behaviours as a way of trying to regulate the uncertainty of existence. The problem is not, however, the unpredictability of the world, but it is our alienation from the non-dual field of experience from which we ourselves cut ourselves off.

You can try this experiment: go into a café or a bar and hold in mind the thought, *"Everyone is looking at me and they don't like me."* Stay for about half an hour looking around and checking if people are looking at you. You will not feel very relaxed. Who is creating the lack of relaxation? You yourself. You're bringing in a particular reading to the situation: you say, *"I am an object, which can be judged and evaluated by other people."* I am at the mercy of the thoughts that other people have about me. People feel shy, embarrassed, and ashamed. This kind of apprehension of the world is very normal. A whole feeling of insecurity and paranoia is generated from the basic supposition, the basic proposition that 'I am an object'. I am a thing, and therefore I can be defined. I can be caught. However, when we are relaxed and open, we can't be caught. Even if somebody expresses a critical opinion of us, we can just say, *"Welcome to your mind. That's you, it's not me."* In that paradoxical way, being open is being protected whereas being defensively closed is an energetic provocation for more grief, worry and anxiety.

Allowing the world to manifest through us without interfering involves a trust, a trust that we are part of what is going on. This is not a proposition of belief. It's not a dogma that you have to adopt in some way. It is something that you can experience directly through the meditation. So we will do a little bit more meditation now. We want to explore precisely for ourselves *"Am I an object?" "Is my mind a thing?"*

FIVE QUESTIONS TO THE MIND

There are five questions traditionally used to examine the mind and see whether the mind is a thing like all the other seeming things in the world.

1. Does the mind have a shape? Is it round or square, triangular?

2. Does it have a colour?

3. Does it have a size? Is it bigger than the body; is it bigger than the house; is it smaller than the body; is it small enough to fit inside the brain?

Then there are two linked questions.

4. Where does the mind rest? At this moment, at each and every moment, where is the mind?

5. Does the mind ever leave? Does it go away some place? We know that thoughts arise, stay and go, as do feelings, and sensations, and buses. But does the mind ever leave?

With all these questions we are asking ourselves whether the mind is in the same family as all other phenomena. Or is it different? What we are looking for is not just an idea about it, but we're looking for direct experience. Small babies are interested in their mouth and when they start to develop teeth, they chew on their fingers. Then at a certain moment, *"Ouch!"* They get the experience of 'this is my finger!' This is not theory. *"Ouch!"* is direct experience. So that's what we want. We don't want an idea about an idea about an idea because they always vanish. In questioning our mind we want to directly taste *"Oh it is this!"* Direct experience is what opens up a new vista. 'Ideas about' belong in one paradigm whereas direct experience opens up another.

MEDITATING IN A DZOGCHEN WAY

As we start these questions we will start by sitting in a relaxed way, releasing tensions through a long slow outbreath. Then we just sit present with whatever is occurring. Gently allow these questions to arise. We want the questioning to be very soft and gentle, not an invasive active questioning but more a passive receptive questioning. By your own availability, allow yourself to see how your mind is, with these five questions just very gently illuminating the area of exploration.

[Practice]

These questions are the great friends of meditators. Through our general education we have gathered a lot of information about how we are. People have told us what the body is, what the brain is, what hearing is, what liking is and so on and we can use this knowledge to organise our own sensory experience. It's normal in Western cultures to think that mind is in the brain and the brain is in the skull. We are educated to think that there is a material basis for the mind, that it arises due to causes and conditions and that it will vanish due to causes and conditions. That is to say, the mind is just like everything else. We have that support and holding that kind of view supports you in the idea that something is coming into your mind and something is going out of your mind. Where was it before it came into your mind? Where is the border crossing from no-mind to mind? We are sitting here; we may hear a car on the road outside. Of course, we don't hear a car on the road outside; we hear a sound and we interpret on the basis of our knowledge and habit formations that there is a car outside on the road. In school we learned about sound vibrating through the air, coming into the ear and setting up vibrations which the brain then interprets. That is a stream of thoughts.

This is a very important crossroad because if the thoughts are right, I am a diminished being in a diminished world and buddha-nature is just a daydream. Or are these thoughts illusory constructs that offer us modes of interpretation, which mean again further thought construction. If we don't push them away, if we don't merge into them, what is here?

When a sound arises, the immediacy of it is in our mind. Where is our mind? Where the sound is? Does my mind move from here to where the cup falls over? *(A cup had just fallen over)* As soon as the cup is falling, it's as if my mind is apprehending or revealing this experience. Going from here to there is a temporal spatial notion starting with the assumption 'I am here'. But the immediacy of the sound has been there before I'd left here. The being-here-ness is an interpretation.

Does a mind have a shape? What do we find? The mind seems to be able to open up. In this room the limit of what we can see is the walls. If we go out of the city or up onto a city roof the whole sky is revealed. Our direct feeling is that we have immediate access to that whole vista. The world shows itself in and as the field of experience. If we keep looking, we notice that sometimes the mind looks big and sometimes it looks very small. When I look in a shaving mirror and my face is quite close to the mirror, it's quite small. But if I take the mirror out into the street, the whole sky can be in the mirror. When the reflection is of my face, this mirror seems quite small so how can all the houses in the street, and the sky and the trees all be inside the mirror when I take it outside? How is this possible? The mirror offers a hospitality which makes it appear big or small according to the reflections which arise. In the same way, if you're reading a book and you focus into it, this is all there is. This small sphere of attention is the whole field of experience. At other times everything is there, huge, vast, experienced.

If the mind were a thing, it would have a fixed shape however it now seems that the mind doesn't have a shape but its quality is that it can appear to *show* us shape. It's like how the sky looks so big on a beautiful summer's day and then on a grey autumn day when the clouds are low, the sky looks quite small. The sky has not become small but it appears small because that is the limit of our experience. The experience of the small grey sky is located within the vast sky. On a difficult day you might think, *"Oh my God, I can't cope, it's all too much."* but then on another day you feel much better. We are neither small nor big but some days we appear to be big and open, and other days we appear to be small and closed. This is the quality, or the shape, which arises inside the openness of the mind. The mind itself is neither big nor small but the patterns of manifestations of mood, feeling, sensation, memory, intention, demand, all the many factors that can flow through us, give a shape to our sense of our self and the world.

Where does the mind come from? Has there ever been a time without the mind? If it's coming from somewhere, where would it come from? Where would it come to if it's coming from somewhere else?

—It comes from there to here, so I'm here and my mind came from there to me.

—But if I'm here, who is the one that is here when my mind is somewhere else?

You can go off somewhere in a daydream and suddenly come back and say,

—Oh sorry, I was daydreaming, I wasn't here.

244

That is to say. you had slipped out from your familiar construction of 'this is me here in this body' and you had gone off into a daydream. However you hadn't actually gone anywhere else, since your body is still here.

The mind itself, does it go somewhere? Thoughts can go, but does the mind go? Try to remember something that happened to us between the ages of five and ten. Take a moment and see what comes to mind. Do you have some memories? Did you all remember something? Sitting here, did you go back into the past? Or did the past come to you? Did you open some little locked box and take out the past? It can feel as if we can be right back in that situation yet we didn't go anywhere. I go to the past; the past comes to me. These memories are thoughts' patterns; they manifest in the space of awareness. Do they come from outside the space of awareness into awareness? Do they then go out and go somewhere else? Nowadays we have to recycle all our rubbish. Is there a similar big recycling factory for thoughts and feelings?

We could speculate on this forever. To have a thought about a thought about a thought... it's quite easy. You might think that rabbits have a lot of babies but our mind is much more productive! Endless thought production is possible.

Regarding the question, 'Where is the mind?', it is clear that trying to address the question through thoughts, through thinking about it, is not the way. That's why when an answer is formulated in a conceptual manner we have to be a bit suspicious. If a member of the Mafia were to come to a police station and say, *"Officer, the murder that happened last night, that was committed by the other Mafia family."* then the police would rightly be suspicious. In the same way, the Buddha has said very clearly that immersion in conceptual elaboration is deceitful. That is why it is not very wise to rely on our thoughts to give us a true answer.

We investigate by allowing the unfolding of experience again and again. When you're sitting in meditation, many different kind of experience arise. Maybe happy, sad, busy, confused, all kinds are arising. You are here; this is what is occurring in and as the content of the mind. What kind of container could allow such a perfect fitting with whatever arose? In your kitchen at home you will have many containers – different jars and cups and boxes to store rice and spices and so on – each with a particular size and shape. When you put the product into the container, it takes its shape from the shape of the container. Think about the variety of experiences that you have, the various moods you have, what is their container? It seems to be a perfect fit!

There is an ancient Greek story about Procrustes, a man who lived in the middle of a long valley. From time-to-time travellers would walk along the valley. In the evenings Procrustes would sit outside and if he saw a lone traveller he would welcomed him into his house. *"It's a long way to the next village"* he'd tell them, *"so you are welcome to sleep here."* He would cook them a nice meal and then show them their bed. It was a big stone bed with a straw mattress. *"However, the rule of this house is that you have to fit the bed precisely"*, he would then add. If the person was too short he would rack them, stretch them out so that they fitted the bed precisely. If they were too tall he would cut their feet off until they were just the right length. It is an illustration of what can happen when the map is more important than the land, when you try to squeeze the world to fit your mental shape.

When you got up this morning you had no idea of all the things that would happen today. You will have experienced all kinds of feelings throughout the day. Ideas move, memories move, sensations move. When you get caught up in an idea, you, as your ego-self, move. Somebody gives you some troubling information and you respond, *"Oh no, that can't be possible."* You get moved about and tired from all that agitation. By the end of the day you go to bed exhausted, telling people to keep quiet, to go away, to leave you alone since all you want to do is just go to bed and sleep.

We get moved but mind doesn't move. This is the thing. The mind, without moving, fits everything. The mind is beyond thoughts, inexpressible. It's not a thing, it's not like anything else. You can talk about it forever but that won't really help, since it will just give you more and more mental furniture. The main thing is to get a sense about the definition. There are now many buddhist books including the book, *SIMPLY BEING* that I wrote some years ago, which set out the view and understanding very clearly as far as words can go. Each of us has to take these words, take these ideas, and massage them into ourselves.

So there is me; there is the idea or instruction; and there is the practice. A triangle. Me, what I have to do, and what I am doing in the practice. This, however, has introduced artificiality since I now have something towards which I should be going: I now have to remember at a certain point in the meditation that there are these five questions that I should take up and examine. But that's not how we do it; it's not like that. We take these questions and hold them, wherever we are, whatever we are doing, and just let them be part of our experience.

By massaging these questions into the texture of our being, they arise easily and we just stay with them. It is as if the question is asking the question, not me. Then it becomes much easier because our mind is always here. Mind is the awareness, the revealer of all experience. The more we allow these questions to be normal, the more they can be. Sitting on the bus, waiting in a café, with a friend, at work, when life is easy, when life is hard. If experience is arising the mind is there. So how is the mind? Since we were born, we have had many experiences. This is undeniable. During many of these experiences we have felt 'this is me' and yet they have gone. What has always been present is the experiencing, the awareness. We spend so much time trying to get a handle on a thought as if the thought were telling the truth. We disregard the fact that thought always leaves. Awareness – which is always there every moment of every day – we don't explore at all. This is quite remarkable.

So what we are doing now in the practice is relaxing into the spaciousness of the mind and allowing it to show itself. Since space can only really reveal itself to space, one instruction or suggestion in the traditional texts is that we should meditate 'sky to sky'. That is to say, when we are opening to ourselves, we are like the sky and what we open to is also like the sky – two spaces within which shapes and forms and colours and memories are moving. Actually these are not two spaces, they're really only one space. The more we practise, the more obvious this is. Within this, all movements are without any substance.

It's like when a beam of sunlight comes into our room on a sunny day and we see lots of dust moving around in that beam of light. In the same way, when we relax and open we become aware of all kinds of stuff moving around in the mind. None of it is very important since the main thing is the space. When we're clear that the mind is space, then everything which appears is the manifestation of the space, devoid of substance and yet there. Emptiness and clarity inseparable.

When the meditation finishes and we start to engage with the world, we find ourself moment by moment responding in co-emergence with the ever-shifting patterns of our environment. It's not as if we were in a meditation and then came out of the meditation into another world. It is more like the meditation being the sea on a calm day, deep and with a surface that shimmers in the sunlight. When the wind blows a little bit the surface of the sea starts to move. What is moving? The water of the sea. Waves are not separate from the ocean. Waves are how the ocean shows its motility, its capacity for movement. Waves are arising as the expression of the movability of the mind.

We do our practice, we stand up, and then something happens. We find ourself feeling a certain way, perhaps a bit anxious, or proud, or shy or whatever. This is a manifesting wave of our experience. It is a shaping of the un-shapeable. We can't catch a wave; it does have a shape but it's an ungraspable shape. In the same way, whether we feel happy or sad, bright and intelligent or dull and stupid, all these are also moments of manifestation, manifestations of the energy embedded in the clarity, which is itself embedded in the spaciousness.

So that is the basic view of dzogchen. The meditation practice is not very complicated however there are many difficulties to be overcome because of our habit formations. Over time many techniques have been developed, which operate as antidotes, and it's possible to teach dzogchen in that way, using these many techniques.

My own main teacher, C.R Lama, would always say to stay with the most simple point, one which is highlighted by the great masters. That point is:

—the mind is always here

—be present with the openness of the mind and with its flow,

—don't follow after past thoughts,

—don't wait expectantly for future thoughts,

—don't try to hang on to what you like and push away what you don't like,

—rest in open spaciousness.

Do this and the dynamic nature of experience will show the self-liberating nature of the mind. Like a snake untying itself the mind will move free. When you become free your mind is like an empty house – if the thief of habitual formation breaks in, it finds nothing to attach itself to.

So this is the practice.

USING GURU YOGA TO ENTER THE PRACTICE

We will continue doing the same practice, but now we will begin by using Guru Yoga. As I said earlier, 'guru' means the teacher, but it also refers to the buddha mind as well as to our own mind.

When we are established in a sense of duality, we feel that we are in here and other people, the world, is out there. So, I pray to the guru. But as discussed earlier, wherever I am, the world is. I come with the world. The world is as much me as my embodied self. In fact, I see the world more clearly than I see my body. From the point of view of dzogchen, the mind sometimes looks primarily like object and sometimes looks primarily like subject. What we are trying to do in the meditation is dissolve the restricted idea that I sit inside my skin bag, that I am separate from the world around me.

We do this as follows. In the space in front of us we imagine a white letter A about two arms' length away. The letter A could be the Roman capital letter or the Tibetan letter ཨ. In the Sanskrit and Tibetan alphabets all consonants take the vowel A. A is said to be the primordial sound with all other sounds arising as a variation on it. A is seen as the basis of all sounds and therefore of all words, and therefore of all conceptual constructions, and therefore of all the varieties of samsara. A is also the essence of the Prajnaparamita teachings. There is a very extensive version of the Prajnaparamita in a hundred thousand verses; there are many shorter versions such as the Heart Sutra; there is a four lines verse in praise of Prajnaparamita; there is the essential mantra of the Heart Sutra; finally all are reduced to just the letter A. AAA, is a sound which is empty, which doesn't signify very much, is not defined very much, and so in that sense it is open and empty. Yet, because it is the basis of all the other sounds, it expresses a rich potential.

When we visualise this letter A, this is the presence of the awareness of all the buddhas, the wisdom that understands the empty nature which is the ground of everything, and which manifests the wisdom of understanding emptiness, the empty nature of all phenomena.

We can imagine that this letter condenses all the awareness of all the buddhas and that it is surrounded by white, red, blue, yellow and green light. Traditionally these are described as representing the five poisons and the five wisdoms. The five poisons are stupidity or assumption, desire, aversion, jealousy and pride. The five wisdoms are their purification or transformation. Stupidity/assumption transforms to the wisdom of the dharmadhatu, that is to say, the natural openness of the mind. It includes all phenomena, all dharmas. The purification of desire is the wisdom of discernment, which sees each thing precisely as it is. The purification of anger is the mirror-like wisdom. The purification of jealousy is the wisdom which accomplishes everything. The purification of pride is the wisdom of equality, that all things are equal in their emptiness.

Dzogchen texts often say that there is one ground and two paths. The ground is the openness of the mind itself. One path is the path of being aware of this, being present in and as this. The other path, the path of ignoring the ground and fabricating illusory forms, generates samsara. Dzogchen texts are saying that confusion and awakening have the same ground, that they are not two separate families coming from two different places. When we are present in this state of A, all the potential of samsara and nirvana is revealed. We rest in an open way and together we will make the sound of A three times. As we make this sound we are releasing all the tensions of our body, our voice and our mind. We simply open to A, the symbol of the mind of the buddha. After we've made the sound, after a few seconds, this A in front of us dissolves into light and into space, and we just sit in openness as we were doing before.

Then, when you can, when it seems right, gently bring up these five questions we've been looking at.

So that brings us to the end of our study together today. However, we can take the practice of it into the evening, into whatever we're doing. Continue without judging, simply observing and allowing our own existence to show itself, without making it artificial.

THE FIRST STATEMENT OF GARAB DORJE

The first statement of Garab Dorje is to open ourself to the truth of our own being. So when we sit in the practice, we become increasingly aware of the movement of the mind. Our mind is like the sky and our experiences are like different kinds of clouds moving through it. Sometimes the clouds seem to pervade the whole sky, and when that happens we may even forget that the sky is there, and that it is the generous hospitality of the sky that allows the clouds to be there. When that happens we sit and just allow the movement of experience until we are clear that the mind itself doesn't move but that everything else is moving.

When we look around this room, we may think that since we were here yesterday it is still the same room. But is it? We have to get really clear about this. Because nothing looks radically different in the room we take it that it is the same but the sky is slightly different, the amount of light coming in through the windows is slightly different. What we see is the illumination, which is different. What we think, is that it's the same room. Conceptually the room is the same. Phenomenologically it is different.

This is the radical point of difference. If you rely on the thought, the thought standardises phenomena and so the signifier seems to stand in a very accurate relation to the signified. We had idea of the room: this is a concept, a verbal sign. The concept 'this room' determines what we see. So 'this room' becomes a grammatical expression; 'this room' becomes like the seal or the guarantee of this room. We can identify what's going on and because we can 'know' that it is the same room, the actual differences seem irrelevant.

So this is what we spoke about yesterday, privileging the map over the territory. Because we believe in the map and because the statements of the map can be repeated, they give a sense of continuity of the sameness of the room. It seems to indicate that there is permanence to the room, that the room has a substantial reality, that there is an essence to it: it is this particular room.

However, the room arises due to causes and conditions. Some of us were here yesterday evening enjoying delicious food and wine. We were in the same room but it was a different room. The mood was different. The room showed itself in a different way. We had electric light not daylight. We were sitting on chairs, not on the floor and so the room was revealed to us from a different position. We are here together now and it's reasonable to say that we are here together in the same room, in the same room *as concept.* Each person here is sitting in a unique place and so from each unique vantage point we all have our own room. The room as revealed to me: this is what I actually get. Plus I also have my idea of the room. The actuality of our own embodied experience can be ignored and the concept of the room privileged. If I go the theatre and get a ticket that places me behind a pillar, then although I am engaged in the performance I don't see quite as much as a person a few seats along. Yes, I was at the theatre; yes, it was a wonderful play but we saw different things. The people at the front pay more money to sit there rather than sit at the back. This is for a reason. They have a different experience. Somehow in the theatre we can understand this but in ordinary life we don't; we ignore it.

Because the conceptual world creates the illusion of permanence it makes the finite seem infinite. We're here in this room, and in fact some of us were in this room two years ago, so we may imagine that it is the same place now two years later. For someone who has been here regularly throughout these two years they will have a whole sequence of memories which I have no sense of. Their version of the room will be different from mine. To get clear about this will be very helpful: the room (for example) as experience is uniquely personal,

The world revealed through linguistic signifiers appears shared in a way that is delusory. It creates a social conventional field in which, by the exchange of shared signifiers, we appear to be inhabiting something that has continuity. When we see that the finite is finite in space and time then it becomes clear that it is unreliable. It is therefore not a true refuge. It is something to be worked within its dynamic revealing, in its showing, but it's not infinite.

What is infinite? Infinite is the mind itself. When something is finite it has a shape, it has delimitation. It has a shape in time – a beginning and an end – and a shape in space – outside and inside, on the left and on the right, and so on. These formations are part of our communication in and with the environment. We are always communicating. Our nature is expressive, connective and communicative. The gift of ourselves, of our availability, needs to find a reception in the other person. Similarly we are hospitable to other people's gift of themselves towards us. When we experience this it helps us see that the duality of self and other, of inside and outside, is an illusion.

THE SECOND STATEMENT OF GARAB DORJE

The second statement of Garab Dorje is to not remain in doubt. Become clear that this is how it is. This is not a cognitive decision. Rather, by staying present, I see that my awareness is always open, whereas thoughts and feelings and sensations are changeable and have different qualities.

Sometimes I feel expansive, sometimes I feel contracted. Although I may feel quite small I am aware that I feel small because my feeling smallness is within my ever-open awareness. Any feeling of being contracted and inadequate is within the openness of our mind. We are open and we are small at the same time. The openness is infinite with no limit of time and space. Any contracted disturbed state of mind is finite and it passes. But while it's there, it's me. As Hamlet said, *"Ay, there's the rub!"* If I think something is awful and that I need to change it, then by thinking this way I split myself. I have introduced an 'I' who is sitting in judgement on the arising experience. 'I' now have to control and alter 'my' experience. However, this internal splitting will always be vulnerable to the arising of new unwanted experiences and so any path which attempts to manage the contents of the mind is a path without end. It won't lead to peace because the contents of my mind are not mine. If somebody tells us something upsetting, we become upset. This upset comes to us. We didn't choose it but now we are stuck with it. *"You've upset me. Why did you do that?"* On it goes, on and on.

In dzogchen practice, no matter how our mind is we remain open and relaxed without judging, without engaging, without trying to change things, without hanging on to the bits we like, and trying to get rid of the bits we don't like. This is the essential difference between dzogchen and other schools in Tibetan buddhism. By resting and relaxing into the infinity of awareness itself, the finite forms which arise and pass are free to come and go as they do.

I can remember when I was small, being with my mum in a town centre and needing to have a pee. My mum took me to the edge of the pavement saying, *"Just go between the parked cars and have a pee there."* But no, everyone will see! That's how I felt at the time but when you have to go, you have to go. In moments like that you feel such shame or embarrassment that it's as if they are tattooed across your heart. You feel that everyone knows what you have done and this finite moment crystalises, becomes infinite, becomes eternal and paralysing. This becomes a kind of fault line in your energetic system which can collapse under pressure. Such splitting and fragmentation continues in adult life. In order to protect ourselves we mark out a territory where we feel safe, yet hanging on to the knowledge that there are certain things that are just impossible for us. *"I wouldn't be me if I did that." "If that happens to me I don't know what I would do."* We restrict ourselves.

From the point of view of dzogchen this is incredibly sad since these situations which seem so terrible and so painful are actually transient. I still have many scars on my knees from my childhood... falling out of trees, falling off my bicycle and so on. Most of us have some marks some place where something happened. Our ego, like the body, gets scars. Sometimes the scar doesn't heal very well and you get sensitive raw nerve-endings. Sometimes the nerve-endings get knocked off and the nerve is dull and dead. It is the same for our ego. We can be hyper-sensitive about some things and completely insensitive about other things. Small children get upset about situations and have not yet developed the capacity to soothe themselves. The mother has to soothe the child and makes the world feel safe for them. Gradually children learn to be better at self-soothing.

A traditional Tibetan example is that of the mother and son. The mother is our original nature, this infinite awareness there from the very beginning, and the child is the way in which our energetic expression seems to have broken free and have a life of its own. When the mother and child meet, the mother contains the child and the child relaxes. Left alone, however, the child cannot soothe themself. The child is the agitation of our ego state, full of hopes and fears. By relaxing and opening into what is always present, into our awareness, we are able to allow all the forms of agitation to self-soothe, or in the language of dzogchen, to self-liberate. Experiences then go by without any trace. Our ego tends to vibrate with the resonance of many past experiences. Awareness however has no such resonance, which is why it's described as being naked and fresh. It is naked because it's not covered over by the accumulation of past experiences or assumptions about future experiences. And it's fresh because it's always open and available to the next moment. Something is important and then it's gone. The fact that it's gone doesn't make it not important.

Very often when people are in a relationship and one goes away, the other phones and asks, *"Do you miss me?"* If the first person responds, *"Why should I miss you? I'm here, you are there. Your life is there, my life is here, good luck!"* then this is not likely to induce a romantic feeling. *"Of course I miss you baby. I think of you all the time..."* this is what we want. The ego is wanting the reassurance that it is important and that other people remember us and think of us with love and affection and so on. Energetically we are trying to weave these strands of connectivity that provide a kind of reassurance: *"Only you can save me."* But all human beings are going to die, our moods are unpredictable, and we don't always feel affectionate.

This is why dharma says that our own actual being, which is always here, is the best refuge – not someone else, even if they do seem very special. Special is nice for a while, and in the Tibetan tradition the guru is referred to as 'Rinpoche', which means costly, rare, and precious. If you lose something rare and precious then it is very difficult to replace it. You can't just go into a Lidl supermarket, third shelf at the back and find another one. You might be better off putting your faith in apples since if you find a worm in your apple you can get another apple very easily. *"Ah, but the special is rare and so it is important."* Maybe not. What is really precious is our own nature which is there all the time, always available. As in the traditional Tibetan example of the farmer who goes out on the hill looking for his lost cow, while it is actually at home in the barn all time, we go looking here, there and everywhere in samsara for something to fill us, something to make us feel better. But we don't look at our own mind.

So this is the second point of Garab Dorje: keep looking and looking until you taste directly and then be clear that that is enough.

THE THIRD STATEMENT OF GARAB DORJE

This takes us to the third point or statement of Garab Dorje, which is to continue in this way. It means to stay with the integration of all experiences in the openness of awareness. This doesn't mean 'continue to be a buddhist'. The practice is not about becoming a buddhist or continuing to be a buddhist. 'Buddhist' is a temporary structure to help you awaken to your own nature or your own being. To be a buddhist and have a membership card is not different from being a butcher in that both function as an identity. Of course you might say being a butcher and killing animals is not a good thing to do but 'being a butcher' gives somebody a sense of who they are and a function in the world. Being 'a buddhist' can also function like that. Both identities are constructs.

All constructs, all compounded things, are impermanent. If you take refuge in the finite you will always be cheated because the finite is unreliable. If, however, you take refuge in the infinite, it will be always reliable. In the tradition they use the word *'vajra'*. *Vajra,* or *dorje* in Tibetan, means indestructible, something that can never be broken. This is the fundamental basis of contentment or satisfaction, referred to as *simpa* (Tib. *Sim-Pa*) in Tibetan. It means 'this is enough'. With this, I don't need anything more.

We have all been alive for some time now and have had many experiences in our lives, both good and bad, and we know that each has its own flavour and that they all pass. If every taste was sweet like sugar it would be a bland world. So although we might say we don't like bitter and sour flavours, they are important in cooking since they provide a counterpoint that highlights certain other flavours. Likewise, we can see that feelings such as sadness, hopelessness, anger, jealousy and bitterness are flavours. It does not mean that I am a bad person for feeling such things. I have a friend who drinks lemon juice first thing every morning. This would not be my choice, but it's a taste, that's all. Just a taste.

Jealousy is a taste, hatred is a taste. If you taste the taste, you know what it is. Then you know, *"Oh, I'm jealous. This is what jealousy is like. This is what it does to my body, what it does to my breathing, what it does to the patterning of my thoughts. It's like this; it's just a pattern of experience, arising due to circumstances, and passing due to circumstances."* But if I split myself and say, *"I am jealous. I don't want to be jealous and being jealous is wrong."* then I'm back with ego control. I may not be able to stop being jealous but I don't want anyone to know that I'm jealous so I put on a forced smile and pretend I'm not. Acting like that we don't allow experience to be experience. Experience is a cloud; it's not a solid truth, not an x-ray of our soul; it's just something that is passing.

This is the great liberation of dzogchen – that we are open to everything because we know that no experience defines our infinite nature, our infinite being, and that there is no duality between the openness of the mind and what arises in the mind. Paradoxically, I can now be jealous! I can be fully jealous and upset since 'jealous' is not defining who I am. I don't have to pretend in any way or modulate my expression; I can just be what I am because I am only like this for the moment and after the moment something else will be there. And after that, something else. Life will go on... Then I will die and all the things that were so important in this life will be gone. What is continuous is the infinite because it doesn't get ended.

AWARENESS AND CONSCIOUSNESS

So, awareness is the absolute central focus. Again and again we have to observe how we cheat ourselves, how we confuse subjectivity with awareness. For example, I am talking just now. This is an energetic patterning; I'm aware that I am talking and I have two aspects to the awareness. I have the grasping aspect of awareness and the open aspect of awareness. The grasping aspect is not really awareness at all. It is a pattern of energy which expresses itself as if it were the ground-clarity of being. Generally, we translate this as 'consciousness'. In Tibetan it is called *nampar shepa* (Tib. *rNam-Par Shes-Pa*). *Nampar* means 'fully' or 'completely' or 'totally' and it also refers to a kind of shaping, to a kind of graspability. So, I know that I am talking; I am conscious of talking; I hold on to the mental idea that I am the one who is talking. This appropriation, this taking hold of the experience, creates the illusory sense that it is a self-existing thing – something in itself – which I can then evaluate. I may say that I'm talking too much, or that what I say is not very clear, or that what I say is fine. Consciousness is the basis for all these judgements and whatever modifications and improvements I make. My subjectivity feels both free – I am what I am – and a bit self-conscious, a bit anxious. Am I doing okay? What do you think of how I am?

Consciousness is the aspect of knowing which takes itself to be positioning. It seems to be located somewhere. We often see it as located inside our body. Somebody may say something to us and we reply, *"Oh, I'll have to think about that."* and we close down a little bit to go into our thinking capacity. This may occur in a meditation when we look for the mind and ask ourselves, *"Where is the mind?"* We find some sort of location. Some sensations arise within us and we say, *"Oh yes, my mind is in my head."* This is a great advantage for us. It keeps us inside the paradigm that we are used to, and in that paradigm we make a definite statement: *"My mind is in my head. I'm not stupid. I know where I am."* The proposition, the statement, seems to guarantee the truth of something but even that thought is already vanishing. Where is its truth? Where is its power? It comes and it goes. It can't be infinite or eternal because it's evanescent. That is to say, consciousness is engaged with the shaping of mental moments.

We are always conscious of some-thing. Consciousness takes an object. It involves a self-recollection which is isolating and supports a reflexive self-commentary. This is very important because it is how we talk ourselves into existence. Our ego is generated by, and exists in, the continuous production of self-narrative.

As soon as a new mother shows the baby to her friends they start covering it in words. *"Oh, isn't he sweet? Doesn't he look just like his dad? He's got your dimples."* Words and words. The baby comes a person through the gradual absorption of these words. The words move around inside this child's body and gradually start coming out of its mouth. Now this is a proper person. Now the child can take, *"Don't do that"* or *"You are a good boy."* and so on. It's like making a little cake. We comment on the behaviour of the child, *"You're doing well. What a wonderful drawing you've done. Be careful. Look where you're going."* The child internalises these linguistic messages and starts becoming self-regulating.

This is the function of consciousness. Consciousness helps us to get a handle on the world by meaning and shaping, and a handle on ourselves by meaning and shaping. This goes on throughout our lives. It is not the same as awareness. One term for awareness in Tibetan is *yeshe* (Tib. *Ye-Shes*). Ye means 'from the very beginning', which actually means 'without ever having had any beginning', that is to say, infinite. *Shepa* means 'to know'. It doesn't mean knowing things; it's more the clarity, or the revelatory quality, of being. 'Being' in this context does not mean being this or that; 'being' here doesn't refer to a defining essence of any kind. 'Being' means 'the given-ness', 'the just here-ness' of awareness itself. It means it's not some-thing. It's very difficult to describe in language because all our language is about grasping and shaping and making.

The mind, like the sky, is just here. It's not created by mental activity. It's not improved by good deeds. It's not destroyed by bad deeds. What is improved or harmed is the patterning of energy. Wisdom is awakening to this unborn quality of presence. Compassion is the movement of the energy, which arises ceaselessly in the field of awareness since when you awaken to your own ground, you don't need to be self-correcting. You can relax and trust you are okay. The energy, therefore, is for the other. Without driving it by making a vow or a conscious intention, we awaken to the very simple fact that we are participants in the field of the environment. The environment is not something other than me, which I enter or don't enter. Tantra expresses this by saying that we are always already in the mandala. Our activity is part of the world, for the world.

When we imagine that we are just ourself, then the orientation is very different because we then think of advantage and disadvantage, what is good for me, what is bad for me. The central point of reference is 'me'. 'Me' is always changing and it's changing in relation to 'you'. There is no essence of me inside me. How you are affects how I am. We have this experience sometimes of being centred in the other person because there is no real 'me' centre. It moves around. It's an ever-shifting movement of the field of energy.

The paradox in the view of dzogchen is that the less hard you try, the more wisdom and compassion are available. Tantra or general mahayana buddhism have a different view, a different meditation and different behaviour. This dzogchen way of practice will suit some people more than others because of their habits and interests. It's not a case of better or worse, right or wrong. However, if you can see the nature of awareness and *be* that nature of awareness, then many problems cease.

PROBLEMS THAT MAY ARISE IN MEDITATION

Three chapters in *SIMPLY BEING* deal with meditation problems. Two were written by Patrul Rinpoche and one by Nuden Dorje, of whom CR Lama was an incarnation. It can useful to read these traditional presentations and see how they emphasise the same thing again and again. They give many different examples of meditation problems people can have and to all of them a single answer is given. Typically they say, "*Many so-called 'great meditators' get upset and cry because they have practised meditation for many years without getting any result. They feel depressed and hopeless. In your practice don't try to change the depression and hopelessness. Stay present with the depression and hopelessness and observe the one who is experiencing.*"

This observer is not a 'me' looking at some-thing: it is to observe it from inside, to be the one who is experiencing it. In Tibetan they use the term *tog tu* (Tib. *Thog-Tu*) which means 'stay on the one'. Awareness is here. Awareness is everywhere and yet nowhere. We don't have to go somewhere else to get to it. It's not like how I have to go to the airport later today and travel from the town to the airport. We all know about this, going from here to there. Awareness is not like that; you don't reach it, get to it, find it. And yet it's everywhere.

That's why if you go looking to find it as 'some-thing', you get lost. You will never find it as something since it's not a thing or a place, you can't say that here is awareness and there is not awareness. Everywhere is awareness. Whatever is happening, be there, be right with whatever is happening.

For example, now we are all in Geneva. Is this the real Geneva? If we go to the town hall of Geneva, and sit on the front steps, will we be more in Geneva? Which place in Geneva is the most *"genevoise"*? Everywhere is Geneva, so you can't actually find Geneva because everything is Geneva when you're in Geneva. In the same way, everything is the mind. There isn't a better bit of mind somewhere else and a less good bit somewhere else. Here, in this room, this is how Geneva is showing itself. When we go out into the street, that is another aspect of Geneva. As we travel around we have thousands and thousands of tastes of Geneva. We might ask, *"But what is the true taste of Geneva?"* That is an illusion; every taste of Geneva is Geneva. The tourist department of Geneva may be highlighting some aspects of Geneva and not others. Probably they won't be promoting the crime statistics for Geneva because they are painting their particular picture of Geneva as a nice place to visit. The police however are very happy to promote the crime statistics because the police always want more money so they can do more things. All of this is Geneva.

When you take a particular view, when you have an agenda, then you have highlighted something as the foreground and other things go into the background. This is another way to understand the difference between the ego and awareness. The ego takes a particular view and wants to maintain its story about what is going on. Awareness says that it's all Geneva.

Whatever is arising in the mind, whether your ego says is good or bad, or it wants more of or less of, just be open to what is there. Have confidence in the vajra nature of the mind – whatever happens will not harm me if I am awareness. However if I am my ego formation then there are many things which can upset me. This is the fulcrum, the balancing point which we need to find and in finding it, relaxing back into the openness. The ego is a formation. It tells you that it is saying the truth but it is unreliable. What it says may be true on Monday yet not be true on Tuesday.

So, when sitting in meditation, we relax, and we open. Perhaps our mind feels dull. Perhaps we feel not quite present. No matter. The instruction is just stay open into however you are feeling; sitting placidly like a cow in a field. The clarity of the mind is illuminating the dullness of the content of the mind. This is the central point – even when our mind feels dull and stupid, or agitated and excited, or if we are itemising all the faults of another person, or if we're full of self-pity – whatever small-minded patternings arise in our mind, we're only aware of them because of our awareness. Awareness is clear; it is the clarity of the mind that shows this horrible petty aspect of ourself.

So, don't fall into merging with the transient content of the mind. Don't stand apart from it in judgement either. Don't try changing the mind's content. Be present as the clarity that illuminates what's there.

This is easy to say but difficult to do. Tibetans say that it's like pulling a hair out of butter. In Tibet people made their own butter. They would have a wooden churn and would move the thick milk around until gradually butter separated out. Traditionally this was the work of women and women had long hair. Sometimes a hair would get into the churn and was moved about as the butter formed. When the butter was taken out and made into butter-pats, you could see how the hair swirled through the butter. In pulling it out care had to be taken in case it snapped inside the butter. Pull hard but not too hard. Likewise in meditation, we are trying to find that balance point where we are present with what is arising, and are not falling into it, nor holding back too far away from it. A 'being with' which is not a 'being apart'.

When a feeling is swirling inside my mind, it feels as if it is really me. However, if we take up antipathy and negative feeling towards it and want to get rid of these thoughts and feelings then many problems can arise in the meditation.

We may think that since our mind is full of obscurations, we shouldn't do any meditation and we need to do purification first or apply an antidote. We may decide to offer lots of butter lamps or go on a long pilgrimage or do lots and lots of Vajrasattva mantras. From the point of view of dzogchen, adopting these antidotes is unhelpful. Why? Because they confirm the true force and reality of the obscuration. *I* have decided that this is a real problem and that *I* have to do something about it. Subject-verb-object, we are back with a dualistic structure. Of course, in having something to do the ego now feels better because it feels it is no longer at the mercy of the horrible contents of mind! Applying antidotes is a reasonable practice; it's not wrong or bad but it is a practice performed from the point of view of the ego.

That is why it is important to understand that the view of dzogchen is different. Dzogchen operates from the view the view that whatever is arising cannot contaminate the mirror. The mind, as the infinite, offers hospitality to everything yet without being touched by anything. This is the meaning of non-duality. It's not that there are two different things. It's not that there is just one thing, but that there is the inseparability of these two, which are not one.

What is arising in the mind and the mind itself are inseparable but there are not the same. What is inside the mind, the content of the mind is moving and changing. However, the mind itself is not moving or changing. Yet the mind and the content of the mind are inseparable. This is the key point.

If we stay with the mind itself, the impermanent contents of the mind go free by themselves. The ego's effort is not required. C.R Lama's text[2] says on several occasions that human knowledge is not necessary, is not required. It means that we don't need to develop highly intelligent thoughts nor do we need to have a great knowledge of the dharma. What we *do* need is to trust our own awareness which is pure from the very beginning, as in the first instruction of Garab Dorje. Open up and be present with who you have been from the very beginning. Whatever different kinds of experiences arise and pass, stay present with the clarity that although the content moves, the mind doesn't move. The third statement of Garab Dorje is that we should continue in that way since nothing is lacking and everything is fine, is perfect just as it is. This is the meaning of dzogpachenpo.

Perhaps we have done a lot of *tonglen* practice, giving out good positive feelings to others and inviting their troubles into us. We may practice equanimity, making no differentiation between friends and enemies. But we are still surprised when we have a lot of shitty contents in our mind? English has the term 'nimby' which means 'not in my back yard'. Let's say a new care centre or hostel is being planned for alcoholic people or people with mental health

---

[2] "The Meditation and Recitation on Vajrasattva" in *SIMPLY BEING*, pp. 49-60. (ARP, 2010. ISBN 9789075710l5)

problems. Usually the locals object, saying that although it is a really good service to have it shouldn't be here, not near my house, not in my back yard. However if everything which arises is Padmasambhava, if everything is the radiance of the mind, how can I then say that I only want bright shiny bits in my mind? How can I say that everything has the same nature yet I still want to have a menu? I want to choose the bits that make me feel good? Here we can see how the ego, or our personal sense of subjectivity, contaminates our availability to the openness of awareness.

We probably all have the fantasy that people should be exceptionally nice, kind and generous if they have been doing meditation for a long time. Whereas actually the key thing is whether whatever is arising is integrated in awareness – is like illusion, like a mirage, a rainbow, something which is there but there is no essence.

Stories about the eighty-four mahasiddhas and other great Indian yogis of the past often describe strange and unusual things they did. They sound strange now and they seemed strange then too. They often lived on the edge of society doing activities which were regarded as dirty or very low status. Again and again we come back to recognising that our strong judgement, our sense that we know the truth about what is right, is in fact only an opinion, a point of view generated by the point from which we view it. If we are looking from the point of view of the ego, at what I like, and at what I don't like, then we will have a very strong view of what is good and what is bad. When we are sitting in meditation, however, we open to however our mind is. Whenever we feel disappointed, frustrated, or blocked, we should take this as a sign not that something should be done, nor a sign that we should be doing something else, but simply note that we are looking from the point of view of the ego and that the ego is just doing its ego job, which is to say, offering a biased reading.

What these great masters point out is, "Don't be misled into taking the current pattern of the content of the mind as being a revelation of a fundamental truth about yourself. Don't be defined by what is arising." This links back to what I began with: how our 'identity' is a process of generating composite formations. This process is in the house of compassion, where our identity is a social function. At work, for example, whatever role we have allows us to do some things and not others, to go into some rooms but not others, to talk in certain ways, with some people but not with others. Identity and role are part of the choreography of social existence, of interaction; they are not a definition of who we are. The more we see that, the more we see, *"Oh this is all the theatre of the mind. Due to causes and circumstances we can speak in a particular way and then due to other causes and circumstances we can't."* It's just like that; identity is not intrinsic.

The meditation is very simple: we relax and open and stay present with whatever is occurring. This is exactly the meditation that Buddha Shakyamuni was doing when he was sitting under the bodhi tree. Many things were moving around him, different maras, different tempting or terrifying demons, and he is not moving, not reacting.

'Not reacting' is not like trying to be brave when you are sitting in your dentist's chair. It's not an act of will or courage. It's just that things don't get to you. It's like in paintings of the Buddha at the moment of enlightenment when maras are painted drawing back their bow and arrow. As the arrow shoots towards the Buddha it turns into a flower and falls to the ground. The arrow is not dangerous because it doesn't arrive. The reflection in the mirror doesn't touch the mirror. This is the great mystery of existence – that we both are and are not the content of our mind. Ignorance and attachment over-fixate on the content of the mind and we take it to be ourselves. With the dissolving of ignorance we recognise the ground basis, awareness, rigpa, within which the content of the mind is moving.

So again and again we simply return to this practice. Whatever is occurring, we just enter into the practice and stay with it. Without hopes or fears. Without selective attention. Without any notion of going somewhere. We are just present in this moment as it is. Undefended and hospitable. This is the heart of Samantabhadra, the great founding buddha of the lineage.

Teachings given at a retreat in Geneva, 19-20 March 2016. Edited by Barbara Terris and revised by James Low in September 2022.

Appendix

1. Getting to know how we are. *Teachings given in Frankfurt, 11 March 1995.*

2. Love and impermanence. *Teaching given in Warsaw, 14-15 December 2019.*

3. Open to life: the heart of awareness. *Teachings given at Brighthelm Centre, Brighton, UK, 2nd December 2012.*

4. Wisdom and compassion. *Teachings given in Macclesfield, UK, 22-24 February 2013.*

5. The natural freedom of the mind. *Teachings given at a retreat in Geneva, 19-20 March 2016.*

Other books by James Low

1. Buddha Shows the Way: a collection of public talks and teachings

(Published by Simply Being, UK, 2022. ISBN:979-8825841762)

This book contains a selection of edited public talks given by James Low. They cover a wide range of topics yet share a common theme: how to apply Buddhist teachings in our complex engagement with the modern world. We are all faced with ever increasing tasks of life maintenance as we struggle to cope with the profound impact of climate change, conflict, economic chaos, environmental and political instabilities. Moreover our own inner life is prey to habitual tendencies, impulses and blind spots so that our sense of the world is often more muddled than we imagine it to be.

The Buddhist view encourages us to see the ungraspable illusory nature of every situation in order that we might avoid being buffeted by samsara's waves of hopes and fears. With this clarity our own potential can be turned towards the benefit of the many rather than towards individual selfish pursuits.

The Buddha shows the way contains eighteen short chapters which can be read in any order so it is a book that can be dipped into according to your mood and time available.

2. Proud Little Cloud: letting in the light

(Published by Simply Being, UK, 2022. ISBN: 978-0956923998)

This illustrated book invites children to see how by collaborating together the sea and the sun and the clouds make our bright and variegated world. Each needs the other and so the key theme is that none of us is alone and we all get along better with friendly and appreciative participation.

The hope is that adults read the book aloud and talk about the pictures and these themes with the child.

3. Me First!: an account of the rise of the Wrathful Buddhas

(Published by Simply Being, UK, 2022. ISBN: 978-0956923981)

This is a traditional Tibetan epic tale of the havoc created by the arrogant entitlement that proclaims, "Me first!". When pride turns demonic, the Buddhas manifest many faces of kindness (both peaceful and wrathful) to tidy up the mess.

The text by James Low is based on the *Padma bKa'-Thang* by Padmasambhava and revealed by the terton, Urgyen gLing-Pa.

4. Sweet Simplicity: Mahamudra doha songs

(Published by Simply Being, UK, 2022. ISBN: 978-1739938154)

The beautiful brief Buddhist songs in this book point towards the inexpressible sweet simplicity of our own minds. This simplicity is usually obscured by the complexity of our reified experience and the conceptual elaboration we employ to try to work out who we are and what our life is for.

The doha songs encourage us to turn towards our own minds as the ungraspable simplicity of the ever-present ground.

The dohas here arose from the minds of enlightened yogis in Eastern India during the 8th -10th centuries. The collection is referred to as the *Asta Doha Kosa* in Sanskrit, *Do-Ha mDzod brGyad* in Tibetan. The collection is supplemented by the famous Mahamudra Aspiration prayer, also known as the Chagchen Monlam (Phyag-Chen sMon-Lam in Tibetan), written by the third Karmapa. The introduction and translation from Tibetan is by James Low.

It has been translated into German, Spanish, Italian and Hungarian.

5. Lotus Source: becoming Lotus Born

(Published by Simply Being, UK, 2021. ISBN: 978-1739938123)

This book focuses on Padmasambhava, the Lotus Born Guru, known in Tibet as Guru Rinpoche. He awakens us to our own lotus source.

All Buddhist practice is concerned with awakening from the illusions which bind us. The lotus represents both this awakening and also the intrinsic purity which is the source of both awakened Buddhas and deluded sentient beings. Forgetfulness of our lotus source has given rise to our experience of being someone real somewhere in a real world.

The wide range of prayers and practices translated and explained in this book provide guidance on how to live in a clear and ethical way. These practices ease the process of dying and guide us to Padmasambhava in his pure realm of Lotus Light, also known as Zangdopalri, the Copper Coloured Mountain.

Texts are translated by C. R. Lama and James Low.

6. The Mirror of Clear Meaning: A Commentary on the Dzogchen Treasure Text of Nuden Dorje

(Published by Simply Being, UK, 2021. ISBN: 978-1739938130)

This commentary by James Low on a traditional authentic Dzogchen text by Nuden Dorje gives a clear and pithy account of how our mind actually is, cutting a clear path through the forest of our beliefs and assumptions, it brings us face to face with the presence of the radiance of our mind illuminating both its open empty ground and the ceaseless appearance of its potential. This text can be a great support for meditators and shows us how to avoid many of the mistakes and misunderstandings that can arise.

The presentation is a personal distillation of Nuden Dorje's realisation in a manner both beautiful and deeply meaningful. Short verses show with pithy clarity how the various aspects of dzogchen fit together.

This book has a conversational style, being a lightly edited transcript of teachings given by James Low in Aracena, Spain over four days in 2019.

7. Longing for Limitless Light: Letting in the light of Buddha Amitabha's love

(Published by Simply Being, UK, 2021. ISBN: 978-1739938109)

This book offers a sequence of key texts in the Mahayana tradition of Tibetan Buddhism. These prayers and aspirations form part of the daily practice for many in the various Tibetan Buddhist traditions. They include prayers, aspirations, rituals and descriptions of a path to enlightenment.

The loving heart of Buddha Amitabha Limitless Light invites all beings into his pure realm of Happiness known as Dewachen or Sukhavati where, say the texts, awakening is easy. Relying on the warm presence of the Enlightened Ones, our lonely struggles can be left behind as we relax into the ever-inclusive ground of our being. These practices are an effective antidote to the sense of alienation and isolation which is so pervasive at this time.

The practice texts in this book offer tried and trusted ways to connect with the Buddhas whose welcome already awaits us. They include the prayers and full ritual for Taking Refuge and for Taking the Bodhisattva Vow and prayers and practices such as the Dechen Monlam for Taking Birth in Dewachen.

They provide a coherent support for developing faith and confidence in this Mahayana method that unites wisdom and compassion.

Each text was translated from Tibetan by C R Lama and James Low together many years ago in India. James Low has recently revised them and written an introduction.

8. This is it: revealing the great completion

(Published by Simply Being, UK, 2021. ISBN: 978-0956923974)

Each section of the book leads into the next, showing how, by peeling away our habitual assumptions and projections, we can directly encounter the intrinsic purity of our own mind. "This is it", Dzogchen, the great completion.

The first facet, *One Thing Leads to Another*, offers sutra texts on dependent origination. The second, *Increased Transparency*, includes the Heart Sutra and indicates that all phenomena, whether seemingly outer or inner, subject or object, are empty and devoid of inherent existence. This leads onto the third facet *Encountering the Other*, the story of how the Buddha Chakrasamvara manifested in order to deal with cruelty and malicious behaviour. The fourth Facet, *Getting Lost Invites Trouble*, offers two accounts of how pride and self-confidence can lead a person astray so that their provocations lead to a display the Buddhas' wrathful power, enforcing transformation and the abrupt end to the careers of heartless bullies.

Next, in the fifth facet, we see how transformation can be elective rather than imposed. *Cutting Free* begins with the story of Machig Labdron, her struggle to free herself from social constraints so that she could pursue a life in dharma. There is a short guru yoga practice and her Chöd practice, The Dakinis' Laughter. Finally in facet six, Just This is *The Cuckoo Cry*, the foundational text of the dzogchen mind series. In just three couplets it sets out the view, meditation and activity which are the inseparability of primordial purity and instant presence.

9. Chöd Khandro Gadgyang by Jigme Lingpa (Sound of Dakini Laughter: The Method for Cutting the Ego)

(Published by Wandel Verlag, Berlin, 2020. ISBN: 978-3942380294)

Chöd (Tibetan: *gcod*) (Lit: 'to sever'), is a spiritual practice found in the Bön tradition as well as in the Nyingma and Kagyu schools of Tibetan Buddhism. It originated in the 11th century and is still practised today. Also known as Cutting Through the Ego, the practices are based on the Prajñāpāramitā or Perfection of Wisdom sūtras, which expound the emptiness concept of Buddhist philosophy.

According to Mahāyāna Buddhists, emptiness is the ultimate wisdom of understanding that all things lack inherent existence. Chöd combines prajñāpāramitā philosophy with specific meditation methods and tantric ritual. The chöd practitioner seeks to tap the power of fear through activities such as rituals set in graveyards, and visualisation of offering their bodies in a tantric feast in order to put their understanding of emptiness to the ultimate test.

Chöd literally means "cutting through." It cuts through hindrances and obscurations sometimes called 'demons' or 'gods'. Examples of demons are ignorance, anger and, in particular, the dualism of perceiving the self as inherently meaningful, contrary to the Buddhist doctrine of anatta (non-self). This is done in a powerful meditative ritual which includes a stunning array of visualisations, song, music, and prayer; it engages every aspect of one's being and effects a powerful transformation of the interior landscape.

According to Jamgön Kongtrül, Chöd involves "accepting willingly what is undesirable, throwing oneself defiantly into unpleasant circumstances, realising that gods and demons are one's own mind, and ruthlessly severing self-centered arrogance through an understanding of the same-ness of self and others."

This has been translated into German.

10. Finding Freedom: texts from the Theravadin, Mahayana and Dzogchen Buddhist traditions

(Published by Wandel Verlag, Berlin, 2019. ISBN: 978-3942380270)

This book offers three approaches to awakening. The first section, *Fighting the Good Fight,* is concerned with how we can commit ourselves to the mindful activity of renouncing our familiar and often comforting limiting habits. Here the orientation is towards leaving our familiar ego-home and going on a journey to seek something which seems only to be available elsewhere.

The second section of the book, *Mistaken Identities,* points to how we can develop the honesty and courage to face our lives as they manifest, resolving our limiting habits and releasing ourselves from misleading identities. Here the orientation is towards recognising how our self-centredness has harmed others and made us blind to our interdependency.

The third section of *Finding Freedom, Sweet Simplicity,* is concerned with how we can relax and release ourselves from all limiting habits and thus effortlessly abide in our limitless intrinsic freedom. Here the orientation is towards awakening to the actuality of our mind as it is.

These three sections are quite different in tone, yet are harmonious and compatible in their underlying message of freedom. The Buddha offered all he was to help us, and if we offer ourselves fully to the path we will awaken with the same smile he offers us.

Finding Freedom contains *The Dhammapada* by Buddha Shakyamuni, the Sharp Weapon Wheel by Dharmarakshita, and four Dzogchen texts by Tulku Tsulo, Gonpo Wangyal, Ayu Khandro and the famous Kunzang Monlam – *The Evocation of Samantabhadra.* All texts were translated from Tibetan by James Low with the guidance of C R Lama and have been revised for this book. Each section is accompanied by a comprehensive introduction that touches the depth and heart of Buddha's teaching and points to the end of sorrow for all beings and the attainment of lasting freedom.

The book has been translated into German and Polish.

11. Sparks

(Published by Simply Being, UK, 2017. ISBN: 978-0956923943)

Sparks is a a wide ranging and accessible collection of short writings and poems arising from James Low's experience of practising and teaching Buddhism for many years. The book's focus is on the dzogchen approach of resting in intrinsic open awareness which is the radiance of our being. In simple and beautiful language it is an expression of the profound non-dual view of Dzogchen, which illuminates the enlivening Buddha potential present in all of us.

Sparks' pithy collection of prose and poems can be entered at any point, enjoyed and reflected upon since each 'spark' or 'snippet' is complete in itself. The topic is profound, yet it is condensed and expressed in simple language using examples and metaphors from everyday life and the living world around us.

The book has been translated into German, Italian, Polish, Spanish and Turkish.

12. Collected Works of C. R. Lama

(Published by Simply Being, UK, 2017. ISBN: 978-0956923929)

C. R. Lama, also known as Chhimed Rigdzin Rinpoche and as Zilnon Lingpa (1922-2002), was an important lama in the Khordong and Byangter lineages of the Nyingmapa School of Tibetan Buddhism. A scholar and also a yogi, he combined these two streams in his work as Reader in Indo-Tibetan Studies at Visva Bharati University at Santiniketan, West Bengal, India. He was a family man who was actively engaged in the world around him.

This book gathers together Rinpoche's writings on a wide range of topics including Nyingma Buddhist Philosophy, Tibetan cultural practices, his life in Khordong Monastery in Tibet and his advice for Dharma practitioners. Tulku Thondup writes, "James Low studied under the Ven. Chhimed Rigdzin Rinpoche for years with incredible dedication in austere conditions to accumulate vast knowledge of Rinpoche's teachings. This volume is filled with those precious teachings, most of which have remained unpublished until now."

The book has been translated into French, German, Polish, Spanish and Portuguese.

13. Radiant Aspiration: The Butterlamp Prayer Lamp of Aspiration

(Published by Simply Being, UK, 2011. ISBN: 978-0956923905)

This was written by C.R. Lama while in retreat in Tso Pema in India and arose as a gesture of love and longing for his teacher, Tulku Tsorlo whom he had to leave in Tibet. While alive he offered 100,000 butterlamps each year with his disciples and this practice continues.

The book offers a clear introduction to the Tibetan Buddhist understanding of the nature of existence, exploring how to free ourselves from all that limits us. It provides a translation of a beautiful prayer which employs the symbolism of the ritual offering of butterlamps, where light is seen as the basis of the non-duality of all experience. Radiant Aspiration contains the full ritual text so that readers can engage in its practice if they so choose. There is an extensive commentary focusing on the development of wisdom and compassion making the traditional text fully relevant to the modern reader.

It has been translated into German, Polish and Spanish.

14. Simply Being: Texts in the Dzogchen Tradition

(Published by Antony Rowe Publishing, UK, 2010. ISBN: 978-1907571015)

Simply Being presents twelve texts collected and translated by James Low, who copied them from the travelling libraries of yogis practising in the Himalayas.

These twelve traditional teachings show us how to recognise our own enlightened being as infinite awareness free of all effort and artifice. Freed from limiting false assumptions, human nature is revealed as a joyful process of open responsiveness.

James often teaches from the texts in this book.

This has been translated into French, German, Italian, Polish and Spanish.

15. The Seven Chapters of Prayer: as taught by Padma Sambhava of Urgyen, known in Tibetan as Le'u bDun Ma

(Published by Wandel Verlag, Berlin, 2010. ISBN: 978-3942380027)

In 1981 C R Lama wrote that *"These prayers describe how … Padma Sambhava promises to come every morning with the rising sun and to come every tenth day of the lunar month and make himself visible to the people. The prayers give protection from war, disease, famine, difficult journeys, dangerous animals, earthquakes, troublesome yeti, robbers and authoritarian police, at the time of death, during the bardo, and from the other results of one's karma."* We have also translated the Bar-Chhad Lam-Sel prayer which saves all beings in the six realms from the difficulties that afflict them. The volume concludes with the prayer listing all the important deeds of Padma Sambhava written by gTer-sTon Nyi-Ma 'Od-Zer.

These prayers are said and believed in by all the rNying-Ma lineages, only the lineage prayers at the beginning will be slightly different for the later period and here we have given the Byang-gTer, 'Khor-gDong and sMin-Grol Gling lineages. All the bKa'-brGyud-Pa also read these prayers and some of the Sa-sKya-Pa also read them, and when they do their Phur-Pa practice, they read the fourth chapter. The prayers are also read in some dGe-Lugs-Pa monasteries, and they are respected everywhere for their great blessing.

The book has been translated into French and German.

16. Being Guru Rinpoche: A Commentary on Nuden Dorje's Terma Vidyadhara Guru Sadhana

(Published by Trafford Publishing, 2006. ISBN: 978-1412084079)

Being Guru Rinpoche shows how to use a traditional Tibetan Buddhist meditation text as a method for transforming daily experience into an unbroken flow of wisdom and compassion.

It contains the tantric ritual practice called *The Vidyadhara Guru Sadhana* and James Low's brief commentary on it. The commentary is the edited transcript of two talks and in no way claims to be a complete account of the text. Rather, it is offered as a way for western people to approach the engagement with tantric practice. The text itself is from the nyingmapa tradition of Tibetan buddhism and is a treasure text of Nuden Dorje. James first translated it with C R Lama (Chhimed Rigdzin Rinpoche) over twenty-five years ago and it has become the most frequently practised larger text amongst his students.

This ritual text is a very important one because of the depth of its content and the shortness of its lineage, in other words, its closeness to Padmasambhava, the root of all the Nyingma lineages.

This has been translated into French, German, Polish and Spanish.

17. Being Right Here: A Dzogchen Treasure Text of Nuden Dorje Entitled the Mirror of Clear Meaning

(Published by Snow Lion, 2004. ISBN: 978-1559392082)

Being Right Here provides a very clear authentic account of the view and essential meditation of dzogchen, the practice of non-dual experience. The presentation is in the Men Ngag style, a personal instruction distilling the author's own realisation, revealing the lived experience of the terton Nuden Dorje Drophan Lingpa in a manner both beautiful and profoundly meaningful... It consists of short verses which, with pithy clarity, show how the various aspects of dzogchen fit together. The text provides both an authentic account of the practice and instruction in how to apply it.

"Giving this commentary was the last time I taught in Rinpoche's (C.R. Lama) presence and re-reading it brings back the facilitating warmth and spaciousness of his empowering and liberating display. The teacher is the site of integration; through the practice of the text the nature of life is revealed through integration with the living presence of the teacher. The teacher is of course not an entity, but a relational field," says the author.

The book has been translated into French, German, Italian, polish and portuguese.

18. The Yogins of Ladakh: A Pilgrimage Among The Hermits of The Buddhist Himalayas

(Published by Motilal Banarsidass, 1997. ISBN: 978-8120814622)

James Low wrote Chapter 15 Practising Chod in the cemeteries of Ladakh which includes a secret biography of the yogini Machig Labdron and the Chod practice which she created. It is unique to Tibetan Buddhism. *The Yogins of Ladakh* investigates the social anthropology of the area through studies of village life. Further it enquires the social organisations, history, meditational practices and philosophy of the yogins who still lived and practised in the remote parts of the area.

In the Introduction, John Crook writes, *"James Low and I undertook long journeys on foot in Ladakh to meet the yogins in their monasteries and 'caves'. Few of these yogins were teachers but they allowed us into their presence and showed us their manner of being. A landscape was set before us which we had to map as best we could. Our book is a map of the cultural landscape of these men. We hope and believe it will help Westerners both to broaden and to deep in their insight into the Dharma. Come with us then in an exploration of these inner landscapes set amongst the highest mountains of the world. It is our belief that what we found there is of great significance in the suffering world of today."*

The book has been translated into Italian.

Printed in Great Britain
by Amazon

23900066R00165